Polite

Polite

The Art of **Communication**
at **Home**, at **Work**
and in **Public**

LOUISE MULLANY

WELBECK

First published in 2024 by Headline Welbeck Non-Fiction
An imprint of Headline Publishing Group Limited

1

Cataloguing in Publication Data is available from the British Library

Hardback ISBN 978 1 8027 9342 0
Trade Paperback ISBN 978 1 8027 9343 7

Typeset in Berling by CC Book Production

Printed and bound in Great Britain by Clays Ltd, Elcograf S.p.A.

HEADLINE PUBLISHING GROUP
An Hachette UK Company
Carmelite House
50 Victoria Embankment
London EC4Y 0DZ

www.headline.co.uk
www.hachette.co.uk

For Abbie and Tommy

CONTENTS

1

Politeness Everywhere

When people ask me what I do for a living, quite often they laugh out loud if I tell them that, outside of lecturing, I spend my time researching politeness. Sometimes this inspires people to tell me a rude joke or results in comments along the lines of 'Oh, I bet you hate swearing, don't you!' Reactions and responses to my research specialism demonstrate that people make presumptions about what a 'politeness researcher' believes and does. Many assume that I try to sanitise language by teaching people they must be more polite, and explain how to rid impoliteness from our lives.

Just for the record, I do not hate swearing. I have been known to swear myself on occasions – just ask my editor. I also do not spend my time trying to force people to be more polite, and it would be impossible to go through life avoiding impoliteness. Instead, I work in the academic field of linguistics to identify scientific approaches which decode the unwritten rules of politeness and impoliteness within society. This decoding shows the significance that politeness rules have in the communication we engage in as we go about our daily lives. The language we use is heavily influenced by these rules, which we begin acquiring in early childhood.

The science of politeness

This book draws on the best scientific knowledge that academic linguists have produced over the last fifty years to explain politeness, impoliteness and the rules that lie behind how we successfully communicate (and miscommunicate) with each other. This comes from the discipline of sociolinguistics, the study of the connections between language, society and identity. Sociolinguists examine different language varieties, the social and cultural contexts where interactions take place, and the different identities and power relationships of those involved.

Since the 1970s, sociolinguistics researchers all over the globe have been creating and refining scientific approaches for analysing politeness in communication in all of its various forms, uncovering unwritten rules of politeness in different situations. Through real-life communication data and peer-reviewed research, I demonstrate how we can become better communicators by learning to recognise our unconscious motivations for politeness and impoliteness, which are fundamentally linked to our identities and the communities in which we live and work.

As politeness is something we readily discuss in general conversations outside of academia (anyone ever complained about the rudeness of a colleague with friends?), you will already have some thoughts and opinions about politeness and impoliteness. Reflect for a moment on the vast array of communication that you have engaged in and witnessed during the past few weeks or months – with strangers, partners, work colleagues, friends, family members. You will likely be able to recall situations in which someone has been especially rude or particularly polite towards you. You may well remember your reaction or have spent time reliving the moment, perhaps wishing that you had responded differently. Parents are frequently praised or criticised for the perceived 'politeness' or 'rudeness' of their child's behaviour by the adults around them. We constantly make value judgements about our fellow human beings on the basis of unwritten politeness and impoliteness rules that exist in the cultures and societies where we live.

Politeness affects our relationships with everyone, from those with whom we have the closest bonds through to complete strangers and everyone else in between. It influences our friendship choices, whom we will pick as romantic partners and how we get on with those whom we work with. Politeness and impoliteness affect all languages and cultures, no matter where you are in the world, from the remotest tribes to the most densely populated towns and cities.

Politeness is literally everywhere, in every interaction we have, whether our communication takes place in person, online, in speech, writing, by phone, via sign language or through gestures. The more we learn about the linguistic rules of politeness, the better we will understand and be able to interpret our everyday social interactions. This includes explaining why we communicate differently with people from different communities and cultures to our own. It helps shed light on why some individuals are more successful communicators than others, and how impoliteness, miscommunication and conflict happen. If conflict escalates and relationships break down, linguistic politeness rules can be drawn upon to mediate, repair and resolve damaged relations between individuals, groups and communities.

This book focuses on politeness in a very broad range of everyday settings. These include: communicating at home, at work and in public spaces, including on the street, in schools, on social media and other online spaces, in community groups, in shops, when playing, coaching or spectating sport, on the telephone, via instant messaging, in healthcare settings, at the airport, and when watching the TV, consuming media and engaging with advertising. It also covers settings when the stakes are high, including difficult and sensitive interactions about life, death, politics, religion and legal matters. It doesn't matter who you are, where you live or what you do for a job, politeness is key to the success of our social relationships as human beings. By decoding unwritten politeness rules and uncovering politeness myths, we will uncover why we prefer the company of some people over others, as well as making our future communications more productive and informed.

Where it all began

A fascination with the importance of politeness in human communication can be traced back as far as 2,500 years ago to ancient civilisations, including in China, Egypt and Greece. Since these ancient times, people have been intrigued by how we judge one another and it seems politeness has always played a crucial part in what we deem to be appropriate and inappropriate in our communication. Since politeness was first studied, there have been accompanying anxieties about slipping politeness standards, as well as moral panics about language decay and declines in manners and 'proper' behaviour. However, language is always changing and, with it, politeness practices change too. This is a natural and inevitable process of language evolution – it does not indicate that people are becoming more uncivilised, discourteous or rude. Deborah Cameron,[1] a specialist in language and communication at the University of Oxford in the UK, refers to any attempts to intervene and clean up language as part of 'verbal hygiene', an unnecessary intervention to try to stop imaginary language rot by demanding that language is used according to unrealistic ideals of correctness, purity and civility.

None of this is to claim that politeness is unimportant in society or that we need to get rid of politeness rules. However, one of the first principles that any student of sociolinguistics learns is that the type of language held in the highest esteem in

6

any society is that which is associated with the group that holds the most power. There is nothing inherently better or superior about it, but it still carries the most prestige and social status. Politeness rules help to keep the status quo in place. Politeness and power are fundamentally linked, and politeness can be used as a tool of social exclusion. But more on that later.

I first came across the scientific study of linguistic politeness as an undergraduate English language and linguistics student back in the 1990s, on a sociolinguistics course. I learnt how sociolinguists investigate the relationship between language, power and identities in different societies, cultures and communities. From that moment on, I never looked at the world in the same way again. For the first time, I encountered scientific explanations based on reliable research of authentic, real-life communication, which finally made sense of the weird, wonderful and sometimes downright unpleasant things that happen to us when we communicate with each other.

Even more exciting was the realisation that people were paid to investigate everyday communication as a job. Thirty years later, as a professor of sociolinguistics at the University of Nottingham in the UK, I still find it just as fascinating and as compelling as ever to decode linguistic politeness and impoliteness to show exactly how humans are communicating or miscommunicating with one another. And it is this obsession with politeness and impoliteness in language which has led me to write this book.

Whilst my office is located directly under a literal ivory tower, in the university's ivory-towered Trent Building, I am most often found outside campus recording and decoding language in a range of real-world settings. Over the years, I have researched the language of business leaders, police officers, firefighters, healthcare professionals (including physicians, nurses and patients), sporting figures, CEOs, lawyers, politicians, teachers, journalists, NGO leaders, insurance providers, technicians, engineers, chemists, astrophysicists, geologists and climate change scientists, as well as the language used by members of the public.

My sociolinguistics research focuses specifically on how our identities influence the language choices that we make when we communicate with each other, and how these language choices are influenced by politeness and impoliteness. Topics that I have researched have included miscommunication, how impoliteness and offence are caused, and managing conflict and verbal abuse, as well as the positives of using linguistic politeness to create effective teams and ensure strong, trustworthy interpersonal relationships. I have also examined how individuals, groups and communities are represented through a politeness lens in the mass media, including in radio and television broadcasting, newspapers, magazines, posters and billboards, and on global social media platforms, including YouTube, Twitter (now X) and Instagram.

The impetus behind the research I conduct is to improve knowledge and understanding of exactly how language works, including how it evolves and changes, and to explain how language is interpreted differently by people with different identity characteristics.[2] My overarching motivation is to work collaboratively with people to increase their understandings of language and politeness to enhance their lives in some way. My research experiences over the last thirty years have continued to shape my views on the study of politeness, and they have made it into the pages of this book in one form or another.

Politeness and popular culture

There are other books out there which are traditional manuals of politeness, focusing on the importance of learning etiquette to improve oneself, or insisting on the need to improve politeness through better courtesy or manners. Young people are often blamed for such alleged declines in standards. However, many of these books are not supported by rigorous linguistics evidence and they are frequently written by those who have no formal training in linguistics or social sciences. We wouldn't expect to read a book on physics or maths written by someone who had never studied these subjects, and language and linguistics should be no different.

Language is infused with power, status and prestige in complex ways that cannot be easily overridden. It is unfeasible to read a book one day and then wake up the next as a perfect communicator who then has amazing social relationships with everyone and never again experiences impoliteness or conflict. To pretend that such a transformation can happen, as some self-help books quite happily do, is disingenuous and devoid of any scientific knowledge as to how language really works.

Sociolinguists do not try to sanitise language or prescribe that language standards are slipping, and nor do they proclaim that people have to change the way they speak and abandon their original identities. So, instead of telling you all of the things that you are doing wrong when you communicate and how you need to improve, this book will instead help you to recognise politeness rules and norms, how they vary, and what power they have based on different identities and the different communities and cultures in which communication takes place.

This book also presents evidence of how to recognise and pull apart long-standing myths and stereotypes around politeness and impoliteness. There are many of these out there in the world; some of the most persistent include that the youth of today are lacking politeness and respect, that women are biologically hard-wired to be more polite than men, and that swearing is a sign of a limited vocabulary and intelligence. These deeply ingrained fallacies surrounding politeness and impoliteness can do a great deal of damage to social relationships. While, conversely, gaining knowledge of how to identify language myths about politeness and impoliteness immediately raises awareness of the stereotypical value judgements that we make about one another, which, in turn, makes us more informed and knowledgeable communicators.

It is important to know that we can unlearn habits and assumptions, just as we learnt them in the first place. Politeness is not something that individuals or groups inherently possess or are born with. Access to the rules and norms which are held in prestige in any society will depend on privilege and social class background – this is a theme that we will return to throughout the book.

The art of communication

When we understand how politeness and impoliteness in language really work, we can become more informed and knowledgeable communicators. It teaches us to recognise how language is deeply connected to our identities and the societies and cultures in which we live. In this book, I will present different strategies and show how others have achieved communicative successes and navigated communication failures. I want to help you to be able to spot ingrained myths and stereotypes about politeness and see how these can be unpicked to enhance overall awareness of language, politeness and power.

We are constantly negotiating and grappling with politeness and impoliteness subconsciously. Whether we like it or not, politeness is truly everywhere. Once we learn how to interpret politeness and impoliteness using academic knowledge from sociolinguistics, we become far more aware of the communication strategies we use. This then enables us to play a much more active role in enhancing our communication, with the aim of bringing a much greater depth of harmony into our future relationships with others.

2

Communicating Politeness and Impoliteness

From the moment we wake up each day and start our first interactions with others, we are constantly presenting different versions of ourselves through our politeness choices. Linguist Penelope Brown[3] has described politeness as so fundamentally important that it is a pre-condition for human co-operation to exist. Politeness reduces tension and friction, and it plays a foundational role in how we express our feelings, concerns and attitudes towards one another. It is a way of avoiding confrontation and conflict with others, as well as being key to maintaining strong interpersonal relationships. In contrast, impoliteness is when behaviour is judged to be inappropriate and offence has been caused. How much offence is taken will depend on what was said, who said it, whether there is any attempt to repair the relationship and whether the impoliteness was perceived to be intentional in the first place. Relationships may be damaged or break down as a result, if situations cannot be defused and rectified.

Politeness principles

Politeness is encoded in everyday language use, such as in how we are tactful towards each other, show approval, compliment, give praise, express modesty by not appearing egotistical or bragging, use humour and express sympathy when it is required and/or expected. The exact ways in which these politeness features are used will vary from culture to culture, but the overall aim will be to maintain harmony and good interpersonal communication, which strengthens social bonds and solidarity between people.

Politeness includes respect and deference, and it can be seen as part of a moral act, with adherence to politeness norms seen as a way of upholding the morality and civility of a society. The terms 'politeness' and 'etiquette' are often used interchangeably in popular culture. In this book, 'politeness' is used as an overarching term and 'etiquette' is defined more distinctively as a specific type of politeness which is very formal, with a strict system of rules and codes which are associated with accruing power in specific contexts and cultures. Decorum and manners are a key part of social etiquette. Access to social etiquette rules and codes are based on power and privilege, and most often on social class background. Linguist Sara Mills[4] is an expert on the connections between politeness and social class and she traces this relationship back to key points in history. She argues that, historically, only upper-class men were afforded access to politeness norms in society, acquired through wealth, social privilege and power. She draws on the work of Richard Watts[5] to show how politeness traditionally belonged to 'the innate gentleman' who had a certain *'je ne sais quoi'*. Watts provides a cutting assessment, arguing that it is little wonder that such 'innate gentlemen' kept the secrets of politeness to themselves, as it brought them an immense amount of power and privilege from which others were completely excluded.

Today, in popular culture, politeness norms associated with deference, manners and decorum are typically associated with middle-class speakers, who hold the most power and status in public. Australian sociolinguists Keith Allan and Kate Burridge[6] argue that there is a 'middle-class politeness criterion' which dominates. It excludes those who are uneducated, poor or socially deprived, who are either unaware of or cannot afford to observe the social 'niceties' of politeness. Middle-class politeness norms therefore play an important role in our consideration of politeness and impoliteness throughout this book, as these are what the average person is evaluated and judged against in public, and in contexts where politeness is synonymous with decorum, manners, civility and social etiquette codes.

However, another key part of politeness is how we express solidarity, friendship and social bonds, and how we communicate to others that we like them, admire them and want to be around them. People from different social class groups and communities may do this in different ways, but everyone draws on politeness principles. As Mills points out, it is important to investigate what politeness looks like in all its forms, not just from a middle-class, elitist perspective of decorum and manners.

With her colleague Stephen Levinson, Penelope Brown[7] divided politeness into two categories: 'positive' politeness and 'negative' politeness. It is essential to emphasise straight away that these two terms *do not* equate with good and bad – in other words, negative politeness does not imply impolite, or bad behaviour. Instead, positive politeness refers to how we show solidarity, friendship and social bonds with one another, whilst negative politeness is how we show respect and deference towards others, how we signal formality and social distance, and how we avoid intrusion. This distinction between positive and negative politeness is very useful and it has endured the test of time in sociolinguistic politeness research. It has been used to research politeness in the widest range of contexts for the last

15

forty years, from conversations between intimates in the private setting of homes, through to very public contexts, including in courtrooms and parliaments. It will be applied to the range of different places where we examine politeness in this book.

Other considerations which influence the level and type of politeness we use include the cost or benefit that any act will have for others, such as when we are asking for a favour. To demonstrate this, it's worth comparing the difference between borrowing a pen versus asking to be lent a large sum of money by a friend. In addition to their categories of positive and negative politeness, Brown and Levinson[8] refer to the cost-benefit process as 'weightiness', when speakers 'weigh up' how much politeness they need to use for the outcome they desire. This process of weighing up draws on an assessment of the power relationship between speakers and how much solidarity or social distance there is between those communicating.

A request to borrow a substantial amount of money from a friend comes at quite a cost, with very little benefit to the friend, and so it will need far more politeness work than just use of the explicit politeness marker *please*: 'Please can I borrow X?' just won't be enough. This simple politeness request would be completely appropriate for borrowing a pen, as the imposition and obligation of the pen is small, status is equal and intimacy between friends will be stronger than social distance. However, asking to borrow money is far riskier. The request needs to be longer and more complex to do more linguistic work. Consider the following: 'I'm so sorry, I really don't want to have to ask you this, but I'm in a really tight spot paying our mortgage and I think I'm about to lose my job. Is there any way at all that you would consider lending me £200 just to tide me over? I promise I'll pay you back as soon as I can.'

This longer and more complicated request includes an apology, a statement of reluctance to ask in the first place, a justification of why the request is being made, details of what the money would be spent on and a promise and reassurance that it would be paid back swiftly. This extra linguistic work is needed to justify the weightiness of such a request to a friend and it also increases the requester's chances of success in gaining access to the much-needed cash. Using such detailed politeness strategies to borrow a pen would be very inappropriate and most likely be viewed as laughable and over the top.

These useful concepts of weightiness and ranking of the imposition have been key features of Brown and Levinson's work since the 1970s, alongside positive and negative politeness. Their work has been very influential and they have been credited with establishing politeness as an international area of linguistic enquiry in its own right.

Their research, and the work of those who have followed in their footsteps, has tried to provide answers to complex questions, including: why don't people say exactly what they mean when they talk to each other? Why do some people get offended when certain things are said to them, but others do not? Why do some people find humour in banter, but others get offended by it? Why do some people swear, whilst others find swearing objectionable? Why is there so much variety in the terms of address that we use for each other, and how do we decide on what terms to use?

Early politeness research in the 1970s and 1980s focused on co-operation and harmony, and all of the ways in which we try to protect and be considerate of one another in communication, including how we show power, deference and formality through the ways in which we address each other. From the 1990s onwards, researchers also began to examine impoliteness, as there was a realisation that impoliteness was far more commonplace in everyday communication than linguists had first assumed. Researchers developed practical frameworks to explain what happens when conflict and disharmony occur in communication and offence is caused, as well as focusing on co-operation and harmony. And so it became important to analyse exactly what impoliteness looks like, how it happens, the impact it has and how it can potentially be resolved.

Impoliteness is critically important in showing us where the boundaries of politeness rules lie – observing what happens next when impoliteness takes place tells us a great deal about a society's morality and civility. It can also tell us a great deal about ourselves, how we display our identities when we are under pressure and how we see ourselves as conversationalists. If we think about times when we have encountered impoliteness in our lives, it is useful to consider what was said, whether we assessed the impoliteness to be deliberate or not and whether there were any attempts to repair any damage that had been done – for example, an apology for causing offence. The ways in which the encounter ended is also an important consideration – how serious was the offence? Did harmony get restored? Did the relationship suffer or break down? How were things finally resolved, if at all? Did the situation escalate beyond impoliteness to law breaking, through verbal abuse, threats or physical violence? Did anyone lose their job or get prosecuted?

UK linguist Jonathan Culpeper[9] is an impoliteness specialist who has mapped out various ways in which impoliteness can be delivered and responded to. He argues that it is crucial for impoliteness not to be from a common stereotypical perspective in popular culture as a 'debased form of language' or as something that is an uncontrolled 'emotional reflex'. Impoliteness is just as strategic, creative and powerful as politeness. Impoliteness can be shown through insults or abusive terms of address, using scorn or ridicule, being condescending, deliberately disagreeing with someone, telling inappropriate jokes, staying silent in cultures where talk is expected, acting uninterested or being unsympathetic. Other strategies are: threatening or abusive language, including words and phrases known to be taboo, using sarcasm or irony, making rude gestures, invading the other person's space, being verbally aggressive through shouting, swearing at someone in a threatening way or interrupting and preventing another person from talking when they wish to speak, or by using overpoliteness – being excessively polite so that it stands out as breaking a social norm.

People respond to initial acts of impoliteness in various ways, depending on whether they are willing to enter into conflict with another person and the severity of the situation. Culpeper[10] points out that, as impoliteness causes offence, there will be negative consequences for those involved, including sadness, suffering or hurt experienced by the person who has been offended. In terms of what happens next, Culpeper and colleagues[11] argue that one option is not to respond at all to an impolite comment, choosing instead to keep silent. If a response is given by the person on the receiving end, then they could apologise if they feel responsible, which will likely de-escalate the situation and signal that they are trying to repair the relationship. Alternatively, they may 'counter' the initial impoliteness by either going on the offensive and lashing out with their own impolite comment or going on the defensive, where the recipient of the impoliteness tries to defend their original position.

Culpeper and colleagues[12] give the following as a typical example of how impoliteness can escalate. On a street in New York, the driver of a car has been attempting to park and ends up in an altercation with a pedestrian about who has the right of way. The argument descends into a series of insults, showing an offensive–offensive pattern (the car driver is noticeably overweight):

Pedestrian: Oh, shut up you fat pig!
Driver: Go fuck yourself!
Pedestrian: Go on a diet.
Driver: Go fuck yourself! [13]

In situations like this, when someone replies to one offensive comment with another offensive comment, conflict typically escalates. Conflict between road users is a very common cause of impoliteness between strangers. This is partly because driving is such a high-risk activity – people's senses are heightened because serious physical harm can occur, either to oneself or to one's family and friends as passengers, as well as the fact that financial loss can instantly take place if things go wrong on the road. There is also a sense of moral outrage that is invoked when other people break the rules of the road, which arguably makes people more inclined to react more impolitely than they normally would, especially when another road user has done something risky or dangerous.

Chances are that you will have either been involved in or witnessed impoliteness whilst out on the road as a driver, pedestrian, cyclist, horse rider or other sort of road user. Impoliteness is typically delivered through a combination of language and gestures, with hand gestures (including those that are non-verbal signals for swearing) favoured if speakers cannot hear each other or if used for additional emphasis. Impoliteness, annoyance and frustration can also be communicated using a car's mechanics, including flashing of lights, braking very quickly if someone is travelling too close behind and aggressive honking of the car horn, which goes beyond any legal use of the horn to signal one's presence. More significant altercations on the road where impoliteness escalates can result in impoliteness tipping over into illegal behaviour if verbal threats or physical violence results.

Staying with the theme of driving and traffic, as it is a rich area to explore when thinking about impoliteness, Culpeper and colleagues[14] give an alternative pattern of response: the offensive–defensive pattern, drawing on the communication strategies used by traffic wardens towards motorist offenders in a fly-on-the-wall TV documentary series called *The Clampers*. In the following exchange, a traffic warden had put a clamp on the wheel of a car for a parking violation. The driver returned to his car whilst the traffic warden was still present and so he decided to confront him. The driver engaged in impoliteness, using an offensive strategy in the form of a challenging question to call out the traffic warden's ticket as showing a lack of intelligence: 'Don't you think this is a bit stupid?' The traffic warden chooses to respond defensively with, 'Well you see, I'm just doing my job.'[15] By blaming his job role, the traffic warden sidesteps any personal accountability – this is a very common and rather useful strategy for those who work in professions where they are regularly subject to impoliteness as they come into conflict with others as part of their everyday job role. The traffic warden example is a typical de-escalation strategy which can be used as an attempt to defuse conflict. It maintains the traffic warden's status and their position as a good, competent professional who is just doing their job and who won't be drawn into verbal abuse.

Those who work as traffic wardens, police officers, bailiffs, debt collectors, security staff and bouncers, amongst many other roles, have clear professional responsibilities based on unequal power relationships and social distance between them and members of the public. It is important that those in such professional roles avoid offensive–offensive patterns and do not descend into slinging insults at members of the public if they are to maintain their professional status and avoid reprimands or accusations of inappropriate conduct.

Of course, not everyone will be able to abide by the politeness rules that are in place for their job role. In Cardiff in 2016, a member of the public who had just received a parking ticket filmed a traffic warden telling him to 'fuck off'.[16] The member of the public decided to release his video on social media and it went viral. He claimed that he started filming because he wanted to explain the reason he didn't have a ticket to the traffic warden, but the traffic warden wouldn't listen. The traffic warden is first recorded telling the member of the public that he will have him arrested for filming him. He then goes on to angrily shout, 'You're the person who parked their fucking car there, so fuck off!' The member of the public then ironically replies, 'Nice language; well done, sir.'[17] His use of the formal term of address 'sir' draws attention to the lack of respect the warden has just shown him as a member of the public. As the traffic warden walks away, he sticks two fingers up at the camera and at the person he has ticketed. Once the video had been watched by the traffic warden's employers at Cardiff City Council, an official statement was released confirming that he had been removed from duty with immediate effect. A spokesperson stated that, 'The council does not condone this type of behaviour and has guidelines which we expect our employees to adhere to.'[18] This case epitomises how failure to abide by the politeness rules for one's profession when interacting with members of the public is newsworthy if caught on a recording device; it can result in disciplinary action and job loss, and so the stakes are high in situations where individuals need to keep their impoliteness under control and instead, on the face of it at least, appear polite.

Many fly-on-the-wall reality television programmes such as *The Clampers* focus on real-life situations where conflict is expected to take place due to the job role. Other programmes have been deliberately staged to provoke people into being impolite to each other. There are multiple versions of these franchises broadcast in countries across the world, translated into many different languages. Such programmes have become a dominant form of popular entertainment over the last two decades and many impoliteness researchers have used such programmes for research data and analysis. Culpeper[19] has focused on the hugely successful and long-running TV quiz show programme *The Weakest Link*, which originated in the UK. From 2000 to 2012, contestants were constantly subject to ridicule, scorn and derision by the show's host, Anne Robinson. Most often, the impoliteness was targeted at the contestants' incorrect answers and their perceived lack of knowledge and intelligence. The show has had significant global success, having been adapted in over fifty countries internationally.

TV celebrity chef Gordon Ramsay is another high-profile example of someone who has turned impoliteness into a highly profitable entertainment genre in his various TV series of 'kitchen nightmares' on both sides of the Atlantic. The show involved him going into failing catering businesses and challenging them to turn their fortunes around, which Ramsay did by often being very rude and challenging to the staff, using insults, scorn, ridicule, derision and condescending remarks, accompanied by multiple expletives, to emphasise his anger and frustration at those who are doing a bad job. Some of the appeal of reality TV programmes such as *The Apprentice* also comes from an expectation that impoliteness and conflict will occur, as individuals are pitched against each other in a divisive competition format, particularly where there is the chance to win a highly prized career opportunity.

Clearly, then, all of these examples show us that members of the general viewing public are fascinated by watching norms being broken and conflict unfolding in other people's lives. But what does the popularity and success of these television programmes tell us about politeness and human behaviour more broadly? Culpeper points out that part of the popularity of impoliteness in entertainment is due to a voyeuristic pleasure that people derive from watching impoliteness and conflict on TV, where a sense of enjoyment and gratification is gained from watching the pain of others. It is also popular as audience members can feel superior to the people who have been drawn into the impolite exchanges that they are witnessing. Culpeper further points out that the audience watching conflict unfold on television has the added advantage of knowing that they are safe (unlike if they were witnessing an argument or a fight in a public place). When impoliteness and conflict happen to us, our emotions run high and we may well be upset, fearful or angry. However, if we are watching other people in conflict with each other on TV or via social media videos, we are at a safe physical and emotional distance. We are free to derive a sense of gratification and satisfaction in watching conflict unfold, from a position of superiority. There is also a sense of escapism from our own lives – we can criticise the impolite behaviour of others and pass moral judgements on their rudeness without any fear of personal rebuke or impact on ourselves or our own interpersonal relationships.

Such media can also be enjoyable because it grants us special access to parts of people's lives which are not usually seen in public. In some shows and videos, the audience is given access to observe impolite and rude behaviours which people try their best to hide. Another aspect which draws large audiences back to watch is the desire to find out what happens next with conflictual relationships and/or to see how different people react in difficult situations, such as getting a parking ticket. Precisely because this access is so privileged, these shows make for compelling and addictive viewing. As human beings, we are fascinated with watching and observing politeness and impoliteness in the social behaviours of others, and so mass media producers have capitalised on this and created a number of successful formats which allow easy access without having to leave the comfort of our own homes.

If you enjoy these programmes and social media videos, the next time you are seeing impoliteness unfold on screen, consider why you are watching it. Whose behaviour do you like or dislike? What kinds of moral judgements are you making about the people involved? What are you finding enjoyable and/or humorous? What is it that draws you back to watch? How do your views compare with the opinions of your friends and family? Your answers here will tell you a great deal about your own moral attitudes to impoliteness, and where your own boundaries of polite behaviour lie.

Finally, when we are considering impoliteness, one note of caution is that it is important to acknowledge that people with neurodiverse conditions including autism, ADHD, Asperger's syndrome and Tourette's syndrome may struggle with politeness norms and conventions. For example, being able to maintain eye contact, or speaking at the culturally expected speed or volume, may be very difficult for neurodivergent individuals and such behaviour may be mistaken for impoliteness, even if politeness norms are not being intentionally broken. This book focuses on the experiences of neurotypical individuals, defined as the majority of the population who process information in ways that are typical within their cultures. This is not to suggest that the experiences of those who fall outside of this category are unimportant; rather my research expertise is with neurotypical populations, and I wish to leave space for others with specialisation in neurodiversity to tell the story of how neurodiverse populations interact with societal politeness and impoliteness norms to do this justice.

Here, then, we have gone through the different ways in which politeness and impoliteness norms have been defined and recognised by sociolinguists in their research. I have emphasised how politeness is essential in enabling human beings to co-operate with one another and make meaningful relationships. I have also defined politeness and given an overview of different politeness terms and the most important approaches to politeness from sociolinguistics. Additionally, I have outlined the importance of defining and examining *impoliteness*, to ensure that a more comprehensive picture of politeness is presented from different angles, including when politeness fails and when impoliteness takes over. We will now move on to add identities, communities and cultures into our consideration of politeness and impoliteness in everyday communication.

Identities, communities and cultures

When we engage in polite or impolite behaviour, we are displaying a particular version of our identities, which links directly to the beliefs, values and morals in the communities and cultures where we live. Sociolinguists have studied this extensively, and a useful way to think about identities when considering politeness is to split them into three core strands: 'personal', 'social' and 'organisational'.[20] These categories can aid us as individuals to reflect on our own sense of self and who we think we are, but also how we come across to others, given the different types of identities that we will display to one another in different settings.

'Personal' identities refer to the different personality traits that we have, such as being extrovert or introvert, as well as our personal skills and experiences, including our competence and abilities to fulfil particular tasks. 'Social' identities include our sex, gender, race, ethnicity, age, sexuality and social class background, as well as identity features that are related to geographical identities, such as local, regional and national identities. These geographical categories will be assigned at birth, but they may well change if we relocate to other places and become members of new communities in different geographical locations. Our social identities do not exist in a vacuum and they continually intersect with each other – we are simultaneously aged, raced, gendered and classed by others based on assumptions and value judgements that are made about us, including the countries and cultures of where we are perceived to be from.

'Organisational' identities refer to the more formal identity roles and categories that are allocated to us by the different organisations that we are connected to during our lives. This can be as part of education, healthcare, work and any other formally organised groups that we may interact with – in schools, colleges or universities, in hospitals or doctors' surgeries, in workplaces, sports clubs or community groups. Within these organisations, we will be assigned specific named roles, such as student, teacher, nurse, doctor, patient, CEO, group leader, coach, instructor. And when we communicate in these organisations, these roles come with their own politeness rules and expectations. For example, swearing may be completely appropriate in some workplaces and yet highly stigmatised in others – such as in a school classroom from a pupil directed to a teacher or in a courtroom from a defendant to a judge. On occasions, certain aspects of our identities will be more important than others. For example, if someone starts to talk about age in conversation by introducing the topic of ageism and discrimination in the workplace, then the age of those present in the conversation will be foregrounded.

Reflect for a moment on your own personal, social and organisational identities, as well as the identities of others with whom you interact. This can be family members, work colleagues, friends, acquaintances or complete strangers. How do your identities become more/less important in different situations? What politeness rules are in place for you but not for others who have different identities? How are these identities evaluated according to the politeness rules and norms in the communities and cultures where we interact?

When we are thinking about culture and communities, it is really useful to follow a definition used by politeness researchers Helen Spencer-Oatey and Daniel Kádár.[21] They assert that culture refers to 'patterns of traditions, beliefs, values, schemas, norms and symbols'. These patterns will be shared by members of the same culture and they affect how we behave and how we evaluate the behaviour of others.

It is also useful to split culture into 'large' culture and 'small' culture categories, following Adrian Holliday's[22] work. Large culture refers to ethnic, national and international identities and how individuals are affected by culture at scale – such as at the level of governments, education systems, the media or a country's

27

economy. In contrast, small cultures refer to the activity of much smaller groups of people who come together within large cultures to form communities and establish their own politeness norms which bond the group together. This can be at the level of families, friendship groups, sports teams and clubs, workplace teams or groups created via social media networks, all of which we will cover in this book.

At the level of large culture, politeness research has focused a great deal on observable differences between politeness in Eastern and Western cultures. In Western cultures, a sense of self is based more on autonomy, independence and individualism. However, politeness research conducted in Eastern cultures, including Japan, China and Korea, has instead shown a much greater emphasis and importance placed on collective identities and group reactions instead of individuals.

Although there are noticeable differences between Chinese and Japanese cultures, they both value group harmony more than individual autonomy, and this leads to different politeness norms and conventions. Respect and a sense of self in East Asian cultures stems from being included as part of a collectivist culture. Often, communication strategies are self-effacing, and more orientated to the other rather than the self. Communicative behaviour really gains social value when people come together and interact as part of a group with collective social roles and responsibilities, as opposed to communicating as an individual.

We do need to be careful not to over-simplify here, as there will be occasions where group identities are really strong in individualistic cultures and vice versa, but, overall, it is useful to emphasise that politeness can have different meanings and manifestations for different cultural groups.

At the level of small cultures, there have been multiple studies in which politeness researchers have investigated politeness rules and how they are developed within groups, asking how these different groups use politeness effectively to strengthen social bonds and enhance their interpersonal relationships. I have spent time analysing politeness norms that develop within particular groups as an important part of my business consultancy work, looking into how different workplace departments work effectively (or ineffectively) with one another to get tasks achieved.

In one large organisation, two departments had very different politeness norms and expectations. The sales and marketing group favoured a very direct, competitive communication style. In contrast, the design group favoured indirect, co-operative styles. Whilst this worked fine when they were communicating within their individual departments, when they got together in larger, company-wide meetings, they clashed because their politeness norms were different. The design group perceived the sales group to be impolite because they favoured banter and gave orders directly. The sales group viewed the design group as unassertive complainers who didn't say what they really meant in meetings, which they found confusing and frustrating. We'll consider the consequences of such differences in team politeness norms when we investigate workplace talk in detail later in the book.

The groups with which we feel the strongest sense of belonging, whether at home, at work or in public, are known as our in-groups, and we share communicative patterns with other members. This can be our family members, friendship groups, workplace colleagues, fellow players on sports teams or, on a larger scale, as supporters of the same team when spectating together in a stadium. These contrast with out-groups, the groups from whom we wish to dissociate ourselves, or with whom we feel like outsiders. Our language styles will diverge between the two. Sociolinguists have devised theories around group membership to show how our feelings towards others affect our language choices. One of these is called 'communication accommodation'.[23] If we want to be included in the group, then we learn to adjust our language styles to the politeness norms for this group to make sure that we fit in as legitimate members. For example, we will learn what jokes or types of humour are appropriate and which are not. If we wish to dissociate from a group, then we will use strategies that differ from these group norms – for example, being too formal. Politeness is key here in conveying solidarity and a wish to be included or, conversely, conveying social distance and a wish to be dissociated from certain groups.

In addition to the language choices that we make, our identities play a part in our body language and communicative gestures. This is part of the overall 'demeanour' of how we present ourselves to those around us. 'Demeanour' was defined by influential sociologist Erving Goffman[24] as how we perform our identities through body language and gestures when communicating. It includes how we dress, how we style our hair, how we move our bodies – including our stance and how we choose to walk, talk and sit. In part, this will be influenced by our socio-economic class background and how we have been taught to behave politely in public, as well as age, race, ethnicity, gender identity, sexuality, peer group, religion and any other social features that may be relevant in a particular situation. If we are interacting in public, it may also include additional organisational identities that come with their own rules or norms for demeanour – for example, many workplaces or sports teams will have their own uniforms or dress codes. Value judgements based on politeness and etiquette are consistently applied to different demeanours, with individuals making assessments based on who is deemed to be desirable to be around.

Value judgements based on politeness and etiquette codes are constantly applied to different demeanours. We make assessments about whom we most want to associate with and whom we least want to associate with based on desirable demeanours. Consider the last time that you went to a formal social occasion, such as a wedding, a birthday party, a workplace night out or a social event of a sports team or a community organisation to which you belong. How did you show group membership through your choices of dress, body language and stance? How did you converse with others? What types of humour were used (if any)? Did you feel that you had legitimate membership of your group? Why/why not? Did everyone behave according to the politeness norms of the occasion? If not, consider how and why politeness norms were broken and what the short-term and long-term consequences of this were for those involved.

Decoding politeness in adolescence

To get us thinking in more detail about the connections between politeness, appropriateness and demeanour, it is useful to consider one particular stage in our lives when demeanour is really acute: adolescence. Adolescents frequently push the boundaries of politeness rules and acceptable behaviour. They will often use language innovatively, including different pronunciations for their in-group and the creation of new words and slang terms to show membership. As they try out different identities and strive to find their own styles and unique demeanours, they will alter and experiment with how they present themselves and their bodies. This innovation often involves adolescents dissociating themselves from the identities and communication practices of older generations, particularly voices of authority, including parents, caregivers and teachers.

For example, secondary schools in the UK (ages eleven to eighteen) often choose to have stringent uniform codes, including avoiding hair dye, not wearing jewellery or having piercings, as well as prescription in terms of length of skirts and length of ties, based on what the school deems to be an appropriate demeanour to show politeness and respect for the school and its rules. Pupils often create innovative workarounds to try and break the politeness rules for dress as small acts of rebellion and rule-breaking, for example, rolling skirts up at the waist or fastening ties the wrong way around. Schools employ sanctions for dress code infractions, often in the form of detentions.

In countries where schools do not have such widespread uniform policies or dress codes, such as the US and Canada, there's arguably a greater degree of freedom for adolescents in terms of the demeanours they display through appearance, with students having more freedom to choose what they wear. Sociolinguists Penelope Eckert and Sally McConnell-Ginet[25] studied high schools in California and focused on how adolescents used their demeanour through dress, gesture and stance to signal strong in-group membership, as well as how adolescents are language innovators. In their research, they describe the very strict dress codes of girls who belong to the self-described 'Asian Wall'[26] – which refers to a brick wall in the school where Asian students hang out together during their break times. To be a legitimate member of the 'Asian Wall' you firstly need to be of Asian descent. Eckert and McConnell-Ginet observe how the Asian-American students who belong to the Asian Wall congregate at the wall and display very similar demeanours and language styles to display politeness, solidarity and a strong sense of group membership with each other. Eckert describes how they have 'high platform shoes, skinny bell-bottoms, and very small T-shirts, with hips cocked. As they toss their heads, their long, sleek black hair (in some cases tinted brown) swishes across their waists, the slimness of which is emphasized by shiny belts. Some of them talk to, some lean on, quiet-demeanoured boys with baggy jeans and baggy shirts, with hair long on the top and shaved at the bottom.'[27]

They then introduce us to one of the adolescent girls, known as Linda. They observe Linda talking to one of the boys, asking him a direct question about his identity, described as follows: 'Linda turns away from her group of friends with a characteristic tilted head toss, bringing her hair around her shoulders; and with an exaggerated high-rise intonation on the pronoun, she calls to a boy who's standing nearby. "What are you?" Another girl answers for him, replying that he is "Japanese Filipino".'[28]

Their observation contains a great deal of information about identity labels and the broader performance of adolescent identities for this ethnic group, particularly how this shows solidarity and inclusion. Group solidarity is actively displayed through dress, stance, language style and gesture. It also shows how components of our identities are very difficult to pull apart, with gender, ethnicity, heterosexuality, life stage and social status all visible and being simultaneously displayed here. Because adolescence is a time when identities are particularly acute, it is a popular area of research for sociolinguists who specialise in the role that language plays in displays of identity, group membership and language change.

Think back a moment to your own adolescence (or if you have teenage children in your family, you could also consider them) and how membership of different groups, including friendship groups, is displayed. How did you display politeness through solidarity and belonging? How did other groups display different behaviours? What language features, dress and demeanours strengthened or weakened solidarity and social bonds between you? What created distance with other groups? Have any of these communication features transferred into adulthood with you?

Whilst the acuteness of such identity displays and the desire to be different and rebellious arguably diminishes for many as we venture into adulthood, a sense of group belonging is still critical in our adult lives, and our ability to use politeness to show solidarity and social bonds through our language, gestures, dress and demeanour is still crucial, as we will see throughout the chapters in this book.

Tattoos and piercings

In discussing demeanour, it is also interesting to consider tattoos and body piercings as part of politeness. Tattoos can be visible markers of identity, and can also signal group belonging in some cultures and contexts. However, tattoos can also provoke assumptions of uncouth, inappropriate behaviour that break taboos and even the law in others. In the vast majority of countries, you have to be over eighteen to get a tattoo, partly to prevent adolescents getting tattoos which they later regret. Reactions to tattoos and piercings vary greatly, depending upon cultural rules of what is deemed appropriate and attitudes also change over time. In countries including Iran and Saudi Arabia, tattoos are illegal for religious reasons; in Japan, there are long-standing cultural associations of tattoos with gang members and criminality and so tattoos are not allowed to be on display in public places including swimming pools, saunas and spas. In Denmark, it is illegal to get a tattoo on your hands, neck or head, including your face.

Academics have investigated tattoos in the workplace, and how a worker's professional competence can be called into question in some professions if they have visible tattoos or body piercings. Selena Au and colleagues[29] found that, in Canadian hospitals, thirty per cent of family members with relatives in intensive care reported that it was important to them that their physician did not have visible tattoos, as this damaged family members' confidence and trust in a physician's clinical competence. Thirty-nine per cent also said it was important for clinicians not to have visible piercings for the same reasons.

In a US study investigating parents' reactions to paediatric healthcare practitioners with visible tattoos, Scarlett Johnson and colleagues[30] surveyed over 300 parents to assess whether they would trust a doctor treating their child who had a visible neck tattoo or facial piercings. Their participants consistently gave tattooed healthcare practitioners lower confidence ratings when compared with non-tattooed practitioners. Some parents even considered going to an alternative emergency room that was fifteen minutes further away to avoid their child being seen by a tattooed clinician. The research participants also reported feeling greater degrees of discomfort with practitioners who had facial piercings. Johnson and her colleagues concluded that these factors negatively affect clinical confidence ratings of health-care practitioners with visible tattoos and piercings, regardless of age, gender or geographical location of participants. These findings emphasise how people have strict expectations about what someone *should* look like if they are to be viewed as professional, competent and trustworthy.

In the UK, the BBC[31] reported that financial services, law and healthcare tend to have the strictest rules about employees not having visible tattoos. However, some other workplaces have recently relaxed rules, showing a shift in some professions' views of appropriacy and decorum in relation to where and when tattoos can be displayed. This includes Virgin Atlantic allowing their flight attendants to display tattoos and police forces across England and Wales relaxing their rules. A recent YouGov survey[32] found that a quarter of people in the UK now have tattoos and for one in nine people these tattoos are visible.

Other decoders of politeness

The body language and gestures that we use in our everyday interactions are part of the study of paralinguistics. We have seen the importance of body language and gestures in our consideration of adolescence and it is useful to explore these categories in more detail to gain a fuller understanding of how they can be used to decode politeness and impoliteness in different cultures. Paralinguistics is technically defined as the scientific investigation of non-verbal features that are used *alongside* the words that we speak to convey important information. Paralinguistics includes touch, the physical space that exists between us when we are interacting with each other, how loudly we speak and the use of silence, along with facial expressions, eye contact, and the tone and pitch that we use. Let's now look at some of these features in more detail.

Touch and physical closeness

The scientific investigation of touch is known as 'haptics'. In many cultures, people use touch to show positive social connections with others. In countries including the US, UK, Canada and China, it is usual to shake hands as part of a ritualised greeting routine, especially in more formal situations, such as the workplace.

In other cultures, including Japan and Korea, a bow will be given instead of a handshake – directly touching each other and encroaching on the other's personal space is avoided. The angle, length and style of the bow will depend upon whom is being greeted, and it is important not to get the bow wrong. The levels of social distance and formality that exist between those bowing and the context where the bow is taking place are crucial – a deep bow is often only appropriate for an emperor or a very senior dignitary.

Another useful category to consider when decoding politeness is the physical closeness that exists between us, known as 'proxemics'. All cultures have unwritten rules on how physically close we can get to each other for the interaction to still feel polite and respectful. If one feels that one's space is being invaded, then this will lead to negative value judgements and may well be seen as potentially threatening or intimidating.

Body language and greeting rituals

During the Covid-19 pandemic, in cultures where handshaking was a standard way of introducing yourself, some people started greeting each other by touching elbows instead, to try to minimise the spread of germs. The 'elbow bump' had previously been mooted for use by the World Health Organization[33] a few years before the Covid-19 pandemic, during an avian flu outbreak. The desire to rapidly replace a handshake with an alternative form of physical contact shows the importance of having at least some form of touch to show connection as part of a greeting for many in the West. However, elbow bumping during Covid was very short-lived, as it soon became illegal to get close enough to touch anyone who belonged to a different household to one's own, with the implementation of stringent social distancing laws.

Outside of pandemics and epidemics, making physical contact with each other – through giving 'high fives', cheek kissing, hugs, holding hands or patting someone on the back – is an important politeness marker of intimacy, friendship and solidarity. However, if these forms of haptics are used incorrectly, then they can quickly become negatively evaluated as impolite, signalling disrespect, rudeness and a potential threat. This can also depend on the context, the relationship between those communicating and the cultural setting. For instance, whilst handshaking is acceptable in China, hugs or kisses as greetings are not. In many parts of Europe, such as Italy, Spain, France and Belgium, cheek kissing is a key part of a ritualised greeting, but this may well be questioned as being too intimate in other countries, including the UK. Haptics are imbued with politeness and it is really important to be aware of different cultural norms when interacting to avoid becoming accused of inappropriate behaviour.

Volume

There is also the volume at which we speak which we need to consider. Noisy behaviour may be viewed by out-groups as rude, inappropriate and uncivilised – politeness rules for what is appropriate vary from culture to culture, which can become an issue when members of different cultures are interacting together. Linguist Deborah Tannen[34] reports that in New York Jewish communities, speakers have a high involvement style, which includes talking loudly and interrupting. No offence at all is meant or taken by members of the same group; however, if others are present who do not share these norms, they may view being loud and interrupting as impolite.

Silence

As another paralinguistic feature, silence and attitudes and reactions to being silent can also tell us a great deal about politeness and impoliteness in any culture. Canadian sociolinguist Ronald Wardhaugh[35] has drawn together studies of cultures in different areas of the world to illustrate how silence is valued very differently. Wardhaugh reports that, in certain North American indigenous cultures, it is perfectly acceptable and completely appropriate for community members to visit one another's houses, stay silent for almost the duration of the visit and then return home again. There is no need for talk to take place, as this is not the expected cultural norm; silence will not be interpreted as a sign of awkwardness or rudeness.

Wardhaugh tells of similar behaviour in Denmark; he warns that many Danes negatively evaluate guests who insist on talking as rude and overbearing. In contrast, for the Roti people who live on Timor in Indonesia, talk is considered a great pleasure, as is the ability to be able to show off one's verbal skills in debating and arguing. Silence there is viewed very negatively. In fact, it is so rare that when it happens it is seen as signalling acute distress or confusion. And so talk almost constantly takes place.

Filling silences: Talking about the weather

In the UK, it is traditional to gabble on and fill silences in order to abide by politeness rules and avoid the discomfort of sitting without talking. Having conversations on neutral topics is very common to avoid silence and such talk is known by sociolinguists as 'phatic communion'.[36] According to Janet Holmes,[37] phatic communion refers to an interaction on a neutral topic. It could take place in any context, and talk must primarily serve a social function, to establish common ground. The neutral nature of this form of communication minimises risk to anyone's status or image within the group.

Probably the most iconic example of phatic communion in the UK is talking about the weather. Whilst this may seem like an unfair cultural stereotype, weather talk is undeniably common in the UK. In a study on British culture, social anthropologist Kate Fox[38] found that 94 per cent of British people had spoken about the weather in the last six hours, with 38 per cent reporting having talked about it within the last hour. She uses this observation to decree that at any one point in the UK, people are either currently talking about the weather, have just finished talking about the weather or are going to start talking about the weather in the near future. In 2018, British newspaper the *Independent*[39] reported that, on average, British people will spend over four months of their lives talking about the weather, including spending an average of eleven minutes a week looking at weather forecasts on TV or on their phones. The average British adult will also post six times a month about the weather on social media.

The weather is an ideal phatic topic to fill silence not only with strangers but also to reconnect with people you know, even those you know intimately. Conversations about the weather are enduring for many reasons. Weather talk often takes place at the openings and closings of conversations, where politeness strategies are more ritualistic. Weather is a topic that can be shared with multiple conversationalists. It is important for those interacting phatically to avoid disagreeing with one another – and so if someone starts to argue about the weather or disagree with another's assessment of it, then talk immediately ceases to be phatic. The British obsession with talking about the weather to fill silences is so well recognised that it has become common material for many comedians and satirists, such as the Instagram account and website known as #verybritishproblems,[40] which has a range of T-shirts dedicated to the weather, with slogans including the ironic phrase 'I love rain'. And this is all just down to the cultural discomfort within Britain to sit with another person in silence.

To summarise, it is not just our language but also our body language, gestures and demeanour that work together to display politeness or impoliteness in communication. As communicators, we are constantly using all of the clues that are available to us to try to decode politeness and impoliteness in our interactions. If we wish to be evaluated as polite and our behaviour seen as appropriate, then we need to ensure that it is not just our language that is suitable for the particular contexts in which we interact, but all of the other communicative behaviour that goes along with it too.

Frontstage and backstage: Knowing your audience

If we really want to know how to decode politeness, we need to bear in mind not only our own actions, but also the audience that we're communicating with and the environments we find ourselves in. Public settings including workplaces tend to have more formal rules compared with how we interact within our own homes. However, it is also important to acknowledge that politeness rules are not set in stone. They are fluid and they do change over time.

One other factor to take into account is who could be potentially listening to us or reading our language (in letters, email, social media posts etc.) when we communicate and how broad our potential audience may be. Again, the work of Erving Goffman[41] provides a theoretical approach to considering how audiences may affect politeness choices. Goffman brings in a metaphor of life as a staged performance, drawing a distinction between 'frontstage' and 'backstage' performances. This has been a really useful tool in decoding politeness as we think about our identities and how we shape our language depending upon context and our knowledge of who we think is listening, or who is paying attention.

Goffman defined 'frontstage' as situations where we are on public display. We are fully aware of the presence of a public audience and therefore we adjust our politeness norms accordingly, including our language styles, dress and demeanour, to abide by public politeness rules. This may include: presenting ourselves in attire that abides by workplace dress codes, such as dressing formally in a suit or wearing a particular uniform; making sure that we do not talk too loudly, so that we avoid disturbing others around us; ensuring that we do not take up too much space in shared areas, such as when using public transport, or abiding by the correct etiquette for eating in public, such as not making excessive noises that others would find annoying or rude. In contrast, 'backstage' is where we are not on show or public display, so we can engage in much more informal talk. If we are in private settings, such as the home, with family or close friends, then we may also have a more relaxed approach

41

to dress and demeanour (unless it is a special occasion). Being backstage can also take place in more public arenas, such as a workplace, but it is distinguished as a setting where no one else is around to cast judgement. So, two workplace colleagues can drop the personas they present in public by engaging in gossip about colleagues in a private office because they know no one else can hear them. The differences between backstage and frontstage are usually clear-cut. However, on occasions, unexpected (and unwanted) changes in 'staging' can happen – there may be eavesdroppers or encounters may be recorded without interactants realising. This can be particularly damaging in public settings where backstage talk is taking place despite professional identities being on display.

One famous example is an exchange accidentally caught on a microphone between the UK Prime Minister Tony Blair and US President George W Bush in 2006 at a G8 summit in Russia. The conversation between the two was later released to the public via the media. It offered an unusual opportunity to observe politeness norms between them that were never meant for public consumption.

The exchange took place during a lunch break in a public conference room. As far as the two leaders knew, there was just the two of them in the conversation and they were out of earshot of the rest of the delegates – very much a 'backstage' situation. They were unaware that the microphone on the table in front them was still turned on. Their private conversation ended up very frontstage, being broadcast on media channels around the world, and so we got to see language styles and politeness.

George W Bush had been sitting talking to Russian president Vladimir Putin when Tony Blair came over and put his arm on Bush's chair. In terms of proxemics, Blair also leaned towards him, signalling through his body language and gesture that he wanted to have a private conversation with Bush, without the other delegates listening in. Bush turned towards him to signal his engagement and started the conversation with the informal greeting and question: 'Yo, Blair, what you doing?'[42] Bush's use of last name only as his term of address signalled an established personal relationship and pre-existing solidarity between the pair. The common informal greeting 'yo' is also used to signal solidarity, informality and intimacy between interactants.

The media homed in on the informality of the greeting; 'Yo, Blair!' It figured heavily in newspaper headlines, partly because the general public had never before seen this side of their relationship. It was newsworthy precisely because it contrasted heavily with the carefully choreographed, frontstage politeness norms of formal political communication between leaders in public. T-shirt companies even had the greeting emblazoned on to shirts soon afterwards. Listening to the recording very carefully, it is unclear as to whether Bush said 'yeah' or 'yo', but ultimately this did not matter – 'yo' was much more newsworthy. The greeting even became part of the title of a biography covering Blair's ten-year premiership.[43]

As well as the greeting and conversational opening, other parts of the interaction between the leaders that stood out as unique insights into the positive politeness that existed in their private relationship include Bush telling Blair to get German Chancellor Angela Merkel to call on him when the topic of trade comes up: 'Tell her to put me on the spot. And thanks for the sweater, awfully thoughtful of you.' He makes a swift transition from a core business topic to a conventionally polite 'thank you' for a gift, which invokes humour. Blair laughs in response and states, 'It's a pleasure.' Bush continues the humour, joking, 'I know you picked it out yourself.' Blair builds on this, stating, 'Oh, absolutely. In fact, I knitted it,' followed by simultaneous laughter from them.

One other part of the conversation that drew media attention was the use of swearing by Bush when talking about trying to bring about a ceasefire in the Middle East. Bush states his view to Blair: 'What they need to do is to get Syria to get Hezbollah

43

to stop doing this shit and it's over.' This very informal evaluation of foreign policy strategy, complete with an expletive, would be completely inappropriate in a formal, frontstage setting; it would be deemed impolite and offensive, with politeness rules dictating that political leaders are not permitted to swear or talk in such an informal style in public. In this informal, backstage context, however, there were no such rules.

It is difficult for politicians when they are caught out like this, as inevitably their backstage language styles will differ from what is deemed to be polite and appropriate frontstage. As elected officials, politicians are held to high account and so broadcasters and the public can be rather unforgiving when glimpses of how politicians really speak to each other behind closed doors when their guard is down are released in public. These instances provide us with excellent illustrations of the different identities portrayed by our backstage and frontstage selves. It is perhaps a useful lesson for us all in being careful about not blurring the lines between frontstage and backstage in public settings, as well as being aware that there could be unseen audiences or recording devices present.

Eavesdroppers: Can impoliteness bring down a prime minister?

The scientific insights given to us by sociolinguistics, outlined in this chapter, can provide a practical guide as to how we can use politeness to communicate effectively in the communities and cultures in which we live. Sociolinguistic approaches help us unpick the way in which politeness encodes a great deal of information about our identities and how we are judged by others on the basis of how we use politeness strategies. To bring together all of these different elements of how we communicate politeness and impoliteness, I want to finish the chapter with a final illustration, focusing on another political faux pas. What we have learnt here can be applied to any setting when communicating with anyone, but I've picked politics again as it provides a particularly rich area when illustrating the importance of verbal and nonverbal communication, dress, demeanour, staging, the role of audiences and of the media, and how politeness and impoliteness can affect evaluations of people's identities and careers. In this specific case, it can be seen as a contributing factor to bringing about a change of government.

The incident in question took place in the UK and involved the then Labour Prime Minister Gordon Brown. He was on the campaign trail during the general election of 2010 and was talking in public to members of a local community in Rochdale, a town in northern England. It was a very frontstage setting – Brown was surrounded by members of the public and journalists with TV cameras and microphones.[44]

During general election campaigns, politicians are forced out of their carefully scripted comfort zones and into having unplanned conversations with members of the voting public in important constituencies – these tend to be unrehearsed, unscripted and unpredictable encounters. These contexts can pose threats to politicians' reputations as they need to come across as competent and respected communicators who are genuinely in touch with their voters, proving themselves as authentic leaders, with no pre-prepared script to rely on. The very public nature of these interactions, with large media audiences, significantly amplifies any negative behaviour.

Gordon Brown was visiting this traditional Labour voter area to talk about the government's achievements in crime, health and education. He had just finished visiting a youth correction centre when one of his press officers decided to get him to meet with an older female voter, sixty-six-year-old Gillian Duffy, who had approached them to say she wanted to talk to Brown in person.

At the start of their conversation, Gillian Duffy told Brown that she had voted Labour all her life, but then, in front of the TV cameras, said that she was now 'absolutely ashamed' to say she was Labour. She went on to criticise and challenge Brown and his party about ineffective policing, being taxed too much as a widow and, in her view, too much immigration from Eastern Europe. The latter issue was particularly contentious as she used the following problematic language to pose a challenging question to Brown: 'All these Eastern Europeans what are coming in, where are they flocking from?' In sociolinguistic analysis, application of a verb to humans that is designed to describe birds or animals ('flocking') would identify this as a form of language prejudice.[45]

Brown looked very uncomfortable at this point as the topic had drifted into an emotive and very controversial political topic. He hesitated and then replied, 'Er, well, a million people come from Europe, but a million British people have gone into Europe.' He then attempted to repair the conversation using multiple politeness strategies and steered the conversation away from immigration. He tried to bring the encounter to a positive resolution to minimise the damage to himself and his party, in terms of how the media would portray the encounter on news bulletins. At a surface level, he did this successfully. He complimented Duffy, positively evaluated her as belonging to 'a good family', asked if she had grandchildren and patiently listened to stories about them. After remaining polite throughout various turns, he managed to bring the conversation successfully back to his main political arguments from his election manifesto. He stated three principles: 'Education, health and helping people. That's what I'm about. That's what I'm about.' He repeated the last part of the statement of his own identity to emphasise the importance of these principles to him as a politician and as the current prime minister.

Duffy responded positively, expressing her approval of Brown. She congratulated him on his political achievements – 'Well, congratulations, I hope you keep it up.' Haptics then came into play: she shook his hand and patted it affectionately with her other hand.

Brown followed with a ritualistic phrase for polite conversational endings with strangers, saying that, 'It's been very good to meet you.' Which Duffy reciprocated with, 'Yeah, nice to meet you.' Brown repeated his positive evaluation and then brought in humour by making a joke: 'Very good to meet you and, er, you're wearing the right colour today.' Gillian Duffy had a bright red collar on her coat, the colour traditionally associated with the British Labour Party. They both laughed together at this, and then Brown moved in and put his hand affectionately on Duffy's coat to continue the joke and show a sense of solidarity with her. He finally brought the conversation to a close by saying, 'It's very nice to see you. Take care.'

And so, this unplanned frontstage conversation came to an appropriate and harmonious close. When Brown left, the watching journalists asked Gillian Duffy what she thought of Gordon Brown. She replied that he was 'very nice' and confirmed that she would be voting Labour.

After waving goodbye to the crowd of people who had gathered, Gordon Brown then got into his official prime ministerial car. But, unbeknownst to him, he was still wearing a radio microphone from a major TV channel, which was still turned on. This is what was then said in the car, which Brown had presumed was a private, backstage space between only him and a member of his team:

Brown: That was a disaster.
Team member: Why, what did she say?
Brown: Well, just, should never have put me with that woman. Whose idea was that?
Team member: I don't know. I didn't see her.
Brown: It was Sue's, I think. It was just ridiculous.

Team member: They took pictures. I'm not sure that they'll go with that one.

Brown: They will go with it.

Team member: What did she say?

Brown: Och, everything. She's just a sort of bigoted woman that said she used to be Labour. I mean, it's ridiculous.[46]

Brown's private evaluation and language use contrasted markedly with the frontstage interaction he had with Gillian Duffy at the end of their conversation. The transition from Brown's public, polite persona was swift. He negatively evaluated the exchange as a 'disaster' once he believed he was backstage. He expressed anger and frustration. He then made what the media later construed as a 'rude' evaluation of Duffy, with his choice of the phrase to negatively evaluate her as a 'bigoted woman'. The sound then cut immediately when they realised that he was still wearing the microphone.

What Gordon Brown said in the car is not unusual in terms of how we often have a public mask that slips the moment we go backstage and allow our real thoughts and feelings about a person to whom we have just been talking to come out. Once speakers think they have entered a backstage space, they may well act in ways that are inconsistent or contradictory to how they have just communicated. We can probably all think of similar examples, where encounters have been painful to endure and/or damaging, but we have upheld politeness norms and engaged in white lies or used formulaic, ritualistic phrases to maintain politeness – such as 'good to see you', 'nice to meet you' and 'take care' – until the space becomes backstage. Once backstage, we can say what we really feel, which may often include being insulting to or derogatory about an individual or a group. We do this to let off steam and work through difficult encounters. Sociolinguists have long argued that variations within individuals' linguistic behaviour in different contexts are crucial for us to have a perceived sense of wholeness, and in that sense, we should embrace this other side of ourselves. The problem for Gordon Brown, though, was that, despite thinking this was a safe, personal exchange, it was then broadcast to the whole world. A journalist listening in decided to make the private conversation public and so the audience for Brown's comments immediately shifted from one trusted confidante to a large, international public forum.

To give the revelation its full resonance, news reporters went to Gillian Duffy and played the recording to her. She said she was 'very upset', would no longer be voting Labour, could not understand why he had called her a bigot and wished for Brown to apologise to her. There then followed many other calls from the public and media for Brown to apologise. In a national radio interview during the afternoon of the same day, Brown defended himself by saying that Duffy had made a comment about Eastern European people to which he was reacting. It is this part of Duffy's conversation that Brown referred to when he tried to explain why he used the word 'bigot'.

However, a great deal of criticism ensued, including from within Brown's own party. On an official Labour Party blog, Brown's comments were described as offensive to Duffy and others like her because they were 'obviously rude and unfair'.[47] By the evening of the same day, Brown had ended up changing his campaign schedule to travel back to Rochdale to go to Duffy's house and apologise to her in person. In a press conference outside the house immediately afterwards, he evaluated the 'bigoted' comment as a 'miscommunication' and 'misunderstanding', which had now been resolved with 'Gillian' – with Brown using her first name in an attempt to show a transition in their relationship from one of conflict to one of solidarity.

Journalists still cite this encounter as the event that significantly damaged Brown's political career and subsequently changed the course of British politics.[48] The Labour Party was already slightly behind in the opinion polls, so the impact of the Duffy incident on the election is somewhat hard to gauge. However, it clearly had a very damaging effect on Brown and his popularity. Some voters were angry with him for apologising, as they agreed with his initial assessment that Duffy was bigoted and saw the apology as a capitulation that then gave licence to people to express xenophobic attitudes. Others thought that Brown had unfairly insulted Duffy and took it as evidence that he had lost touch with core Labour Party voters. And the public, having witnessed the contradictions between his frontstage politeness and backstage impoliteness, punished him.

Summary

And so, what have we found in our focus on learning how we communicate politeness through sociolinguistics? Well, politeness is much broader than just a focus on etiquette, manners and decorum. It is also about appropriacy, respect and deference, as well as building solidarity, friendship and strengthening social bonds and interpersonal relationships. It necessitates paying attention to one another's needs to be desired, liked and wanted. Politeness is also concerned with our rights to not be unfairly taken advantage of or unreasonably imposed upon by others. Politeness rules vary from culture to culture, and what's polite in one context may be impolite in another. Cultures can be large, at the level of countries or geographical boundaries, but they can also be small. Specific cultures can be developed within small groups of people who come together to fulfil particular activities.

If we become embroiled in impoliteness, then it is important to quickly assess how this can be de-escalated, particularly in situations where insults or abuse are being thrown. It is a good idea to consider how strategies of repair, such as apologies, can be brought in to defuse a situation and try to re-establish a connection; we will discuss at length strategies for doing this later in the book. The many TV programmes focusing on impoliteness can be used as learning tools for us as viewers, to see how impoliteness can be successfully defused and resolutions can be made. Viewing impoliteness on social media, TV and any other media sources can also enable us to safely witness the consequences of what happens when situations explode and become non-resolvable, with the hope of avoiding similar situations where relationships break down. Those who occupy professional roles need to be especially careful to ensure that they behave appropriately, even if they are subject to insults and abuse from members of the public, customers or clients; otherwise, they may well need to face the consequences of breaking codes of conduct for their job, which can include being reprimanded, fined or fired.

As we have seen from the two examples from politics, we need to know who our audience is when we are interacting; if we are unsure if anyone else could be in earshot, it is advisable for us to exercise caution and try to avoid communicating anything that would be deemed impolite by an overhearing audience. If we do happen to insult someone who overhears then there will be a good deal of repair work needed if the relationship is to mend.

Similarly, in order to have a coherent sense of ourselves, we may contradict our frontstage identities backstage with those whom we know well to let off steam and process difficult conversations. But in doing so, we may engage in behaviour which would be considered impolite or taboo frontstage, including many of the classic features of impoliteness, such as insults, name calling and swearing. It is also important to exercise caution in case we are videoed or audio-recorded without our prior knowledge – as we've seen with Gordon Brown, the negative consequences of this can be serious and long-lasting. This can be particularly difficult to control in the age of social media,

51

where smartphones are everywhere and videos of inappropriate behaviour that takes place, often in backstage contexts, can go public on global social media sites very rapidly, often without the knowledge or consent of those being recorded.

Next, we are going to look at terms of address, as they form a crucial part of politeness norms and identities in all cultures.

3

What Did You Just Call Me?
Politeness and Terms
of Address

W hat we choose to call someone when we are addressing them is a classic indicator of politeness in any culture. Terms of address directly encode information about the politeness norms and rules in the communities and cultures where we live. They can tell us a great deal about power, social status, formality and appropriacy in interactions. When sociolinguists first became interested in mapping out scientific approaches to politeness, they started by analysing the words that we use to refer to others, as well as our own preferences in how we wish to be identified. They catalogued multiple words and phrases which show whom we are directing our communication at when we interact. These include the use of titles (Ms, Miss, Mx, Mr, Dr), proper nouns (Max, Louise, Chris) and pronouns (you, we, they). Terms of address range from very formal titles, which would be expected in official public settings, such as countries' parliaments (Sir, Lord, Lady, Right Honourable), through to very informal nicknames and terms of endearment used in the home with families, close friends and intimates – these names may only be known and used by a handful of people.

Politeness and birth names

Let's think firstly of the formal names given at birth, so those which appear on official documents, including birth certificates and passports. Formal names are an integral part of our identities and they play significant roles in how we are addressed and identified during our lives. Whilst these names are not fixed for all time and can be legally changed, the thought that goes into birth name selection and any subsequent official name changes involves navigating norms of politeness and cultural appropriacy, as well as legal requirements. Parents across different cultures often spend a great deal of time deciding on the names they will give their offspring at birth – a lifetime of teasing and derision can potentially await if a naming choice is made that sits outside the norms of appropriacy for the naming culture where a child grows up.

To consider where the rules of politeness and the boundaries of cultural appropriacy intersect with naming choices, it is useful to begin with what is permissible in law. In the UK, the government's Deed Poll Office[49] issues all legal naming documents, including birth certificates. Its trained examiners will deny an application if they think it's demeaning, thus putting a child at risk of losing dignity and respect in society, two key components of linguistic politeness that affect status and reputation. This can include a name being too long (a maximum of 300 characters) or containing symbols or punctuation marks other than hyphens or apostrophes. Names can also be rejected if they are against the law, which includes anything seen to encourage hate, or taking illegal drugs. There is an opportunity for parents and caregivers to make a case to justify the chosen name, but ultimately, a name can be refused if concerns remain about it causing offence by not meeting standards of dignity and respect, or if it breaks the law.

Furthermore, the UK government's Passport Office has an even more specific set of rules than the Deed Poll Office, and it will refuse to issue passports for names that its officials deem to be inappropriate. From an impoliteness perspective, this covers names that the Office categorises as being vulgar, offensive or blasphemous,[50] including names that are considered to be taboo, swear words, words that are sexually explicit, and names that may have religious connotations.

Regardless of these official guidelines that are in place to protect people's dignity around naming, children regularly tease and insult one another by deforming proper names into vulgar and/or offensive terms instead – politeness and language taboo researchers Keith Allan and Kate Burridge[51] point out that even the most 'normal' or conventional names can be deformed through rhymes and/or word play. And if there's an opportunity for children to associate them with taboo topics, all the better. Whilst authorities such as the UK's Deed Poll and Passport Offices have their rules and boundaries for excluding names evaluated to be demeaning or in bad taste, to maintain polite-ness, civility and naming standards, children are very adept at corrupting any name in their interactions with each other.

The shortened version of my first name, Lou, was a source of much mirth for some of my contemporaries at school, who thought it was hilarious that I was named after a slang word for a toilet. I have been called 'toilet', 'toilet-head' and 'bog-face' more times than I care to remember. The Huffington Post[52] recently reported on survey results from the US National Institute for Research, cataloguing the top ten names most likely to see a child bullied at school, with Dick and Fanny being top. Names associated with sexual body parts stand a high chance of a child being subject to teasing and derision. That said, children can and will corrupt any names in their interactions with friends, siblings and parents to create humour. When my son was nine, he thought it was hilarious when he came up with the nickname 'little baby mummy poo' for me. These deviations from using polite, conventional terms of address in their proper forms are very common ways for children to play around with the boundaries of politeness and impoliteness. It enables them to explore how deforming terms of address can affect the identities of those being derided (positively and negatively) and how this can then affect their relationships with them.

In cultures including Chinese, uniqueness is highly valued. Parents and grandparents tend to decide on a strong symbolic name at birth. As sociolinguist Susan Blum[53] points out, the name should be in harmony with the time and place of birth. The chosen name will also be seen as directing the fate of the child, so names that represent future aspirations, including success or prosperity, will often be given. Evason[54] gives the examples of 'Kang' (healthy), 'Yong' (brave), 'Mei' (beautiful) and 'Ling' (wise). Parents may take inspiration from the natural world, including trees, animals, flowers and astronomy, or be influenced by works of literature or philosophy. Chinese given names can also include place names, or children can be named after significant historical events, for example, the Beijing Olympics. There is no convention for married couples to take each other's names in Chinese, though the vast majority of children will take their father's surname. There is also no established custom in China to name children after older relatives, as this can be seen as impolite and disrespectful to elders.[55]

Blum observes in her research that, in interactions with family members and before children enter the school system, they are nearly always referred to by nicknames, most often derived from part of their formal name. These are called 'small names' or 'milknames'.[56] Names can also be changed if there is illness or difficulty. In fact, unlike in many Western countries, Blum summarises a crucial difference – in Chinese, people are referred to by a range of different names and 'they do not necessarily retain any of them as their "real" name or as the one that they feel reflects their identity'.[57] Identity can be seen as very fluid as terms of address will vary from context to context, as names change depending on politeness conventions of formality, status and the audience. Naming includes kinship terms, nicknames, pronouns, social and occupational titles, pen names, dialect names and names in other languages (for example, an English name when learning English), as well as their proper names. Blum goes on to point out that even when talking with family and intimates, Chinese politeness norms are such that terms of address will be chosen that signal a formal relationship, showing hierarchy and respect, but not a relationship of social distance.

In contrast to naming practices in China, in many other countries it is appropriate to give children names from older relatives – this can be a way of showing politeness through respect and honour by carrying on a traditional family name. A classic example of this is the first-born son inheriting their father's name. In several countries, including the US, Latin America and Brazil, there is a tradition of adding 'Junior' or Roman numbers (e.g. III) to show the generational layers of the same name. For example, Brazilian footballer Neymar shares the exact full name of his father, Neymar da Silva Santos, and so the suffixes 'Senior' and 'Junior' are added to distinguish them. Some cultures have a historical naming tradition of using only one word for a name at birth, known in linguistics as a mononym. This was the case in ancient societies, with Plato and Aristotle being two famous examples from Ancient Greece.

Changing formal names

As we've seen already in our example of Chinese culture, names can be changed if they are seen to be unlucky or become associated with misfortune or ill health. Changes to naming practices can also be due to prescribed state intervention following major historical events. This is part of what is known in sociolinguistics as language planning, and often politeness conventions are changed during such times of prescribed language shifts. For example, in Turkey, mononyms were dominant until the collapse of the Ottoman Empire in the 1920s and the population did not have surnames. Popular mononyms included the name of a profession or a place name, and they were written in the Arabic alphabet. When Turkey became a republic in 1923, President Atatürk changed the language script from the Arabic to the Latin alphabet. He then also passed a Surname Law in 1934,[58] which declared that the male head of all Turkish families was legally obligated to choose a formal family surname. To abide by the new rules of cultural appropriacy, these surnames needed to be created, and could be based on either ancestor names, the man's profession, personality traits or historical events. These new names were then legalised in Roman script, as a first name and last name. This symbolically represented the legal formation of new identity markers for all citizens, signalling social change for every individual's formal identity. The Surname Law additionally forbade people to refer to each other by titles only, in order to fit in with these newly created politeness norms and changes in lessening power and status differences, signalled by the new naming practices. President Atatürk also passed an additional naming law that only he could take the surname Atatürk, which translates as 'father of the Turks'. Even members of Atatürk's family were legally not permitted to share his surname.[59]

In current-day Turkey, married women keep their maiden name and take their husband's surname. Babies take their father's surname, which is seen as the official family name. State intervention in naming at such a large scale shows the power of changing terms of address and how changing rules around politeness, appropriacy and naming can directly affect the identity labels of all individuals within a nation.

Formal names can also be officially changed at an individual level for a variety of reasons, including marriage, civil partnership, divorce, gender reassignment, or for other practical or preferential reasons. Self-selected formal name changes represent distancing oneself from the past and taking on a new name for a different identity in future. The term 'deadname' has recently entered the *Oxford English Dictionary*[60] as both a noun (with the first recorded entry from Twitter in 2010) and as a verb ('deadnaming', first entry, again from Twitter, in 2013). Deadname and the act of deadnaming describe the act of causing offence by using the wrong name to address a transgender person who has stopped using their birth name in favour of a new name which they have chosen to be more compatible with their gender identity.

In public life, there has been much discussion about transgender actors' rights to get their names changed in credits for films they starred in prior to their gender transition, which still list them by their deadname. For example, transgender actress Laverne Cox argued that deadnaming on sites such as the Internet Movie Database (IMDb), which catalogues all films and actors, was insulting and offensive.[61] In response to such criticisms, from 2019, actors have been allowed to replace deadnames with their new names in previous cast lists.

Politeness scales: Formality, intimacy and status

Let's move beyond proper names now to give a much fuller consideration of different terms of address and how they are used according to politeness norms. Selecting appropriate terms of address helps us follow politeness conventions and avoids disharmony or neglecting our fellow communicators. They are usually first used at the very start of conversations, often as part of greetings, so it's critical to get them right from the outset to help get the communication off to the best start. It is important to use a term of address that is the most appropriate for the context in which the communication is taking place, including considerations of the power (im)balance and social distance that exists between speakers.

Our choices in how we address someone can depend on the culture in which we are interacting, whom we talking to and our relationship with them (compare, for example, work colleagues, friends, family members, intimate partners), how long we have known them, any age differences that exist (for example, an adult talking to a child, a member of an older generation talking to a member of a younger generation). Formal titles directly encode information about gender identity and/or marital status and can convey respect, status and honour. They are known as honorifics and include, in the English language, Miss, Ms, Mr, Mrs, Mx, Lady, Lord, Sir, Doctor, Captain and Your Majesty. If address terms are used with too much or too little formality to the wrong person in the wrong situation – for example, addressing the leader of a country as 'mate' at a formal state occasion – then politeness norms will be broken, offence may be taken and behaviour will be negatively evaluated as impolite and rude.

Linguists have devised different politeness scales that help to decode our language choices and how they are influenced by politeness rules, based on the amount of power and distance that exist between people in any setting. There is a scale of formality, with high formality at one end and low formality at the other; an intimacy scale, with very intimate at one end and socially distant at the other; and also a scale of status, with high status at one end and low status at the other. Our language choices move along these scales depending on whom we are talking to, where we are, how long we have known each other and the language and cultural setting in which we are interacting. Terms of address are also influenced by the medium of communication that is being used – there will likely be noticeable differences between the address terms used in an official written letter from a formal organisation (such as a utility company or a bank) and the address terms used between very close friends during an informal face-to-face conversation.

At the informal end of the formality scale are the most familiar terms used by those with whom we have close relationships and the highest solidarity, including address terms that can only be legitimately used by good friends or family members. Diminutive forms of people's first names (Lou, Ted, Tom, Abbie) tend to only be used by those who know each other well, while some people will have nicknames or other variations of their first name that have emerged from interactions with intimates and would not be appropriate if used by anyone less familiar. Other terms explicitly encode specific family relationships (Auntie Audrey, Uncle Ron, Dad, Mum). Terms of endearment can signal informal relationships with high solidarity and are used by close friends, as with the examples, 'pal', 'love', 'duck', 'bab'. There is UK-based regional variation here with some of these examples: 'duck' is associated with the East Midlands, 'love' is associated with Yorkshire and 'bab' with Birmingham. These are common terms of endearment used by speakers in these local cultural settings and there are many more, depending on geographical location. As well as being used between friends and intimates, these regional terms of endearment can also be used as politeness markers between strangers of any gender as greetings in public settings, including service encounters in shops or on public transport between drivers and passengers.

Address terms with regional variation work effectively as politeness devices in British English to indicate shared group norms and in-group solidarity with strangers who are from the same geographical area; however, these may be unintelligible and confusing – and can thus be interpreted as impolite – to those from other regions and countries who do not share the same local cultural knowledge.

63

Also at the informal end of the scale are familiarisers, terms of address which mark out familiar relationships between speakers, such as 'mate', 'cuz' (cousin), 'bro', 'sis'. Familiarisers can play important roles in team building, solidarity and strengthening social bonds in different groups. Speakers use familiarisers to enhance solidarity and bring a clear sense of in-group identity and cohesiveness within teams, including friendship groups and sports teams.

If we think now in more detail about terms of address at the high formality, high-status end of the scale, it is useful to look at an example of honorifics from the East Asian languages of Japanese, Korean, Vietnamese and Chinese, through the term *sensei*. *Sensei* translates as the one who came before and is used in these cultures to refer to teachers, along with any other high-status professionals, including doctors, police officers or lawyers, where someone has acquired mastery in something, including martial arts. It is used as a formal marker of status and its use is essential for students or subordinates to show deference, respect and honour to their superior, whether it be their teacher, boss, a professional superior or an instructor.

Since the end of the Second World War, martial arts have been successfully exported to countries all over the world. This has seen formal language practices, including the use of honorifics, also reaching other cultures. And so, regardless of which language students may speak, *sensei* is an essential term of address to use to address the most senior instructor(s) who holds the highest rank when training in many *dojos* (martial arts' training halls). Students are expected to use honorifics to show respect and courtesy when training, to ensure that the right amount of deference and honour is shown. Adopting these terms of address is part of a very long history and tradition. As someone who is a practitioner of aikido martial arts, I have first-hand experience of this term of address. Use of the honorific *sensei* for my teachers is an essential part of our sporting community's politeness norms to show respect and deference and to avoid impoliteness and causing offence.

As one of the most internationally renowned and respected martial artists in the world, Joe Thambu Shihan[62] points out, in an interview for this book, a *sensei* must not break etiquette by demanding the title, nor should they ever refer to themselves as *sensei* in any form of communication, spoken or written; instead, the naming should come from the student, and their strong desire to give status and respect to their instructor, signalling formality, and emphasising their different positions in status and social distance. When students do this, it demonstrates respect, trust and adherence with politeness.

Many students will choose to refer to their *sensei* by this title not just when training in their martial art, but in every other context when they are together, regardless of how informal the setting may be. This continuity of naming shows the same level of respect, deference and status difference between them and their instructor, even if they are in public settings such as pubs or restaurants or in the private setting of each other's homes, and even if there are others present who know nothing about martial arts' politeness rules.

Any sense of potential embarrassment is overridden by a desire to be consistently respectful. In such cases, terms of address go way beyond the training hall to encompass all aspects of a student's relationship with their instructor. This illustrates how shared principles around terms of address can signal strong membership of a group that is firmly bound by adherence to traditional etiquette. It is a way of signalling belonging to an historical tradition and practice that is held in high esteem by its participants, built on respect, deference and enhancing the status differences between students and head instructor(s).

If any students fail to do this when it is expected, then important *dojo* etiquette will have been broken. And whilst such individuals can still participate in martial arts, in traditional *dojos* they will not be able to gain status as an authentic martial artist if they do not adhere to honorifics. As Thambu Sensei[63] points out:

'People who call me Joe on the mats, off the mats, I will still teach them because I've taken their money and I am honour-bound and duty-bound to teach them, but the people who do show the proper respect, and I'm not talking about false etiquette, but etiquette from the heart, these people tend to learn and exemplify *budo* [the martial way, leading to harmony] more. You can learn all the techniques well but you'll never be a *budoka* [an authentic martial arts practitioner] unless you understand etiquette.'[64]

It is also common practice for senior instructors to refer to one another as 'Sensei' as a way to show mutual respect. Thambu Sensei further points out that calling an instructor Sensei then signals an obligation from the Sensei not only to teach but also to protect and take care of the student who has chosen to give them this respect. The Sensei needs to honour the role of responsibility that they have been given by their students:

'Sensei also means someone that's going to protect you. To protect you 360. Protect you from other people you train with, protect you from teachers who might be abusive, protect you in hierarchical situations. It is then you have to speak up. And if you don't, you're not worthy of the title. That to me is etiquette. You earn the right to be called Sensei, and you have to exercise that right.'[65]

The etiquette therefore goes both ways, initially from the student choosing to give the instructor respect and deference by using the title, and then from the Sensei back to their students to protect them as part of their way of being.

Martial arts present an excellent example for considering broader issues of politeness and etiquette rules and breaches, and we'll come back to this topic and *budo* later in the book when we consider sport in more detail (see chapter six).

To wrap up our thinking around the roles that politeness scales play in determining terms of address and to bring these ideas together, consider an average week in your life, including your time at home, with family and friends, at work and in public, including sports groups, or any other organisations or settings where you spend time. Think of the wide variety of terms of address that you experience and those that you choose to use for others in conversations, in writing and in online communication. What do these terms tell you about the power relationships that exist between you and your fellow communicators, based on the politeness scales of formality, intimacy and status? How do your terms of address change for the same person as you enter different settings or groups? What are your own preferences for naming and why? What external factors (including changes in setting, or audience), trigger any changes that you make in how you address others? How are these preferences linked to the identities, beliefs and cultural norms of the speakers, including yours, the setting and the audience?

Changing attitudes to terms of address

Attitudes towards address terms change over time. As sociolinguist Janet Holmes[66] points out, in Western cultures, politeness norms started to shift during the second half of the twentieth century and nowadays, in many contexts, solidarity is given greater weight than status. So, for example, in New Zealand workplaces, where Holmes and her teams have conducted research, secretaries now tend to address their bosses more informally, by their first name only (and not a formal title) in everyday workplace conversations, if they have worked with them over a period of time; Holmes observes how civil servants use first names for senior policy makers if they work with them on a regular basis, and factory floor workers also address their regular supervisors by their first name. These shifting patterns are observable across Western cultures. However, in Eastern societies, in cultures including Japan, Korea and Indonesia, the overriding need to clearly emphasise status differences with terms of address to maintain politeness norms remains.

Language change for terms of address can also depend on the medium of communication. Whilst there have been observable transitions in conversation, with official written letters or documents, formal titles are still expected to show politeness, respect and formality, with someone's title followed by their last name still used as standard openers to begin a formal letter (Dear Dr Smith, Dear Ms McLeod). With social media, there is much more freedom and creativity. Terms of address are often included in one's profile. Some may directly correlate with someone's real-life first names and last names, others may be completely fictional and unrelated to their legal, formal name. The anonymity that is afforded by adopting a username/handle that bears no relation to one's official name can be powerful. On the positive side, it can be quite liberating as it frees up one's identity from the constraints and assumptions that people make based on gender, age, race, ethnicity, etc. during face-to-face communication. On the negative side, it can lead to impolite behaviour through a lack of accountability for one's actions. In the worst cases, anonymity can lead to people engaging in highly abusive and illegal behaviour because they think that their names and identities cannot be traced.

Politeness rules can also change in response to transitions in political thinking and awareness of changing cultural attitudes towards social identities, such as gender. For example, in the

UK state school system, it is generally deemed polite to call male teachers 'sir' and female teachers 'miss'. More recently, in response to movements towards bringing greater awareness of gender equality into schools, some schools have started changing their politeness rules and policies so that all teachers are instead addressed by their first names to get around female teachers being referred to by the inferior title 'miss', which has significantly less social prestige and status attached to it than 'sir', the term used to denote someone who has been given a knighthood. For example, in 2023, British newspaper the *Guardian*[67] reported on a school in London that had dropped these terms of address in order to fight 'cultural misogyny', with teachers to be referred to as Mr or Ms plus their surname instead. The sixth form had contemplated using *'sensei'* or 'professor' instead, but in the end decided to go with an honorific plus the teacher's last name to attempt to eradicate the use of sir and miss.

The headteacher originally tried to make the same change almost a decade earlier, in 2014, but on this occasion, teachers could not make it stick. The change has now been implemented. The need to address outdated naming practices has grown significantly in education and other professions in recent years. The BBC[68] reports that historically, the use of 'sir' began in private boarding schools. It then spread to grammar schools and eventually into secondary state schools. It also reports that in some state schools first names are now used, and this is standard practice in schools in many countries including Sweden. This approach also gets around gender binaries, though for many (and presumably Mr Handscombe) this could be seen as too informal and disrespectful. The use of 'miss' stemmed from the fact that historically, if women married, they were not allowed to stay on as teachers (until the Education Act in 1944 was passed) as it was seen as being incompatible with attending to their wifely duties. Bringing things back up to date, the crucial point here is egalitarian use of terms of address, so that one group of teachers is not being accorded more deference and social status than another on the grounds of gender and historical politeness stereotypes.

In other contexts, if there is any uncertainty about which term of address to use in English, then speakers are lucky enough to have a get-out clause as English allows us to avoid using an address term altogether without breaking any politeness rules. For example, speakers can say 'good afternoon' to each other without any address term and it will still be viewed as formal and polite. In many other languages, this luxury is not available – in Spanish this would need to be accompanied by either an honorific – 'Buenos tardes, señor' – or by also adding in a proper name, as in 'Buenos tardes, Señor Emery'.

Indeed, in Spanish, French and many other languages other than English, including Italian, German, Greek and Russian, politeness is also encoded in address terms through formal and informal versions of the pronoun 'you', known as the *tu/vous* system, (based on the French pronouns). Whilst English used to have this pronoun distinction in the form of thou/you, it died out. There are also observable changes here in more traditional attitudes to terms of address. Historically, languages that have these pronoun systems encode the power and formality between speakers within the grammar of the language. Speakers need to take great care to make sure that they get the pronoun correct to avoid causing offence and impoliteness. Originally, the distinction was to show the difference between singular (*tu*) and plural (*vous*), but their meanings became more complex as the terms were loaded with social value and meaning: *vous* became used by higher classes as a form of respect, whereas mutual use of *tu* showed solidarity amongst lower-class speakers.

Asymmetrical use of the terms then developed to emphasise a difference in power relationships: those in positions of power addressed powerless speakers with *tu* but received *vous*. These distinctions have been used historically to signal unequal power differences in relationships, such as those between a parent and child, a boss and employee, etc. However, asymmetrical *tu/vous* use has been declining in more recent years. To maintain formality and politeness, mutual *vous* can be used, as is frequent between strangers, though mutual *tu* is now more common, as language norms in Western cultures have become more informal. It is now not uncommon for mutual *tu* to be found in workplaces, particularly those with flatter power structures.

Through the *tu/vous* system, communicators need to make deliberate choices about the level of formality that they perceive to exist between them and their fellow communicators. You cannot use the English language strategy of avoiding using a name or pronoun in languages that maintain the *tu/vous* distinction, so the pressure is on to make the most appropriate choice and not read the relationship incorrectly. Getting it wrong by being too formal or too informal can be deemed very impolite and even cause offence.

Summary

In this chapter, we have considered the cultural and social rules behind how we name each other, the legal ways our names can be changed and what this means in terms of politeness, status and how our identities can alter over time. When we name others, our choices are influenced by a number of politeness rules, which are part of ever-evolving culture. This can include state intervention in language planning to change politeness and naming culture very rapidly, as was the case in Turkey in the 1930s, or it can be in response to particular cultural trends. Naming practices differ all over the world and if people stray outside the boundaries of acceptable naming in any form, be it proper names, nicknames, terms of endearment, formal titles, pronouns, kinship terms or social and occupational names, then recipients may experience negative evaluation. If naming choices are deemed to be too inappropriate or demeaning, then the law can intervene and names can be denied official or formal status.

We encode large amounts of information about power, formality and status in naming, even though it is expressed through such a small part of our language use. When individual names are legally changed, often this is due to social expectations or a personal desire to leave one's old identity behind and to move on to inhabit a new one. Nicknames and terms of endearment are critical to our interpersonal relationships and will be common with friends, family members and others with whom we are intimate. All this is part of an incredibly important first step in remaining polite to those with whom we communicate.

We will now move beyond smaller chunks of politeness in language to look at politeness in conversations in our homes and more backstage settings with families and friendship groups. This begins with a consideration of how, where and when we first begin to learn politeness as very young children within our families.

4

Politeness with Family and Friends

The family unit, however big or small it happens to be, plays a fundamental role in how politeness is initially learnt by children in all cultures. Children are taught to use words, phrases and gestures that convey politeness long before they can even begin to understand the meaning behind them. This is unlike the ways that children acquire other areas of language, such as learning individual words for objects that are physically in front of them (for example, banana, spoon, light, door). English-speaking two-year-olds will frequently produce 'please' because they are consistently told to do so, but at this age, they do not know what it means. Because politeness is so deeply ingrained in all of our communication to show that we take into account the feelings of others, parents and caregivers start teaching children politeness skills as soon as they are old enough to be able to articulate such terms.

One of the prime ways that caregivers teach politeness is by consistently commanding that children speak certain words and phrases as part of their everyday routines at home, and then eventually children will start to do this by themselves. Consider the very common instructions that caregivers give their children to speak so that they can express politeness, including greetings and partings: 'say hi!', 'say bye bye!', often accompanied by waving a hand. Or commanding them to use politeness markers when asking or receiving something: 'say please!', 'don't forget to say thank you!' or 'say excuse me!', if a social faux pas is committed. Learning how to behave politely begins with learning these types of routinised speech from caregivers when children are between two and three years old. This initial training provides a foundation for acquiring more sophisticated forms of politeness in conversations as children get older and continue their language socialisation journey.

In a study which looked at how children are taught to ask questions within their families, Haruko Cook and Matthew Burdelski[69] examined English-speaking households in North America and Japanese-speaking households in Japan. They found that parents in both locations consistently teach their children to say 'please' to family members and others as a politeness marker when asking questions. English-speaking parents used 'please' when making requests of their child to model this behaviour and Japanese parents similarly talked to their children using 'X-te kudasai' ('please do X'). They also taught children to use please when they are making requests to adults or to their peers and friends, as in 'doozo, suwatte kudasai tte', ('Say, "please sit down"').

Dinner-table conversations act like a microcosm for family manners, and so some linguists have focused on the dinner table as a productive social space to investigate politeness in everyday family settings. In a study from the US, Jean Gleason[70] and her colleagues observed eight middle-class families with children aged three to four during mealtimes in their homes in Boston. They found that the children were consistently asked by their parents to rephrase their utterances in polite ways during dinner-table conversations. Favoured parental phrases included giving direct orders, such as 'what's the magic word?', or 'say please!',[71] with the child's request for more food or drink only being fulfilled if they articulated the desired word or phrase. At this young age, although children do not understand the social requirements of the dinner-table context or the meaning behind these utterances, they learn these polite phrases as complete units and they use them to get what they want. The research team reported children learning both the word order and the correct timing of the politeness routine, as in the example 'may I be excused',[72] to get the reward of being able to leave the table.

Gleason and colleagues also observed how some adults will insist that children rephrase their original speech, and they will refuse to comply with their child's request until they do so. In one example, a child is taught to completely reformulate her original pleading for some more milk to a more complex, polite utterance. She first said: 'Mommy, I want more milk.' This was rejected by her mother as impolite, and her mother kept saying 'no' until the child repeated the exact words in the order that her mother had told her to speak them: 'Please, may I have more milk?'[73] When the child eventually said this, she was then rewarded by being given the milk. By engaging in this process with her mum, the child learnt a more polite way of getting what she wanted. The takeaway message for the child then is that using 'please may I have' is *the* version that worked. The vast majority of children's activities are based around routines and so, by learning the politeness phrases that work in these everyday situations, children will learn politeness phrases as complete units, which plays a productive role in more complex language acquisition.

Very similar evidence is found across cultures in many different geographical locations. For example, Elizabeth Bates[74] found that, in a study of Italian-speaking children aged two and a half to four years old, those as young as three used more indirectness, including hints, when they were told to ask a puppet for sweets in a really nice way. She concluded that the connection between indirectness and politeness is present from as early as three years old, even though, at this age, children still do not understand what politeness means or why it is important.

In a study of older children in Jordan based on the use of politeness and requests in Arabic, Linda Al-Abbas[75] observed politeness in the speech patterns of eighty children, forty of whom were aged six and the other forty were aged ten. Al-Abbas found that, by the time they had reached the age of six, children were able to understand politeness, but the connection between polite expressions and requests was still not clearly understood. However, by the time children were ten, they were able to use politeness far more accurately when making requests. She observed that indirect requests and the use of explicit politeness markers without any prompting, such as 'please', became frequent between the ages of six and ten years old.

Sometimes, caregivers can communicate messages to other adults whilst they are simultaneously teaching their children about politeness. Often these messages may be unfavourable, so adults may choose to use a child as the addressee as a form of indirectness. A good example of this from Cook and Burdelski[76] is taken from Japan and a mother and daughter's visit to the house of paternal grandparents. Here, the mother told her two-year-old daughter exactly what to say to her grandmother: 'Say to granny, "Please look at your newspaper over there."' Although the child did not comply with this request – in fact, she did not even attempt to say it – this did not matter because the request had already been indirectly delivered to the child's grandma, who had moved from where she was originally sitting. This is a creative way of politely gaining complicity from adults in situations where a request may well be unfavourable. It simultaneously teaches and models politeness norms and the use of 'please' to children.

Cook[77] found that socialisation practices around appropriate dinner-table talk can also apply to young adults when learning a different language. In a study of politeness and Japanese families hosting US college students (aged seventeen and eighteen), she found that Japanese mothers encouraged these older exchange students to align themselves with assessments that the mothers themselves made about the food that they were eating. The mothers would use *desho* to do this – in Japanese, *desho* works like a question tag, designed to get agreement from the speaker. In this instance, *desho* was used to encourage a form of positive politeness about the food from the visiting student: *'This is delicious, desho?'* Cook argues that this illustrates the host mothers socialising US students into how to engage in politeness norms when having dinner in Japan.

Furthermore, in another of Cook and Burdelski's[78] projects, they demonstrated how a Japanese father used hints and a series of indirect utterances to help his son Ken understand politeness and empathy with one of Ken's friends, Ami.[79] This talk took place in a playground in Japan outside Ken's home. Ken was playing with Ami's ball. Ami said, *'Ami-Chan kaeru Wa'* ['Ami-chan is going home].' Ken's dad used a combination of touch (moving Ken in Ami's direction) and indirectness to help Ken understand that Ami was using an indirect request to him to get her ball back. He started with a hint – *'Ken-chan Ami-chan no daro?'* ['Ken-chan it's Ami's, right?'] – to help Ken understand that Ami was asking a question and not just making a statement that she was going home. When Ken still did not start to give the ball back, his dad became more direct: *'hai Ken chan oide kaeshite'* ['Okay, Ken-chan, come return it].' This directness worked and Ken returned Ami's ball. Ken's dad uses the diminutive form of Ken's name (Ken-chan) as a term of endearment throughout. This is also the naming strategy used by Ami to self-refer (Ami-chan), which helps to keep the encounter friendly and harmonious.

A clear power imbalance can be seen in all of these conversations through the language that is used, based on age, family status and culture. Adults have substantial power over children in their care and they can therefore issue direct orders and demands without breaking any politeness norms or rules themselves. Adults can also use 'please' to attempt to gain compliance.

Part of the reason for doing this is also to model polite behaviour. In every family, there will be hierarchies of power that are visible along age, gender and cultural lines, and this will affect the different politeness strategies that are used.

Primary caregivers feel a significant amount of social pressure to bring up a polite child. Impolite children are heavily stigmatised across cultures, which emphasises just how important it is to show that you are taking other people's feelings into account, even for society's youngest members, who don't yet understand what politeness means. Researchers have found that this pressure for primary caregivers is felt regardless of social class background – politeness norms are incredibly powerful and come with a great deal of cultural and social value, which people from all class backgrounds can recognise.

The fact that there is so much consistent evidence in terms of how politeness is taught and acquired by children at the same ages across different languages and cultures tells us how important a priority learning politeness is to human communication, wherever children are growing up. Because it provides such an important foundation to paying attention to others, those responsible for teaching the next generation prioritise politeness as a fundamental part of language learning as soon as children are cognitively developed enough to cope with articulating the words – even if the meaning and social significance of politeness comes later. Of course, different cultures, communities and groups all have different rules that children will learn as they get older and become more sophisticated language learners and users. This variation shows us how different groups will have different politeness priorities, depending on how politeness has developed historically. As children get older, they become more specialised in learning politeness norms in conversations, in writing and in digital communication, where text and images are often creatively combined.

A good deal of the work that we do with children throughout

the socialisation process in terms of teaching them politeness is subconscious. Regardless of whether you have children, consider what your own expectations are for children's behaviours, particularly in different public spaces. How does this differ based on your perception of the child's age? If you have ever been a caregiver to a child, then it is likely that you will be able to recall experiences of when things may have gone well according to societal politeness norms and expectations, and when things really have not gone to plan at all.

If even very young children do not participate in politeness routines when they are instructed and/or cajoled into doing so, parents and caregivers will often experience a strong sense of social stigma and negative judgement from others. I can still clearly remember the acute feelings of embarrassment caused by my then two-year-old daughter who refused to greet the cook at her nursery every morning, despite what felt like a million prompts from me to do so ('say hello!') in response to the cook's happy chimes of 'hello, lovey!' Stony silence was my daughter's response. This seemed to be accompanied by a number of similar-aged children clearly saying hello and waving as a paralinguistic part of their perfect, polite greeting as they skipped on by the nursery kitchen. My daughter has no memory of this and thinks it is hilarious that I still remember the feelings of embarrassment so strongly. But the sense that a social faux pas was continually being committed, as well as the feeling that I was a terrible parent because of this, was enduring.

I initially felt compelled to apologise to the cook daily, including an explanation of why my daughter hadn't said hello. However, before too long, I ended up clutching at straws after going through the obvious, 'Sorry, she's a bit tired this morning', 'Sorry, I don't think she heard you', 'Sorry, she's teething' as a set of increasingly pathetic excuses. It is precisely the strength of the social imperative to have polite children that makes parents and caregivers constantly ask their children to comply with

81

politeness norms before the children can comprehend what politeness means. As greetings are part of paired speech that demand a response, any silence will be noticed and it will feel like a snub due to our social expectations that a greeting needs to be followed by a greeting. Silences can be painful to endure and the cook's daily looks of disappointment made me feel like we were consistently hurting her feelings.

As abiding by politeness rules is so deeply ingrained in all of us, as a clear signal of living in a civilised society, negative judgements about children's lack of politeness can be made by total strangers in public, through to people who are well known to us in backstage settings, including in the home. In reality, children will acquire politeness at slightly different rates, as with any other form of language development. However, the social pressure on children to consistently perform politeness and on their caregivers to constantly teach politeness as soon as it is possible is very strong.

Older children acquiring politeness

With older children (aged ten and over), parents and caregivers will still engage in politeness monitoring. The unequal power relationships between children and adults are still present, although children will now have acquired more conversational power for themselves. Children are old enough to understand what politeness is and why it is important, and so the broader cultural rules of politeness can be learnt.

Older children become more fully-fledged participants in many family contexts, partly because they are asked questions that invite them to take the floor and speak – such as 'How was your day?', 'How was school?', 'How was football practice?' – though this will only work harmoniously if children's responses to such questions are seen to be appropriate and of sufficient length. Replying to the question 'What did you do at school today?' minimally, with uncooperative one-word answers such as 'stuff' or 'nothing' is clearly not abiding by politeness norms.

It is a caregiver's role to intervene if the politeness behaviour or the social etiquette of their children needs correcting. One place where this happens, where there are social rituals, including politeness conventions and strict social etiquette rules, is once more at the dinner table. Common dinner-table etiquette reprimands, which are likely familiar to all of us, include 'Don't speak with your mouth full!', 'No phones/electronics at the table!', 'Don't play with your food!' or similar. These commands may often be accompanied by politeness markers such as 'please', depending on cultural practices and whether the adult wishes to mitigate the force of the command to the offending child somewhat by simultaneously modelling politeness markers in their own speech.

Very similar reprimands will be used, both at the dinner table and in wider family conversations, to teach children about turn-taking norms specific to their culture. As adults, caregivers can jump into a conversation at any point without the need to apologise. They also do not have to use indirectness to criticise, correct or reprimand. This means that family dinner-time conversations are never neutral or equal. Conversations can move very quickly from relaxing, enjoyable talk that interests family members to adults disrupting and interrupting the conversational flow, with corrections to behaviour and commands and requests for children to change their language. For example, sociolinguist Shoshana Blum-Kulka[80] analysed different types of talk at family dinner tables, including those with teenage children in the US and Israel. She cites a father who reprimands his son for interrupting him: 'I'm talking . . . yeah, so you don't interrupt, okay?'[81] Similar utterances will be frequently used at dinner tables and in wider family conversations to teach children about turn-taking norms. In many cultures, it is deemed impolite for children to interrupt adults, or their siblings for that matter. Additional unwritten politeness rules can include letting the person who is speaking finish first, to show respect. This teaches children how turn-taking rules relate to different amounts of power that people have in conversation, which governs how much politeness one should use.

As part of gaining more conversational power as they get older, Blum-Kulka points out that children become able to start conversational topics themselves. Though again, the topics they bring up must be seen as culturally appropriate and permitted by the adults present. Judgements made around topic suitability are governed by strict politeness norms and etiquette codes within societies. As with any setting, it is important to think carefully about audience and which topics may be appropriate for some family members but not for others. If grandparents or elderly relatives are present, then the topics need to take their presence into account. Part of the test of politeness norms is to avoid topics that anyone might find uncomfortable, offensive or inappropriate so that family harmony is maintained. If topic violation takes place, then caregivers may well step in with an immediate topic shift and reprimand for crossing a politeness boundary. It is a good idea to keep topics neutral and uncontroversial, particularly if there are multi-generations present. Topics that are best avoided would be those that divide people and could cause conflict or offence, so depending upon who is present, topics such as politics, religion and finances should be given a wide berth.

Blum-Kulka argues that a good deal of dinner-table conversation where interpersonal relationships are harmonious work to enhance social bonds and closeness between family members. Telling stories, using humour and engaging in gossip about others who are not present are very common politeness strategies to use at family dinner times to enhance intimacy and trust. However, there is also a risk that speakers may become too emotionally involved in conversations and, if this happens, then enjoyment and social bonding may stop. Blum-Kulka draws attention to when children gossip about teachers at school, arguing that often children expect to be censored by their parents for complaining about their teachers, as they know that bringing up such a controversial topic is risky. Blum-Kulka illustrates how some parents are critical of teachers and show solidarity with their children. Others agree with the teacher and so uphold the moral order of the schooling system. Or parents may avoid aligning with the teacher or their child as a more neutral option.

A potentially safer topic for dinner-table gossip is talking about famous people in public life, including sporting figures, television personalities or celebrities, who are not known to the family personally. Blum-Kulka argues that older children will often have a much broader knowledge base than parents on these topics, which again enables them to accrue conversational power for themselves as they will have greater freedom of expression, within politeness boundaries. As celebrities are at a social distance, this can often make topics less personal, thus decreasing the chances of arguments or disagreements – providing of course that the conversational topics remain appropriate for the cultural context.

Think for a moment about talk in your own family gatherings, past and present, where you have engaged in conversations about other people who are not around, such as fellow family members, friends, neighbours, people at school, teachers or work colleagues. What topics have been discussed? Have people been spoken about in a disparaging light, with 'not nice' things said about them? How does this help build solidarity with those who are present? Have there been any adverse consequences?

In summary, then, caregivers never really switch off in their role as educators at the dinner table or any other settings, and children generally understand that they may well be reprimanded in this setting for any inappropriate behaviour, particularly when

85

an etiquette breach or impoliteness takes place. Caregivers are consistently making value judgements about children's behaviour for socialisation purposes. Reprimands for politeness breaches may shift between different caregivers, depending upon the family's cultural practices, including how status and authority are distributed. By experiencing reprimands in family settings, children will ideally learn politeness norms in a safe, backstage space, and then hopefully take this knowledge with them into multiple frontstage settings, such as schools, community groups and, eventually, into workplaces.

Dinner-table talk is rife with information about politeness, etiquette and family relationships. If topics are appropriate, then social etiquette norms will be reinforced and conventional social power will be increased. In addition to topics being carefully regulated in dinner-table conversations in a close family setting to avoid politeness and etiquette breaches, formal dinner tables are occasions when social class and background are really put to the test for children and adults alike, adding in another layer of social etiquette that needs to be learnt: middle-class politeness and etiquette norms include specialised knowledge of table settings and the correct use of utensils demanded in formal settings, such as family weddings. There will also be expectations about how to dress, sit and place your body appropriately to display respect and decorum. For example, in some cultures, it is very rude to have elbows on the table. Where there are special types of cutlery for particular types of food, and where tables are set out with a number of different place settings, failure to know which cutlery to use first or which glass is your own can cause etiquette breaches. This can be the source of much anxiety and embarrassment for anyone who has not been taught these rules during socialisation. It is highly likely that value judgements will be made about those who breach etiquette in formal dinner-table settings, including whether they are found to lack manners, decorum and/or civility.

As linguist Sara Mills[82] points out, knowing how to use table utensils properly is a part of middle-class behavioural codes in the UK, expected to be taught in family settings. Not knowing these codes – including dress, demeanour and table etiquette for formal occasions – can work as powerful tools of social exclusion. This can potentially hold people back in their adult lives; for example, in their careers if they end up in workplaces where they are expected to know these norms, but they do not. As one example of this, in consultancy work that we have conducted, we have found evidence of people from lower socio-economic backgrounds avoiding workplace events, and so missing out on potentially valuable networking and career development opportunities, because they have been concerned about being embarrassed and humiliated for not displaying the right social etiquette. As Sara Mills[83] argues, through formal etiquette practices and guides, politeness becomes 'ensnared in ideological beliefs about the *best* way to behave'.

The 'best' way to behave then will be the way that is associated with those who have the most power in societies. The family plays a central role in influencing behaviours around these class-based etiquette practices, acting as a training ground for adult life. This can work to disadvantage anyone who has not been exposed to such social etiquette practices during socialisation, such as those from working-class or different cultural backgrounds – we will come back to this in the next chapter when thinking about the effects of a lack of access to social etiquette during socialisation as an adult in the workplace.

It is also worth pointing out that the valuable setting of the dinner table as a politeness learning platform presumes that all families will have dinner tables, chairs, cutlery and other equipment required, and will be able to use their dinner table in this way. This is a middle-class norm and other families may not eat in this way. Some families will regularly sit and eat in front of the TV; children and adults may eat at separate times or alone – for example, if parents work shifts – which limits the amount of conversational time and learning opportunities that can take place. In the research that we have drawn upon here, the data are all taken from conventional nuclear families that have two parents and children present. However, there are a wide variety of family types and sizes in the world, which will give children different opportunities to acquire politeness norms and engage in social bonding.

To summarise so far then, in this chapter, we have considered how, why and when children learn politeness, covering a range of issues, including the variety of language strategies that adults use to teach children politeness norms from a very early age in homes and public spaces, such as nurseries or playgrounds. We have seen how dinner tables, as ritualised social settings, are powerful learning spaces for younger and older children to acquire politeness norms, including manners, decorum and respect, and for families to build social bonds and enhance intimacy with each other. Norms that are learnt include suitable topics for conversation, how to eat and act appropriately at dinner tables, and what to do in situations where a social faux pas is committed. We will now change activities in the home and examine what happens when family and friends watch TV with each other.

Politeness when watching television

Another very common shared activity in the home in many countries is watching television. Consider first why and how you watch television with family members or friends. What social roles does watching television together fulfil? What kinds of things do you talk about whilst watching television programmes? What role does politeness play in all of this? We will examine the ways in which families and friends draw on a range of creative, positive politeness to build solidarity and enhance relationships when watching television together as a leisure activity.

Researcher Alla Tovares[84] made a series of audio recordings of families whilst they were watching TV to assess what type of talk takes place around this shared cultural practice. She demonstrated how families enhance bonds with each other by taking vocabulary and catchphrases from their favourite shows, along with the accents and dialects of key characters, and then performing or mimicking these amongst themselves as ways of creating humour, building solidarity and signalling a strong family group identity through creative language play. She argues that these repetitions of language styles from TV programmes can also be used to educate children in families, as well as showing that, as a family, you have a shared perspective on the world, which acts to reinforce social values.

Again, if you think for a moment about your own family's TV watching habits, you should be able to come up with examples of cases where you and/or other family members have used the content of TV programmes as a way to educate and show that you have shared perspectives, which all work to preserve social bonds. There may also be times where you disagree and do not share views, which is fine, providing that conflictual views are expressed with respect. Otherwise, impoliteness may ensue, and conflict can take place if family members feel like they are being unfairly singled out for their differing views.

In another example from Tovares' work, a mother (Clara) and her child (Jason) are watching cartoons on TV together. Jason is not feeling well and he is off school. Earlier in the week, they had been watching a TV advertisement which featured a woman borrowing someone else's toothbrush. Jason's dad Neil was also present at this earlier point. Jason's parents reacted very differently to the advert, which caused a disagreement between them. Neil thought it was funny whereas Clara thought it was gross, showed bad etiquette and, most importantly, was a health risk. The family then talked about the etiquette of sharing each other's toothbrushes, but Neil and Clara did not agree. Neil told Jason that he could use his mom or dad's toothbrush if he didn't have his own. Clara strongly disagreed with Neil's viewpoint and so said to Jason, as an indirect command, 'You never use someone else's toothbrush. It's icky.'[85]

Neil openly disagreed and threatened Clara's position of parenting authority: 'Yes, you can, you can do that' to which Clara replied, 'No, you CAN'T, you can catch Hepatitis C doing that.' Neil disagreed again, saying to Jason, 'Mine or Mommy's but no one else's.' Clara countered once more: 'No, you can't! I'll always make sure you have a toothbrush, buddy.' This level of impoliteness through disagreement with each other would arguably result in confusion at best for Jason, though his mum undermines his dad's views in the end and promises that she'll always have his own toothbrush for him.

Later on, during the same week, one of the characters in a cartoon that Clara and Jason were watching talks about the importance of not sharing a toothbrush due to spreading germs. This cartoon character evaluates sharing a toothbrush as 'disgusting'. This prompts Clara to bring up the toothbrush topic again with Jason: 'See, I told you, you don't use other people's toothbrushes.'[86] Clara's viewpoint has now been expressed on TV in a children's show, which her son Jason enjoys. Watching the cartoon together in a socially bonded space gives Clara a great opportunity to reinforce her earlier parenting message, allowing her to deliver her view calmly, with extra credibility, without the disruptive disagreement and arguing that was taking place when Jason's dad was also there.

The television programme *Gogglebox*, which originated in the UK, has made a highly successful franchise out of an idea that is not dissimilar to one that lay behind Tovares' linguistics research – this time with cameras instead of just audio and broadcast to a mass audience on national broadcasting channels.

Gogglebox operates as a fly-on-the-wall reality television show which captures the immediate reactions of family members and close friends who are in the living rooms of their own homes watching television programmes and spending time together.

In the UK version of the show, the families who take part are either couples, adult siblings, best friends or families with teenage children. The programme makers of *Gogglebox* argued that they sought to get normal, ordinary people as their cast. They deliberately avoided using people who were interested in fame or in becoming a celebrity. They wanted to find people with whom the general public would find a genuine social connection, so there would be a sense of solidarity and empathy between audience members and cast members, even though they were strangers and were never likely to meet face to face.

The central feature of *Gogglebox* is the way that family members and close friends talk when they watch TV; through this communication, we can see significant ways in which politeness features of solidarity, empathy and social connection are successfully built. Knowing they are being recorded will inevitably change the way that people act, but one of the reasons why *Gogglebox* is successful is that the footage nonetheless comes across as natural, informal conversation that is taking place pretty spontaneously. Although the cast are fully aware that they are being recorded, it is not scripted. It is edited, but it stays true to its overall aim of giving audiences a privileged insight into the private, backstage spaces of family members and close friends when they watch television together.

Linguist Mary Talbot[87] talks about a 'synthetic sisterhood' that the media can create, which bonds disparate groups of women and girls together by creating feelings of connection and sisterliness. Talbot uses the example of teenage magazines being a prime way in which readers feel as if they are being spoken to personally, by a supportive, sisterly voice, whereas in reality, a mass audience is being addressed by advertising producers. In

91

a way, *Gogglebox* does something similar regardless of gender, creating what I term a 'synthetic family'. Audience members feel strong affinities with cast members as they share in their humour and their emotional reactions to watching the same TV programmes. The shows watched by the cast range from dramas through to fly-on-the-wall documentaries about intimate and sensitive topics, such as childbirth and embarrassing health conditions, as well as the news. Producers of *Gogglebox* must turn around the show's production really quickly so that the audience watching at home will have seen the same programmes that the cast are watching only the week before; therefore, everything feels current and the emotional connections between the cast and the audience can appear stronger. And so, by watching the same TV programmes at almost the same time and sharing in their private insights, the watching audience can feel a very strong sense of affinity with cast members, like they are a part of the same family, as they have been given privileged access into very private settings. The camera angles and the way that *Gogglebox* is filmed makes it feel like the viewer is in the same living room space as the cast members and so, I would argue, this adds to the feeling of being included as a synthetic family member or friend.

It is clearly a winning formula as it has gained huge popularity as a TV franchise. *Gogglebox* in the UK has been running now for twenty-two series and it has been broadcast in over twenty-five countries, including Australia, Canada, Finland, Poland, Russia and the US. The original *Gogglebox* producer Farah Golant[88] acknowledged that the formula for the show is not really about people watching TV – it is instead about 'people's lives, their relationships, their living rooms and the ways children and parents talk about TV . . . that's quite priceless. It captures a cultural response to something that's happening in the world.'

Usually, we only have our experiences of life in our own homes to draw on, but *Gogglebox* gives us access to acts which are usually deemed to be impolite or even taboo if others are present, which creates humour and entertainment precisely because they are socially inappropriate – such as social faux pas, including passing wind, burping, itching and scratching, accidentally tipping food on oneself or each other, having tea kicked in your face by a pet dog or accidentally flicking off a shoe, only to see it land in a family member's takeaway food. Some of the most humorous parts aren't when the cast members are watching the TV – for example, in the UK version, during the Covid-19 pandemic, cast member Jenny covered her hands in her best friend Lee's sexual lubricant thinking it was antibacterial hand sanitiser and the two of them strengthened their social bond by engaging in a lengthy period of humour about this accident.

The unique and privileged insight that *Gogglebox* allows into those private, backstage areas of other people's lives and worlds that are usually off limits to us is a big part of its success. Similar to what we saw in chapter two when thinking about impoliteness as a form of TV entertainment, we can watch the politeness and impoliteness practices between family members and friends play out in a way that is much safer and far more relaxing for the viewer because we are emotionally distant from what's taking place. And despite feelings of empathy and shared perspectives on the world, there is still a safe social distance, as uncomfortable moments are not happening to us, but we can join in and take part in the humour.

And so, watching programmes like *Gogglebox* can tell us a great deal about politeness and TV in our own families. Who gets the final decision about what to watch and how these decisions are made reveals much about power and politeness in families, as does who has control over the remote control. Watching TV together as a leisure activity can create safe backstage spaces where reactions to world events and emotive subjects such as topics from the news can be worked through, discussed and rationalised in private. In many households, watching TV provides a time for people to physically relax in close proximity to each other, which may often also include pets sitting or lying with us while we watch TV. This proximity often involves positively polite activities where each other's wants and desires are taken into account, which can include sharing snacks and food. If our families are socially close, like the families featured on *Gogglebox*, then watching TV can be an activity that strengthens emotional connections, gained from sharing the same experiences. It can also involve social bonding by talking not just about the TV programmes, but also about the physical environment where TV watching is taking place. Family members may ask others to co-operate and help them by passing them food and drinks or getting things for them from other rooms in the house. Overall, a sense of social bonding and learning can take place in strong family units who enjoy each other's company.

Family pets and politeness

I now want us to move on to something slightly different in our consideration of politeness in families by focusing on pets. Humans have domesticated animals and integrated them as family companions and part of their households for thousands of years. Pets can be a source of great comfort, joy and companionship for many, and given how prevalent politeness is in the routines of our everyday lives, owners will treat their pets as interactional partners in different politeness routines as part of their inclusion in the family.

Pets are very often included in family conversations, despite them being unable to use words or speech. Most dog and cat owners regularly talk to their pets. They will likely give orders ('Get down from there!', or just 'Down!' or 'No!'), as well as expressing praise and affection towards them ('Who's a good

94

boy!' or 'Good dog!'). This can become like a monologue, as in the following example of my daughter talking to her pet cat: 'Oh hello little baby bum bum! You're so cute and fluffy. Who's cute and fluffy? You are, aren't you? [Stroking the cat] Yes you are. I love you.' Such talk, whether in the form of greetings, terms of endearment or praise, are most often delivered using baby talk or at a much higher pitch than 'normal' talk.

Importantly for us, though, pets can play key roles as vehicles for the delivery of polite and impolite messages in family talk. One of the most fascinating parts of analysing politeness involving pets is when owners communicate messages to other human beings who are present through their animals. US linguist Deborah Tannen[89] has studied how people communicate with their family dogs and what happens in pet interactions when it is other humans who are the real targets of talk. Tannen examined how pet owners talk to other family members by ventriloquising their pets, with owners putting on an assumed 'dog' or 'cat' voice. The owners pretend to be the voice of the pet to fully include them in conversation.

In one of Tannen's examples, the mother of a young child adopted the voices of both family dogs to tell her child off and to indirectly criticise his behaviour when he failed to clean up his toys. The dogs supposedly said, 'We're naughty, but we're not as naughty as Jason; he's the naughtiest!'[90] Jason's mum used a baby voice register to deliver her dog voice criticism to her son. The high-pitched tone and the fantasy dog voice minimised the threat, allowing her to successfully deliver her criticism indirectly as a form of humorous teasing. This is less confrontational for her son and had the advantage of being funny, and so would be more likely to be more memorable to him. It is a strategy that she adopted to try and change her son's behaviour, without being too direct or threatening in her parenting style.

In the following example taken from one of my friendship groups, a couple, Sam and Chris, are talking and their dog starts

95

whining in the other room. Chris asks Sam, 'What do you think he's whining about?' Sam replies, 'He's saying, "I'm hungry. Feed me now!"' Owners may interpret their pet's vocalisations and then make them into a feature of their conversation by using reported speech to project what they think the dog is trying to say. Again, the owner is ventriloquising the pet, with Sam pretending that he has the powers of dog translation.

Coming back to Tannen's work, she gave a further example of a married couple, Nora and Greg, and their dog. Nora had forgotten to tell Greg that she had already taken the dog out for a walk. Greg left work early so that he could walk the dog and he was not best pleased. However, he did not directly complain to Nora, but instead used their dog to indirectly register his complaint to her. He turns to the dog and says, 'Well, why didn't YOU tell us?' By speaking to their dog as if he is a fully-fledged human, Greg found a creative way of conveying a potentially impolite message to another family member via the indirect route offered through the family's pet. He also invoked humour, a mitigation strategy which worked as a way of minimising the damage to Nora's sense of self-worth by taking the sting out of Greg's complaint.

In summary, pet owners project politeness on to their pets to include them as part of their family's communication and culture, which works to increase the amount of emotional connection between them and their pets. Some domestic animals, especially dogs, can be trained by humans to engage in acts such as holding out a paw as a greeting, akin to a human handshake, which further integrates them into politeness rituals for family and friends, as they can physically partake in such politeness rituals by mimicking human paralinguistic behaviours. The ways in which dogs can be taught to beg, sit, etc. are akin in a way to humans learning to abide by politeness norms as they demonstrate an ability to control behaviour and perform rituals to get requests fulfilled. Pet owners can gain a great sense of pride and social kudos in some circles if their pet is seen to be intelligent and trainable in these skills. It is often not too dissimilar to what we have described earlier in this chapter, when young children display politeness in their speech and behaviour in public settings to the gratification of adults around them, even though they don't understand the behaviour they are performing.

Politeness in friendship groups

We will now move on to analyse the different politeness techniques that people use in settings with their friends to assess the art of friendship. Linguist Jennifer Coates[91] has investigated close-knit groups of friends in settings in the UK to see how they use backstage talk to work through difficult things that have happened to them when they are in public in frontstage settings.

Coates[92] introduces us to the friendship of Ann and Jude. Ann has told Jude that she has had a bad day at her job in a shop. Jude invites her to explain why. Ann responds, 'I got all the bloody snotty customers, stupid people,' issuing two insults and an expletive to give her evaluation of what happened. She then develops her story, explaining that one customer waited for her to wrap up six glasses before she said, 'Can you take the price off the bottom of them?' Ann evaluates her as a 'stupid cow' and tells Jude the actual, polite language that she had said to the customer: 'Yes, certainly, madam,' which humorously contrasts to her backstage 'stupid cow' evaluation.

This example provides a great illustration of how, when we are frontstage, we are performing politeness to fulfil specific roles, and our genuine feelings and reactions will often not be displayed. However, when we are with trusted close friends or family backstage, we can talk through what has happened to us, particularly if we have been offended, annoyed or upset by something someone has said or done to us, and which we believe is out of line with our social entitlements. It is in these contexts where we do important identity processing, to work through the differences between how we perform frontstage and how we can then consolidate this behaviour with how we *really* feel behind closed doors. In the backstage setting with Ann and Jude, Ann can be as rude as she likes about the difficult customer – it is a safe environment in which to deride the customer's behaviour towards her as her only audience member is her trusted friend and the customer is no longer anywhere in earshot.

Ann's insulting evaluations contradict the 'super-polite' persona that she has used frontstage, in public. And so in her backstage performance, Ann works through her pent-up anger and frustration collaboratively with Jude. Jude helps her by providing empathy, reassurance and positive affirmation. Coates describes some of the talk in these friendship sessions as acting like a form of therapy. When we share difficult feelings or emotions, such as in this case, solidarity and social bonds can grow and our friendship groups can work to make us feel better (providing that our friends are supportive and kind, and that we feel our wants have been met).

Coates gives another example from a different group of women who negatively evaluate other people's children. This friendship group consists of Bea and three of her closest friends, who have known each other for many years. Bea is talking about an ex-friend of hers who has moved to New York, who is constantly telling her how wonderful her son is. Bea's ex-friend expresses this by continually calling him her 'little star', which really annoys Bea. Bea is sharing a story of when she was visiting in New York and the boy, who was aged seven or eight at the time, offered to make her a cup of coffee, which received the 'little star' evaluation from his mother. Bea says: 'He's so perfect that you just want to jump up and down on him and see if he'll squish, you know, and I'm so hoping that something marvellous will happen and he'll run away from home.'[93]

98

Here, Bea expresses an impolite fantasy sequence of how she'd like to 'squish' the boy because he's far too perfect, followed by her hope that, in future, he'll stop being a little star and become rebellious instead. Bea draws on sarcasm as a form of dark humour, describing the imagined future event of the child running away from home as something she would view very favourably, as 'something marvellous'. Bea's views are not hedged. Bea is reacting negatively here to the bragging that her ex-friend has engaged in; she responds with expressions of impoliteness, constructing an impolite fantasy, with what I would describe as almost cartoon-like, pretend violence towards the boy, through her use of the onomatopoeic 'squish'.

Similarly, in another conversation with a different friendship group, close friends Liz, Anna and Sue are talking about how much they dislike some children – they support each other by building the topic together and simultaneously laughing at the impolite, taboo nature of what they are saying. Sue declares, 'I still quite often don't like children,' and Liz then goes on to say, 'I think you particularly dislike your own.'[94] These expressions of dislike towards children, particularly one's own offspring, are in stark contrast to the stereotypes of femininity, women and motherhood that are frontstage, in public arenas. It challenges a dominant, stereotypical view that women are biologically pre-programmed to be maternal and to like all children. Liz's comment is particularly subversive.

Coates argues that such views would likely not be permitted frontstage because there is more social pressure on women than men to be polite, especially in terms of being seen as a 'nice', 'good' person, due to the deeply ingrained myth that women are biologically hard-wired to be more polite than men. In backstage talk, it is possible there can be a direct challenge to that myth with ample examples of impolite opinions and insults, without fear of censure, as well as breaking down the stereotype of the maternal woman.

However, despite the level of impoliteness and taboo about motherhood and the negative views towards children that are being expressed here, this talk is not evaluated as impolite in this context, as it is a form of solidarity-building between close friends. Coates points out that such opinions are socially risky, and the group does need to make sure that they are still seen as good people at the end of the talk. The level of trust in this friendship group is strong and so they feel that they can drop their guard and express their real feelings. To make sure that they do still see each other as good people, Bea says that their negative feelings about children are 'awful',[95] as well as another friend expressing how it is terrible to take pleasure in or to wish another person ill instead of focusing on their successes. Similarly, another friend, Mary, evaluates herself as a 'horrible bitch' for having negative feelings about others. Overall, these conversations do a lot of important work in making these speakers' identities feel coherent again and they represent important communicative roles that friendship group members can fulfil for one another. They teach us that politeness in successful friendship groups is made up of excellent listening skills, displaying empathy, agreeing with each other, and sharing in humour by showing solidarity and appreciation of one another. These are all examples of positive politeness, where the friends are working together to show how much they like and appreciate one another, and how they care about each other's emotional needs and desires.

In a different study, this time with male friendship groups in the UK, Coates[96] found evidence of her participants using other positive politeness strategies to enhance their friendship, by sharing stories focused on competition and individual achievements, especially when things go wrong, as a form of bonding through shared experiences via storytelling. Often, these narrators will present themselves as the individual hero of the story, as a person who has managed to succeed alone because of their own strengths, often against the odds. They work to build solidarity and strengthen social bonds within their friendship group. Some of Coates's examples show how solidarity is built through the use of expletives and taboo language (see also chapter seven), and focus on stereotypically masculine conversational topics, including cars, driving, football and drinking alcohol.

In one example from Coates's study, two male friends are having a private conversation in a pub in Birmingham. One man shares a story with his friend:

> **Speaker 1:** I had some of them fucking tablets. They're BASTARDS, honest. And I went to the Eagle . . . and I got a little bit drowsy . . . and you know where Sandy Road is?
>
> **Speaker 2:** Ahh.
>
> **Speaker 1:** I was taking that fucking corner and everything went woozy.[97]

In the later part of the story, Speaker 1 is pulled over by the police, but he gets away without being arrested, which he portrays as a personal triumph. This is an example of the ways in which this friendship group share stories as a form of positive politeness to build solidarity and enhance social bonds. However, it is important not to over-rely on gender stereotypes, as women may also talk on these topics. It is a politeness myth that men and boys are born to be more competitive and less polite than women, or that they inherently compete with one another and cannot talk about their emotions.

There is nothing inherent in men's acquisition of language or their use of language that means they cannot talk about emotions. Rather, socialisation teaches young boys from an early age that there is one version of masculinity that has more status and prestige than other versions, where boys and men are

101

heterosexual, brave and strong, and show few signs of weakness or emotion.[98] Talking about emotions is not socially valued in this version of macho masculinity. Discussing emotions and feelings can become negatively and stereotypically associated with either women or homosexual men. However, there are many other versions of how to perform legitimate masculinities out there and changing the narrative away from there being only one dominant version of how to behave 'like a man' is starting to slowly change. However, gender stereotypes are endemic in popular culture and in the mass media. Consider, for example, how frequently the phrases 'man-up' or 'boys don't cry' are used to regulate gendered behaviour, or the many terms of insults that exist for boys if they show emotions, which align them with girls and women or gay men, such as 'sissy', 'don't be a girl', as well as homophobic microaggressions, including 'poof', 'ponce' or referring to someone as 'gay' as an impolite insult, if they show their emotions in conversation.

Another area that has been examined in linguistic studies in all-male friendship groups is the role of gossip. As we've seen already in relation to dinner-table conversations in families, gossip plays an important role in building solidarity and strengthens social bonds. An influential example from linguistics of men gossiping is taken from Deborah Cameron's[99] work on a close-knit fraternity at a university in the US, recorded by one of her students. She observed a group of white middle-class male friends, Bryan, Ed, Al and Carl, who were watching a basketball game – a common pastime of the group being watching sport together on television.

They start their conversation by discussing another male student who is in one of their university classes. Bryan makes him the topic of conversation by marking him out as 'that really gay guy in our Age of Revolution class'[100] and they then go on to utter a series of insults about him, speaking of him with scorn and ridicule. They insult the way he dresses, his trainers and his legs, as a way of othering him, all of which allegedly mark him out as being gay, whilst simultaneously building solidarity with each other to position themselves as a heterosexual group of male students. One of them comments that his behaviour is 'so gay' that he is 'the antithesis of man'.[101]

Cameron argues that this focus on othering through homophobia is common in young all-male groups, but points out that it often has little to do with the sexuality of the people who are being disparaged and insulted. Other researchers have also found this pattern. By applying the label 'gay', the meaning is that others are not living up to the group's ideals of traditional, stereotypical versions of macho masculinity, which dominate in fraternity culture and in many other cultures.

Friendships, talk and mental health

However, close-knit friendship groups are one of the places where more emotionally open kinds of talk can happen and in her research, Coates also captures examples of groups of male friends going beyond masculine gender stereotypes, using positive and negative politeness to tell stories about their emotions and engaging in very personal disclosures, as in the following example. This is taken from a conversation between friends Brian, Tony and Pete, who all work together in a university as lecturers. They also socialise together outside of work:

Brian: If you'd had this conversation with me about a term ago – I mean, I was just about as down as you could get because I, er, really was quite seriously suicidal.

Brian here discloses very personal and sensitive information to his close friends as a way of sharing intense feelings, presumably to gain support, trust and understanding from his friends. One of the most crucial roles that friendship groups can play is to help each other through difficult times, using supportive, solidarity-building talk almost as a form of therapy and catharsis.

In the UK, there are now dedicated mental health campaigns specifically designed to encourage men to talk to their friends and family about mental health issues, to start breaking down dominant taboos and myths that men should not talk on topics relating to their emotions or their mental health needs. In the UK, suicide is the biggest killer of men under fifty,[102] and using talking therapies and encouraging men to open up in friendship groups and with family members to build solidarity, trust and empathy are known ways to encourage men to get professional help sooner. The campaigns are designed to get men to break the taboos around their own mental health needs and to start talking about mental health in everyday conversations with friends without fearing negative evaluation or stigmatisation, gender stereotyping or being emasculated.

Professional football clubs have also got involved in these initiatives and some have started running active campaigns around men's mental health needs. An excellent example of this is a social media video that was created by English Championship side Norwich City,[103] in conjunction with several UK-based mental health charities including the Samaritans, CALM, Heads Together and Mental Health Innovations (Shout). At the time of writing, this video has been viewed over 55 million times and has received positive acclaim. It focuses on two middle-aged men who sit next to each other watching their team throughout the season. At the start of the football season, they appear not to know each other, but over the course of watching the football season together, in the same space, they are seen to establish and then build a friendship. This friendship is instigated by the politeness strategies of one of the men who makes a series of attempts to engage the other. The audience sees all the different emotions that the two men experience together during the course of a football season, as strong social bonds form between them.

The camera frame doesn't move throughout this video, and it focuses only on the two fans' faces, or on their torsos if they stand up. One fan consistently looks depressed and unhappy. In contrast, the other fan always looks happy and jolly – he is very talkative and encourages the other fan to talk to him and join in with the rest of the crowd. He initiates all the conversations between the two of them, most often with conventional politeness markers of greetings and then instances of small talk designed to enhance interpersonal relationships. At the very first game of the season, he says, 'Oh wow! How are you doing? God, it's exciting, isn't it?' He then asks different questions at different points in the season: 'So how's your week been?' The depressed man always replies, but usually just minimally, 'Yeah, okay,' but still they start to bond. On another occasion when the team has lost, the happy man says, 'Well, I hope things are better for you outside of football.' The depressed man shakes his head and smiles.

Towards the end of the video, we see a friendship has formed. They embrace when their team scores a goal and the talkative fan gives the other man his football scarf as a gift. However, the screen then goes black. The next time we see their seats, the talkative, happy man's seat is empty. His friend brings in his scarf and puts it over his seat. It slowly becomes clear that he is doing this as a memorial to him and takes his hat off and covers it over his heart in mourning. The overall message of the campaign then comes up on screen: 'At times, it can be obvious when someone is struggling to cope. But sometimes, the signs are harder to spot.' The realisation that the chatty, happy man has been a victim of suicide is delivered to the audience and the hashtag #youarenotalone appears, followed by details of whom to contact if someone needs immediate mental health support.

The message behind the campaign is that talking with each

other is important and establishing friendships and reciprocating in asking about each other is significant. Making connections with friends through showing care for each other's feelings and well-being is a fundamental role played by politeness in friendship talk, regardless of gender. The underlying message of the video is that, while his friend assumed he was fine because of his very positive communicative behaviour, the seemingly cheerful football fan was not okay, but because the politeness wasn't reciprocated then this unhappiness was never uncovered. The campaign's message is encapsulated in the hashtag – that no one is ever alone, and that support is available. People who are suicidal do not always look or act in a certain way – sometimes outwardly happy people can be struggling. And so the campaign brings home the message that men talking to each other reciprocally in male-dominated, stereotypically masculinised social spaces, such as when watching football together, could help.

Another similar campaign based on a comparable premise has been run by an NHS healthcare trust,[104] which uses humour and word play in its title: 'It takes balls to talk'. It also draws on ball sports, including football and rugby, and aligns itself with traditional ideals of masculinity around bravery and boldness to encourage men to talk to each other in their friendship groups. The campaign title draws upon the common masculine slang phrase of 'having balls', as a literal part of the male anatomy, but also through its metaphorical meaning, to be brave and bold. It places this message in the context of being brave by talking about one's own mental health, so directly trying to challenge the stereotype of men being resistant to disclosing personal and emotional feelings, whilst at the same time including images of literal sports balls (footballs and rugby balls) on their website, using visual humour to attract attention to the campaign, to make its key messages memorable.

What we can learn from all of this is that friendship groups and the ability to engage in the classic politeness strategies of establishing friendship bonds and creating solidarity with other individuals and wider groups is integral to our mental health and well-being. For everyone, and despite strong social stereotypes that are held in place by powerful media, regardless of gender, age, race, ethnicity or social class, being able to have good interpersonal relationships with friends around any topic, but particularly emotions and mental health, is fundamentally important.

Friendships, family and digital media

Over the last two decades, advancements in internet communication, including the development of multiple social media platforms, have opened a series of different possibilities in terms of how we communicate politeness and impoliteness with our families and friendship groups. It has intensified the speed and ease with which families and friends can connect with one another, particularly for those who are separated by geographical distance. It offers many advantages, creating online spaces where we can share photos, videos and other information quickly and easily with large audiences of friends and family. However, this comes with its own challenges around politeness and etiquette online. Online platforms such as Facebook and Instagram enable us to see different aspects of friends and family members as they interact with others in a much broader network than what we will encounter offline. *Guardian* journalist Imogen West-Knights[105] has recently outlined some behavioural guidelines on how not to cause offence when interacting with family and friends on social media. She argues that real offence can be caused by unfollowing someone, or by telling your friends that they are being annoying on social media. Instead of unfollowing, muting is recommended. Instead of calling out friends and family for their inappropriate behaviour, her advice is to be forgiving and let this go, no matter how irritated you may be. Additionally, other advice is to avoid humour when friends and family make big announcements such as posting pregnancy news or photos of baby scans – it is very easy for things to be misinterpreted on social media and so where politeness is concerned it's best to err on the side of caution and not run the risk of making an inappropriate or offensive joke which may result in impoliteness.

During the Covid-19 pandemic, when lockdowns were enforced, the platforms of Zoom and Teams provided the technological capabilities for many of us to maintain audio-visual social connections with families and friends whom we could no longer see in person, in particularly challenging times. In many groups, social activities that had traditionally taken place face to face moved online where possible, as the human desire to communicate, stay connected and uphold social bonds, albeit in a different and often reduced communicative format, continued. The desire to co-operate through seeing and talking to each other on screen became a very important way of enacting positive politeness. Without advanced mobile technologies and widespread stable and reliable internet connections, group social connection of this scale would have been impossible, and instead we would have been limited to audio-only conversations with family and friends via landline telephones.

I now want to focus in on how new technologies have influenced the use of politeness and impoliteness in young people's friendship groups in particular. Whilst digital media has undeniably transformed many adult relationships, media studies researcher Deborah Chambers[106] points out that social media has affected communication practices in young people's friendship groups far more than any other group.

This is because their social media identities and the language and communication styles that they use on these platforms have become a central and very public part of their identities. As we

108

have seen earlier in the book, when discussing adolescence in chapter two, it is a critical time in peer-group development, as young people explore the boundaries, including the communication boundaries, of their individual and group identities.

From a positive perspective, being online together with one's friendship group can build solidarity quicker and open up a much wider range of creative ways in which positive politeness can be shared between those with whom young people already have strong bonds – for example, by telling digital stories and sharing jokes, memes, photos, other images and videos, as well as being able to bond over information that friendship groups with common interests will find appealing, such as news about celebrities, sports stars or musicians, in addition to giving each other compliments, praise or positive affirmation via instant messaging or texts.

However, a downside for young people is feeling pressure to always be available to their friends to avoid accusations of impoliteness by not answering calls or instantly replying to messages, as well as experiencing fears of being left out. Another danger is that impoliteness, insults and abuse can spread rapidly, and to large audiences. And so, if young people's relationships become conflictual, then cyberbullying with a large, voyeuristic audience can sometimes quickly result. Social media sites afford young people a great deal of independence from the adult scrutiny of parents and teachers – which is arguably a big part of their appeal. Chambers argues that, for the first time, social media has meant that young people are able to interact privately with their peer groups, without adults playing a central role or being overhearers.

The lack of adult input and supervision can lead to problems, especially if children are subject to impoliteness and cyberbullying, and it can often take some time before young people will ask an adult for help. Some won't ask at all. Although technically there is a permanent record of behaviour, as impolite messages, such as insults, abuse, rude messages and inappropriate images are recorded, inappropriate communications can be easily deleted and if there are no screenshots then it can be very difficult to retrieve messages.

Many young people are part of large chat groups, using platforms such as WhatsApp and Snapchat and these such platforms can become prime arenas for inappropriate communications to take place. This often takes place with limited, if any, adult supervision or oversight, despite WhatsApp's minimum age for legal use being sixteen years old.

Chambers has argued that social media now takes priority over young people's social relationships with parents, teachers and any other adult caregivers. The separation point between children and adults is happening at a much earlier age, as young people's online peer groups are occupying ever-more important spaces in their lives at the expense of having strong adult social connections. This means that valuable face-to-face opportunities to communicate verbally with adults are now lost.

It can also be difficult on social media to control audiences. A message that was originally meant for one addressee can be easily shared by others. Interactions between friends are public on some platforms, and so young people may start communicating their identities for multiple audiences simultaneously – for example, what is being shared with one's friendship group may also be seen by parents and grandparents. The politeness norms and boundaries that will be expected by different members of these groups will likely be different. If young people do not have their security settings set to private, prospective audiences can stretch much wider, to potential employers or any members of the public, which can potentially pose a threat to young people's safety and security.

Chambers reports that 87 per cent of social media communication between young people takes place within their homes, partly because homes have the most stable internet connections.

Our once backstage spaces are no longer wholly backstage. These previously private arenas are now invaded by mobile phones, with access to ever-evolving social media spaces, via WhatsApp, Snapchat, TikTok, Facebook, BeReal or any other emergent platforms. If the people who are present in these backstage spaces take videos or photos and then post them on social media, large audiences are able to see what is being said or done in a private sphere, such as a family party at home. Communication events that were once personal and open only to the people who were physically present can instantly become available to the viewing gaze of anyone who can view it. This can include instances of impoliteness, insults and abuse, and the use of disrespectful or abusive text and images.

Social media sites thrive on gossip, and impoliteness and conflict occur, as well as a certain amount of intrigue and voyeurism. Cyberbullying can take place very rapidly as social media changes the speed and scale of friendship interactions. Chambers demonstrates this through multiple examples gleaned from a group of sixteen-to-eighteen-year-old A-level students in the UK, whom she interviewed about their experiences. One male student said that, pre-social media, people often never knew if they hadn't been invited to a party. Now, offence can easily be caused as people find out about events that they were not asked to via social media, as photos and videos of the event emerge.

Young people have to manage details of their personal lives in a public sphere in front of multiple audiences, which can often be very difficult to navigate. There is what Chambers refers to as an 'ambient awareness' of each other – they can and do eavesdrop on each other's social media interactions to get abreast of the latest version of current gossip. Often, teenagers share 'private' chats with each other so information spreads quite rapidly and rumours circulate quickly. This can result in cyberbullying. The speed and ease with which inappropriate materials can be spread can also have serious consequences for those involved.

Cyberbullying has a highly destructive impact on young people's self-esteem and confidence; in the very worst cases, it can have tragic consequences, with some bullied teenagers taking their own lives. This is clearly one of the downsides of being able to instantly chat to one another and quickly circulate information without adult supervision.

In the US, a recent study by Emily Vogels[107] found that almost half of all teenagers have experienced some form of cyber harassment and bullying online during 2022 alone. Rude and inappropriate comments about physical appearance are the most common forms of abuse, and older teenage girls the most frequent recipients, with abusive comments most often focusing on women's bodies.

In a study about intimate relationships between young people, 40 per cent of participants reported that an intimate partner had used phones or computers to abuse them, most commonly by coercing them into taking nude photographs of them and then, at a later date, using them as revenge porn, circulating these private images via social media, with the intention of causing distress.

Many young people who'd had nude photographs taken of them reported that they had felt coerced into participating in the first place. Revenge porn clearly crosses the line from something that is impolite to something illegal and now prosecutable. In Vogels' work, three-quarters of young people who took part thought that social media platforms and those in government were not doing enough to address the problem of online abuse for young people. Teenagers who participated in the research suggested that those who are caught engaging in harassment should receive permanent bans and face criminal charges.

Similarly, in the UK, a recent Office for National Statistics[108] study found that one in five children aged from ten to fifteen had suffered cyberbullying. And in 70 per cent of the cases, this was someone who went to their school and was known to them and their friendship group. The UK government has been discussing bringing in new legislation to ban children under the age of sixteen from social media.[109] The perils of social media, its pervasiveness and the ease with which impolite behaviour can quickly escalate into illegal behaviour can have pretty dire consequences for all of those involved and there is much that needs to be done in terms of regulation to protect young people and, more broadly, all other digital media users.

Even with the more positive consequences of strengthening group bonds and enabling users to easily keep in touch with friends, and make new friends through the social networking opportunities that various platforms offer, there are serious issues around the permanency of online communication, and consent around taking videos and photos, that need to be carefully monitored. Traditional distinctions between the home as a private, backstage space for friends and family, and being in a public frontstage space have now blurred quite dramatically, as have the politeness norms that go along with these spaces, since digital media in all of its various forms has fused together our public and private lives.

Summary

We started this chapter by focusing on the importance attached to learning politeness as soon as children are able to do so, and how adults prioritise teaching these principles as a significant part of caregiving. The age at which politeness is acquired is very similar across languages and geographical locations, which shows the pervasiveness of the reach and significance of politeness in everyday communication. We have seen how family interactions involving infants and young children play a significant role in unconsciously setting social expectations for children to be polite in their language and behaviour, reflected through caregivers' constant monitoring of and desire for children to learn politeness. This social aspiration to have a polite child is deeply ingrained, while good manners in a child will be positively evaluated by other adult members of society. Overall, though, the most important message here is that politeness norms and rules play a fundamental part in childhood language acquisition, due to the social value and prestige that is attached to politeness in our societies.

For those people with whom we are genuinely close, social bonds and intimacy will be shown through a range of different politeness strategies, in which harmony is maintained and enhanced in collaborative communication. This includes shared styles of storytelling, humour and jokes, some of which may have been retold several times over. There will be common topics of conversation which the group knows well and enjoys discussing. These may be shared in person, via social media platforms or on platforms such as Zoom. If pets are present, their humans may well use them as addressees to deliver polite or impolite messages to other humans. Pet owners impose human politeness norms on to pets. This can help make owners feel like their pet is a more fully integrated member of a family unit. It can also result in humans trying to teach their pets politeness norms or pretending that they can understand simple, polite commands and questions, most often as a form of humorous entertainment.

We have also seen convincing examples of how strong friendship bonds need to be there for the good times and the bad. To have successful friendships, interactions must be of mutual benefit, and it is important that friends allow opportunities to give politeness and space to each other to talk about feelings and emotions in a way that is genuinely reciprocated. We have seen this in action through the mental health campaigns from Norwich City Football Club and the NHS 'Balls' advert, encouraging men to engage in talk more openly and regularly about emotions, though the message is relevant to everyone, regardless of gender.

This chapter has considered politeness in communication from the backstage areas of our lives, within families and close friendship groups in our homes and other private spaces away from public audiences. However, we have questioned the binary distinction between backstage and frontstage, as social media and the pervasiveness of mobile technology means that these traditional categories are now blurred. Our homes are no longer private spaces if digital technologies lurk within them, allowing videos or photos to be uploaded to social media. As part of this, we have illustrated the clear positives and negatives of digital communication. To maintain politeness, ethics and respect, it is important that all who may be included as participants in photos or videos have consented to such recording and documenting taking place and where it will go next in terms of potentially public view.

If we have strong relationships with our family and friends, then we can negotiate times when our mobile phones are not turned on, demarcating private spaces where we can be more relaxed and more like our 'real' selves. Backstage – at least, when there is no invasion from social media devices, videos or cameras – is where our identities are not on public display, and it is here where we can express negative feelings, reactions and emotions about others when our guard is down, without fear of being negatively judged or sanctioned. This is an important process if we are to consolidate often contradictory forms of our identities, which come under pressure in frontstage settings.

When we are with family members and friends, we can create important, trusted spaces for us to work through different challenges that we face, including our feelings and reactions to the language and behaviour that others have used towards us which may have been impolite, insulting or worse. Interactions with family and friends, regardless of whether these are delivered in person, online or in writing, provide essential spaces to bond, enjoy each other's company and talk through difficult topics.

Overall, this work is important so that we can consolidate different performances of ourselves and develop a more coherent sense of our own identities and our relationships with others, including fulfilling the art of having productive and meaningful interactions with family members and friends.

5

Politeness and Leadership
Success at Work

Being able to communicate successfully is an essential part of any leaders' skill set in today's fast-paced, ever-changing workplaces. For far too long, communication has been seen through the misleading and negative label of 'soft skills'. After all, there's no point having excellent business ideas or creating new inventions if you cannot communicate them properly to an audience. The long-standing association of communication as a soft skill is inaccurate, outdated and potentially damaging, particularly as digital technologies, which rely on clear communication, continue to become more and more prevalent at work. If leaders cannot engage in effective communication, then this is going to negatively affect profit margins, morale and staff retention. Leaders need to be acutely tuned into the politeness norms and requirements of all the different workplace contexts in which they communicate in order to have successful leadership styles.

Leadership can be a tricky concept to define, but here I am using it to refer to how people motivate and encourage others at work, how they ensure tasks are completed on time by giving orders and making decisions, and how people can effectively organise, direct and evaluate the workplace performances of others for whom they have leadership responsibility. Leaders need to be highly attuned into the politeness needs demanded by various contexts, teams and individuals in order to be able to fulfil these tasks effectively and efficiently.

During the last twenty-five years, I have personally analysed how multiple leaders from many different organisations, cultures and backgrounds communicate effectively using politeness, as well as what happens when this goes wrong. I have observed shifts in leadership styles and organisational cultures, and examined how this has affected the ways in which politeness strategies are performed. Decoding unwritten rules around what makes successful leadership communication can help those who are already leaders and those who are aspiring to be leaders in future to inspire and influence others. It will also enhance awareness of how persuasion, influence and decision-making works, as well as promoting a greater understanding of how leaders succeed (and fail) in a wide range of businesses and professional settings.

Sociolinguistic analysis of politeness and successful leadership communication has revealed that being able to deliver the following with respect and emotional intelligence, without causing offence, is essential for leadership success: giving orders and demands, making declarations, appointing, nominating, reporting events, expressing approval, giving compliments, making offers and promises, expressing criticisms, issuing warnings and making challenges.[110] The list is quite long, but in this chapter, we will go through these and detail how politeness strategies enable these important communication acts to be successfully executed. Leaders also need to tailor their styles to the person(s) with whom they are communicating, taking into full account anyone else who may be overhearing, or a reader at a later date, in the case of email, social media and more traditional forms of writing, all within the confines of a company's communications culture.

Understanding politeness, leadership and culture

All leaders are affected by the workplace cultures and traditions of the organisations where they work, which will have an influence on their leadership styles. In many businesses and professional settings globally, there has been an observable shift in recent years from a traditional 'command and control' style of leadership to a more fluid communication style, where leaders tend to be less authoritarian and more collaborative.[111] This means a move away from a system where a leader makes unilateral decisions to situations in which power imbalances between leaders and their employees becomes far less obvious. Collaborative communication encourages others to express their thoughts, ideas and opinions. Collective decision-making and two-way leadership styles are much more prominent in organisations with flatter power structures. Many researchers, including professional communication analyst Stephanie Schnurr,[112] have argued that these newer, lateral workplaces are more suitable for organisations operating in competitive global economies as it means that they can adapt quicker to change. Inevitably, this shift has had an impact on how politeness is used by leaders to communicate with their colleagues.

One of the most frequent and significant ways that leaders need to communicate is by giving orders and demands. We can learn a great deal about the politeness culture of any workplace by analysing the levels of directness that leaders use to deliver these effectively. Getting the level of politeness right is crucial to the success of any order or demand. Even in workplaces where collaborative leadership styles are the norm, direct orders may be perfectly polite and appropriate in some cultural settings; for example, if the order is a routine part of an individual's everyday role. Drawing on their extensive work on language and leadership in New Zealand workplaces, Janet Holmes and Maria Stubbe[113] cite the following direct orders that take place between a leader and her administrative assistant in a government department, which were seen as completely appropriate:

'Check that out.'
'Ring the applicants today and say they've been shortlisted.'
'I need to see that file.'
'That needs to be couriered today.'[114]

They explain that additional politeness strategies were not needed in such instances as the leader had the power to ask, and the tasks are routine, non-controversial and quick to do, and so being direct is not going to cause offence. Direct orders may also need to be issued at particular points in workplace talk due to the urgency of the task or the efficiency with which it needs to be carried out. For example, although recent research has shown shifts away from the traditional command-and-control styles of leadership, even in emergency services communication,[115] in communications training work that we have carried out at the University of Nottingham, leaders who work in emergency services consistently report that directness always takes precedence when the safety of staff and members of the public is paramount, like when rescuing people from a motorway crash. One leader in the UK Fire and Rescue Service reported, 'You aren't going to care about politeness or not offending someone when you have a crew member putting themselves at risk in the fast lane of a motorway.' Leadership communication needs to be crystal clear at these points with no room for ambiguity. In the UK at least, direct orders are the best way to deliver such clear demands. In these high-pressure situations, politeness norms are backgrounded and the urgency of the situation takes over. If there is a need to repair or re-establish interpersonal relationships, then this can wait until an appropriate time later, once immediate dangers have passed. The best leaders are those who can quickly and efficiently adapt their communication styles to changing circumstances. This includes having enough emotional intelligence to gauge when there is a need to repair a relationship, if politeness boundaries have been crossed during a high-pressure situation.

In similar circumstances, when public safety and the lives of professionals are at risk, US linguist Charlotte Linde[116] analysed black box recordings of eight plane crashes and fourteen flight simulator sessions to see if indirectness and pilots prioritising being polite to each other over clarity of messages could have been a factor in what went wrong. Linde found that when a crew member proposes a suggestion to the flight's captain, the captain is least likely to act on this if a suggestion is made indirectly, with mitigation. Therefore, if co-pilots or other members of flight crew who have less status and prestige than the captain know or strongly suspect that something is wrong, Linde's findings show that it is really important that they avoid indirectness and use directness when communicating this information, as the captain will be far more likely to react and act on the concern being expressed. Linde found that this was the case for both black box recordings and simulated flights, and these findings were integrated into future pilot training.

Whilst the consequences of clear communication are not always as severe as matters of life and death, leaders who use indirectness as a politeness strategy for the delivery of orders, demands and a range of other types of communication need to be sure that the information they want to convey has been fully understood and will be acted on. This can be a complex issue and so we will now look at this in a bit more detail by focusing on one business in particular.

The following examples are taken from a multinational corporate business where I spent time observing and analysing politeness and leadership communication over a period of six months, though I have removed specifics and identifying features about the company and its employees to allow for their anonymity. My time with this company included shadowing and observing leaders, recording meetings and interviewing staff at all levels of the business, including senior leaders. This company had fully embraced flatter power structures and the newer, collaborative approach to politeness workplace culture was visible in many ways. All employees, regardless of what job role they had, wore the same uniform, including the CEO. Everyone used the same workplace social spaces – there was one canteen and one staff room. The CEO did not have a private office or a parking space. Instead, he would hire one of the shared, bookable meeting spaces if he needed to have private meetings and he tried his luck with parking every day, just like the rest of the firm's employees.

I focus firstly on the leadership communication of Rory, who is positively evaluated as a popular and successful leader. Here is a typical example of Rory chairing a weekly team meeting where he is the team leader of all those who are present. In this instance, his department has been recruiting new staff and Rory wants them to run their own team induction day, instead of their new recruit attending a more generic (and, in Rory's view, much less useful) company-wide induction:

Rory: Do you feel that we need to do perhaps something like the product department did?

Mike: Set a date to sort it out.

Rory: Cos, as Sue quite rightly pointed out, it's all been done for us. Why don't we take advantage of that? Sue's offered her support with perhaps, John? [long pause] Er, you know perhaps to run that. Why don't we just set a date now?

Matt: Yeah.

Rory: And say, 'Right, okay, let's do it.'

Sue: Just get everybody in.

Matt: Yeah.

Rory: Is that okay, Matt?

Matt: Fine, yeah, fine with me.

Rory: Fantastic.

Rory knew that he wants his team to run their own induction day before the meeting begins – he told me this in a pre-meeting conversation that he and I had where he gave me background information on the meeting and explained his views on members of his team. He could directly order one of his subordinates to fulfil the task of running the induction, as he is their leader. However, he chooses not to give a direct order and instead he does something quite different.

By starting with a question, 'do you feel . . .', Rory shows that he is being emotionally intelligent, asking for the considered thoughts of his workplace colleagues, instead of just telling them what to do. Rory expresses this issue as something they need to collectively decide on and then take action on together. By inviting the opinions of his team, he includes them (superficially at least) in the decision-making process. The order gets re-formulated as a request with collective pronouns ('us', 'we', 'let's') along with hedges to minimise Rory imposing an order on his team. Good leaders will check that compliance has been reached and that relationships are still harmonious, just as Rory does here when he double-checks with Matt that the decision is okay.

Rory will play no part in organising or running the departmental induction day, which he and his team collectively agree on, despite his politeness strategies indicating that they will all be involved, as this has been presented as an inclusive team activity. He actively gains the team's support by successfully minimising the status differences that exist between him and his subordinates. It is theoretically possible that a team member may object to this as a way of delivering an order – it takes longer to do and it could be interpreted as manipulative, as Rory is not going to be taking part in the event itself. However, there is no such resistance in this team. They all value Rory's leadership style, which fits in well with the overall firm culture, and they all buy into his approach. Sue's view of Rory, which she expressed in interview with me, gives an overwhelmingly positive evaluation of him as a successful team leader.

'We all think Rory's great to work for. I feel he listens and I am able to speak freely to him. You're allowed to make mistakes and he puts trust in you, but there's no hierarchical system. When you ask for help you get it and you're never shouted at. I haven't had one negative response from him in the eighteen months I've been here,' Sue explained.

Sue comments directly on the lack of hierarchy that Rory has in his team and lists the traits that make him a popular and successful leader. He pays attention to the needs of his staff very closely and makes his team members feel valued, respected and supported in their roles. They are all happy and none of them wants to leave or move teams.

In another example taken from the same close-knit team, here they have spent a long time in another meeting trying to decide on how to display their new departmental vision. They have just jointly come up with a solution, with all members of the team collectively inputting their thoughts and positively evaluating one another. They've decided to display their vision on their firm's identity cards. Rory closes the decision-making process by issuing multiple expressions of approval:

Rory: Fantastic! I knew we'd come up with a solution. Great!
Sue: If in between times anybody wants any sticky back, I can print some more.
Steve: Good. Great! Fantastic! Okay then.

With flatter structures and more horizontal ways of enacting power, leaders like Rory, who favour collaborative styles of leadership, will frequently give praise and positively evaluate group achievements, building solidarity by recognising how workplace goals have been achieved by working collectively as a team. This company values its staff putting time into making decisions, such as where to display their departmental vision. For leaders and employees in organisations that have more command-and-control structures, these kinds of activities may be viewed as a waste of time and resource. However, for this group, the team bonding and collective sense of identity that comes along with actively engaging in these processes is deemed to be time well spent.

In contrast to Rory's collaborative leadership style, his colleague Amy is known for having a more direct leadership style. She is new to the organisation, having joined six months previously. Her department is similar in size to Rory's and so it makes a good point of comparison between their two leadership styles, especially as Rory and Amy are at the same leadership level in the firm. In an interview with me, Amy reported that she had previously worked for over ten years in a workplace where a top-down style of leadership was dominant, and so more direct speech was the norm for her and her favoured way of doing things. Here, Amy is explaining departmental policy to two new recruits, Kirsty and Eddie. Karen is also present and she is one of Amy's more established team members.

> **Amy:** We are going to be carrying it for more than fifteen weeks.
> **Karen:** Yeah, it's ten weeks for stock and it will be calculated on how many sales within five weeks.
> **Amy:** No. It's longer than that, Karen.
> **Karen:** [sounding surprised and hesitant] Oh, right.
> **Amy:** It's longer.[117]

Here, Amy issues a direct challenge to Karen without using any politeness strategies to soften her critique. Amy is technically entitled to do this, as she is Karen's boss; however, Karen's reaction tells us that she is rather taken aback, signalling that this is not the norm in this workplace's culture. Karen had been attempting to collaboratively build on Amy's utterance, but as Amy directly disagreed with her in front of the two new staff members, Karen loses face and credibility here. In our interview, Karen made it clear that she finds Amy very difficult to work with, telling me, 'Amy is a very strong character, very straightforward. She says what she means, and it can be quite an overpowering experience talking to her.'[118]

In the next example, Amy issues an explicit warning and a direct order to her team. The company has a policy that its leadership team has to do menial tasks around the business as a punishment if absence rotas are not filled out correctly. This can include sweeping floors or doing the washing-up in the canteen. As Amy has just moved departments, she is informing her new team that she will individually give them the punishments, just like she did in her previous department:

> **Amy:** When I got them in [departmental name] I gave them back to the managers who'd let me down, so they ended up doing the forfeits. So be warned. Don't do it.

There is no sense of any team spirit here in Amy's leadership style. She makes it clear that if the department gets punished it will be because her individual managers will have let her down personally. Amy's command-and-control leadership style is quite anomalous in this organisation's collaborative workplace culture, and this makes it difficult for her to gain the trust of her team. Amy acknowledged this herself in an interview with me, commenting that some staff find her challenging. 'I say what I think, there's no cutting corners with people . . . and some people find my directness difficult.'[119]

There is another, interrelated issue here, which emerged as I was observing this workplace. Negative evaluations of Amy's leadership style do not just stem from her directness, but also from another aspect of her identity, her gender. Being direct is not seen as being compatible with being a female leader. We will now explore this issue in more detail.

Leadership, culture and gender

Gender comes to the fore as an issue for leadership in this workplace culture as Amy is negatively evaluated by her subordinates and superiors for her leadership style through the use of gender-loaded terms – she is seen as too 'bossy', 'overly aggressive', 'bombastic' and 'dragon-like', as well as a 'tyrant' and a 'witch'. In a series of interviews that I conducted to assess employees' views on leadership styles in the business, one of Amy's status equals drew on the stereotype of women being more emotional and nurturing, but she marked Amy out as being different: 'Women are naturally more nurturing but some are real tyrants.'

Amy is well aware of how gendered expectations about how women leaders should act negatively affects how she is judged: 'I act and talk more like a man in many of my behavioural roles because of what I've worked with in the past. I'm less approachable than some of the men ... I'm not your typical female manager and people find that hard.'[120]

On the one hand, Amy's direct, assertive style helps us to dispel a deeply ingrained politeness myth, that women are naturally collaborative and nurturing leaders because they are biologically pre-programmed to communicate in this way. Amy is clearly able to lead with a competitive, direct communication style. She dominates the talking time and frequently interrupts others to get her points across. She often places herself and her own achievements at the centre of the workplace stories she tells her subordinates, and so she comes across as a competitive, assertive leader. On the other hand, the dominant idea of women being more polite than men is a very powerful stereotype and it deeply affects the ways in which female leaders are evaluated and judged. Time and time again, the research has shown that female leaders are subject to a double bind in the workplace – if, like Amy, they predominantely use leadership styles that are stereotypically associated with men's speech, which revolve around being competitive, using directness, dominating the talking time, interrupting, etc., then they will be negatively evaluated as overly aggressive. But if they use strategies that are stereotypically associated with women's speech, which are based on facilitative, collaborative talk, then they will be viewed as ineffective leaders, even if this style is valued in the workplace.

Multiple research studies have found that female leaders like Amy are subject to negative evaluations and judgements about a perceived lack of politeness in their leadership styles, especially if their leadership style also does not align with the collaborative workplace culture where they are based. Although Amy was generally evaluated as effective by senior management, she was consistently evaluated poorly by the people who worked for her, which negatively affected team morale and resulted in weak social bonds. Here is a comment from Lucy, another member of Amy's team: 'Amy is very domineering. She is very different from the rest of the females in the company. She can be quite abrupt, you know, as a woman. I can be quite honest with her though sometimes she scares the pants off me.'

A further gender-based aspect of Amy's leadership style that she herself draws attention to is her unwillingness to engage in a classic form of positive politeness, which is talking about her private life at work. She acknowledges that some of her colleagues find this difficult, particularly because she is a woman. Amy, however, views this as being a consummate professional. 'I'm an extremely professional person and nobody knows anything about me because I don't ever think to get into that mode while I'm at work. That switches you off to some degree with people, particularly women, who expect it of you as a woman.'[121]

130

As we will see later in the chapter, small talk about one's private life can be a highly valued part of successful leadership. However, as Amy points out here, it is stereotypically associated with female leaders and so if it is missing, its lack will be more stigmatised. Amy expresses her view that it is unprofessional to mix work life and home life, though many others do not share the same views.

Despite her fierce reputation, Amy does show that she has a broader repertoire in terms of her leadership style, with some members of her team. Here she can be seen engaging in politeness strategies to check in on her new recruits to see how they are doing:

Amy: How are you feeling?
Eddie: All right, yeah. I've been round with Bobbie this morning.
Amy: Good. Okay. Kirsty?
Kirsty: Nothing.
Amy: Yeah, you're feeling okay?
Kirsty: Yeah.
Amy: I was just gonna say, what you just need to remember is there's all of us [pauses], so if there's anything just shout up, you know.
Kirsty: Thanks.[122]

Communicating concern for the emotional well-being of her new team members is evidence of a more supportive interactional leadership style from Amy. However, the overwhelmingly negative evaluations of Amy as too bossy and aggressive predominated in this business. Amy left this workplace shortly after the recordings were made and went to work elsewhere. When leaders' communication norms do not match the company's politeness culture, people will very often move on. When gender stereotypes are also at play, negative evaluation can be exacerbated and female leaders can be seen as 'interlopers' who do not really fit. I have found this pattern several times when conducting workplace research and consultancies.

In contrast to the negative evaluations that Amy received, Rory received consistent praise for his leadership style in this particular business's culture, where a more stereotypically feminine speech style was valued. There was no sign of any negative evaluation of him. The research evidence from many different workplaces and cultures shows that men in leadership positions are not evaluated and judged to the same strict rules as women leaders, who are restricted in the language that they can use by deeply ingrained gender stereotypes.[123]

Leadership, culture and ethnicity

In New Zealand, Janet Holmes and Stephanie Schnurr[124] have examined the importance of ethnicity and what happens when leaders move between Māori and Pākāha businesses which have distinctive cultural communications practices due to different ethnic histories and traditions. To look at how leaders need to adjust to a new organisation's communications culture on the basis of ethnicity, the study looks at Steve, a leader from a Pākāha workplace (people of European descent), who moves companies and goes to work for a Māori organisation. Steve is Pākāha and has previously worked only in Pākāha workplaces.

As Steve introduces a meeting agenda item, two other participants, Daniel and Frank, talk to each other, albeit quietly. Daniel and Frank are both senior leaders – Daniel is the CEO and Frank is the finance manager. Steve finds their talking while he is addressing the meeting to be impolite, and he decides to call them out on this by reprimanding them for their impolite behaviour. When he finishes his turn, Steve comments, 'One of the important things in communication is not to talk when others are talking.' However, as Holmes and Schnurr[125] point out, Steve has inappropriately stated a politeness norm for a Pākāha workplace here. Frank immediately responds, explaining to Steve the different politeness norms of who talks when in Māori meetings: 'One of the things that you learn very quickly is that a sign of respect is that other people are talking about what you are saying while you're saying it.' This is followed by laughter from the team to release the tension that Steve has caused. Steve realises the error of his ways and responds, 'I see, I see.'[126]

Holmes and Schnurr point out that politeness is shown by this active style of engagement in Māori workplaces, with workplace colleagues happily talking at the same time as others to show support. In Māori culture, this is a classic way of showing engagement and interest. In the Pākāha workplace tradition that Steve has come from, silence when another person is talking is valued instead. Turn-taking in meetings happens where it is clear that another person has finished, or when someone invites another person to take the floor. If two or more people talk at the same time, one will cede to the other person to maintain politeness boundaries (unless an argument or conflict is taking place). This example shows how easily miscommunication and conflict can occur if ethnic cultural norms are not shared. At the same time, it highlights the need for any leader not to assume that their politeness norms will automatically transfer to another workplace, especially when workplace cultures are rooted in different ethnicities. Good cultural awareness is required to avoid miscommunication and conflict, as well as to show that proper attention and respect are given to other traditions, so that no one, particularly if they are from a dominant cultural group (as Pākāha are in New Zealand), assumes that their cultural traditions will simply be the communications norm in all workplaces.

Furthermore, Schnurr and colleagues[127] demonstrate in another study that it is completely acceptable for meetings to open just with very short phrases or even one word, such as 'okay, let's start' or 'right', in Pākāha organisations. This is enough to mark out the transition from pre-meeting talk to proper business talk. However, in stark contrast, in Māori workplaces, meeting openings are ritualistic, more formal and much longer. They give a typical example, taken from the opening of a white-collar meeting where Quentin, the respected leader of this Māori organisation, formally opens the meeting by delivering a prayer, known as a *Karakia*. As respect for the dignity of others is significant in Māori culture, it figures prominently in the prayer. Quentin asks 'the Lord to guide them in their meeting and to look after them all.' He prays that their discussion goes well and is right and good. He asks people to pray for their relations, many of whom are going through a hard time or are ill. He prays that they are blessed and looked after.[128] Quentin's reference to people's families and their lives outside of work brings a strong family presence into the organisation.

Schnurr and colleagues point to the potential for friction and negative evaluation when these cultural norms for meeting openings are not shared. Māori participants may view Pākāha meeting openings as rude for being far too short and informal. Similarly, Pākāha participants may view Māori meeting openings as too long, overly elaborate and unnecessary. Again, cultural awareness is key. If leaders are aware of different norms and expectations for meeting openings and closings, then ideally they can use this knowledge to manage expectations and teach their teams about different politeness norms based on varying cultural expectations and practices when people move between different cultures. If people are moving between different cultures or groups, either between or within the same workplace, it is good practice to spend time observing and learning what the current communication norms are before jumping straight in to criticise others for being rude or inappropriate.

Another influential piece of research, this time with participants from different countries, has been produced by Helen

Spencer-Oatey and Jianyu Xing.[129] They examine how rapport is managed in two British-Chinese business delegations in visits to Britain. The first Chinese delegation's visit goes well, but the second Chinese delegation's visit goes very badly, even though on paper the visits were very similar. Spencer-Oatey and Xing uncover a number of reasons why rapport was damaged in the second visit, which resulted in confusion, conflict and damaged relationships.

To try to get to the bottom of what went wrong, they interviewed all participants afterwards to get their thoughts and opinions. Offence had been caused early on but the British delegation was completely unaware that anything was wrong. The impoliteness then spiralled. Initially, the second Chinese delegation was not happy with the seating arrangements for their welcome meeting. As the British team and the Chinese team were of equal status, they expected that both delegations should sit down the two sides of the meeting table, with their leaders in the middle of the table. But instead, the British leader sat at the head of the table. This choice was negatively evaluated by the Chinese delegation leader: 'It shouldn't have been that he was the chair and we were seated along the sides of the table. With equal status, they should sit along this side and we should sit along that side.'[130] The Chinese delegation's leader interpreted this as evidence of the British participants not showing them enough respect and treating them as inferior.

This problem was exacerbated when the British leader made a welcome speech without giving the Chinese leader any opportunity to make a reciprocal speech in response, which would be standard business practice in China. Instead, the British leader asked the Chinese delegates to introduce themselves, which caused confusion. The Chinese leader ignored this request and started to give a speech in response. However, the interpreter unfortunately decided to intervene and cut him off, which added to the impoliteness that the Chinese delegation was experiencing.

135

The interpreter then instructed the Chinese leader to make sure that his team introduce themselves instead, because this was what he had been asked to do and he should not have been giving a speech. The Chinese delegation was also upset because they thought that the British chair's speech had not given them enough credit or respect.

Spencer-Oatey and Xing explained that the Chinese delegation believed a rumour that the British company were in serious financial difficulties (which they denied) and their sales orders had saved the British company from bankruptcy. Because of this, they had expected much more deference and a greater number of compliments, whereas instead, they just got a general welcome. The Chinese delegation then spent quite a few minutes discussing what to do next, in Chinese, as they were very upset. This caused confusion for the British delegation as they did not know what was going on. Spencer-Oatey and Xing point out that as a consequence of all of these perceived politeness breaches, the Chinese delegation cancelled the training that had been specially arranged for them and instead went off and spent the remainder of their time shopping and sightseeing. The British delegation thought they were very rude and disrespectful for doing so.

When these problems were talked through with the research team afterwards, the British delegation said that they did not realise that the seating arrangements would cause such offence or that the Chinese leader would want to make a return speech. They had mistakenly thought they were making things easier by making the meeting more informal for their guests, so they did not have to spend time preparing speeches. The average age of this Chinese delegation was younger than it had been and the British contingent had believed that the two companies had already established a good relationship. These things led the Brits to (mistakenly) presume that politeness formalities had lessened. One of the lessons here, then, is that in any intercultural business and professional context, it's important not to make assumptions about shifting politeness norms and formality.

A key difference between the first Chinese delegation and the second Chinese delegation (which happened by accident, not by planning) was that, at the first delegation's welcome meeting, some of the British team had been running late; this had enabled a valuable period of small talk to take place, led by the British team, where delegates started to get to know each other. None of the Chinese delegates were offended by the lateness of the British delegates; instead, they had enjoyed the opportunity to start to get to know their hosts. As this time for small talk had happened spontaneously, it was not picked up as being an important part of the meeting planning for the next delegation. Also, at the first delegation's meeting, the British company's international leader was there and he was able to facilitate relationships by talking about his visits and experiences of being in China, which made the Chinese delegation feel much more at ease. The international manager was unable to attend the second delegation's welcome meeting and none of the other British leaders present had ever visited China, so there was no opportunity for any sense of bonding or cultural appreciation.

There are a number of takeaways from these research studies on politeness, leadership and culture which can be applied to any workplace settings where people come together to do business. For leaders and those who are in charge of setting up events, it is vital that politeness and etiquette norms from all different cultures that will be represented have been considered. The structure and purpose of any event should also be thought through very carefully – if there is an expectation that social relationships should be better established before core business talk takes place, then this needs to be taken into account to ensure that other, more social activities are built in before moving on to meetings with a more transactional focus. If a translator is required, then they need to be very well versed not only in the languages that they need to use but also in cultural politeness norms, so that they can adapt quickly to changing circumstances and pick up on the communicative subtleties when things may be starting to go wrong.

Spencer-Oatey and Xing's work is a great example of how linguists can get involved in troubleshooting communication problems by gaining extra information in interviews with both parties and then feeding back on the crucial moments where offence was taken. If a more neutral person such as a linguist can come in and do this, then miscommunication and conflict can be defused and explained, and hopefully this can result in better relationships in future. Leaders can then monitor different politeness norms and expectations, such as the connection between seating arrangements and power, and/or the need for interpersonal relationships to be more firmly established from the outset. Hopefully this should avoid situations of intercultural miscommunication and conflict from occurring again.

Linguist and intercultural communication researcher Michael Handford[131] and his colleague Hiro Tanaka worked as independent communication consultants over several years helping to improve international business communication for senior and future leaders in Japan. Their consultancy work demonstrates how it is possible to dispel politeness myths that there are national cultural differences that individuals are pre-programmed to live and work by. One of Handford and Tanaka's clients is a large engineering firm in Japan. The senior leaders at this company wanted their engineers who had been identified as future leaders in international markets to be more confident when communicating with international audiences. As part of this, they were trained to break away from thinking in unhelpful national stereotypes that they held about other groups, some examples of which included the following:

Native speakers of English are very direct.
French people are dishonest in business.

Singaporeans are lazy.
Singaporeans are good communicators.
English native speaker humour is not funny.
Native speakers of English talk too much.
Native speakers of English are very aggressive.[132]

A prime method to question the stereotypes about other cultures is firstly to break down the stereotypes that one has about one's own culture. For the Japanese engineers, this included their deeply ingrained belief that Japanese people are more polite than people from other countries, as well as being more indirect, quiet and shy. They also initially held the stereotypical belief that Japanese people work harder.

To recalibrate, the engineers were firstly encouraged to identify stereotypes *within* Japanese society, to encourage them to think about diversity within their own national culture. Examples that they came up with of groups within Japanese society with different communication styles included Japanese biker gangs ('*bosozoku*'), company 'salarymen', ethnic Korean permanent residents in Japan ('*zainnichi kankokujin*') and Shibuya high school girls, known as '*yamamba*'.[133] Having identified these different groups, the engineers realised there is no such thing as only one 'Japanese way'[134] to communicate – for example, Japanese engineers communicate very differently from members of Japanese biker gangs. This process then helped them to question and rethink the other stereotypes that they had expressed about people from other countries. They started to be able to recognise that there is variation within large cultural categories – people from particular geographical locations such as Singapore or France, or native English speakers are far more than just one homogeneous mass who all communicate in exactly the same way.

Once the leadership trainees had been taught how to question Japanese stereotypes, they could then move on to challenge the stereotypes they had of people from different cultures. This then opened up a model of successful international business relationships in which people adapt their styles to the audience with whom they are communicating. Handford reports that this process allowed the future leaders to consider how the stereotypes they held were holding them back. By engaging in such training, the trainees started to unpick and critique dominant cultural stereotypes, which then helped them to see diversity not just in Japan but also in other groups from across different cultures and countries too. Most importantly, it taught them that they were not pre-programmed to communicate in one particular way and that they could change and adapt their communication styles depending on whom they were communicating with. And the results had a very positive impact on the business's bottom line. In the first two years that the training ran, the company's international sales increased by 300 per cent, attributable to the communications-based training programme, which succeeded in breaking down ingrained stereotypes of Japanese politeness.

The changes to politeness and behaviours are epitomised in a report from one external partner, who told of how a Japanese engineer whom he had known for many years had been transformed by the training, as he had gone from being 'very non-communicative, overly vague and impersonal',[135] to becoming vocal and engaged in meetings. His increased levels of engagement applied to both body language and speech; he explained things much more in meetings and he also engaged in small talk and brought in photos of his family, which greatly improved the interpersonal relationships between them and their ability to do effective business.

These changes may seem quite small but the impact they had was huge. Learning how to identify the stereotypes that one has about one's own culture can bring a significant breakthrough in unpicking stereotypes that one holds about other cultures. National stereotypes are easy to understand, which is presumably one of the reasons they remain popular, but, as Handford points out, they are too often 'absurdly simple' and they obscure what is a much more complex picture of human workplace interaction.

The economic and social value of engaging in work which debunks national stereotypes by breaking down politeness myths is very clear to see from Handford and Tanaka's results. However, business training manuals and more traditional communication training materials still persist in propagating inaccurate national stereotypes. This most often ends up doing much more harm than good as it damages professional relationships by reinforcing inaccurate stereotypes and over-generalisations of how people allegedly communicate at work. A more subtle and nuanced approach to thinking about cultural differences will yield much better results in terms of improving relationships with international markets and opening up real opportunities to understand the subtleties of successful leadership communication. It also enables leaders to adapt and change their politeness styles based on a number of factors relating to context and identity, not just based on misleading national stereotypes.

Humour

Humour has long been seen as peripheral to 'proper' workplace talk in global business communications training. However, when real-life recordings of leaders talking at work are analysed by sociolinguists, they consistently find that humour is far more commonplace and essential in getting workplace tasks achieved than was first assumed. Humour fulfils a number of important leadership functions, including releasing tension, expressing solidarity and collegiality, criticising, challenging and warning. It can also be another useful politeness device for leaders to use to issue their orders indirectly. Humour allows a leader's personality to come through, as they draw on creative language devices, within the confines of the politeness norms for their company culture, gender or ethnicity.

A good leader will use humour strategically to fulfil a range of tasks. They will be able to control the amount and type of humour that takes place, making sure that boundaries of unacceptable behaviour aren't being crossed by their colleagues and subordinates. The types of humour that are acceptable will depend on the politeness norms of the workplace, and these will shift over time. Some workplaces may function well with the darker side of humour, including teasing, banter, jocular abuse, sarcasm and irony. In other workplace cultures, less risky strategies such as sharing funny stories or telling jokes which don't threaten individual reputations or the self-esteem of colleagues may be dominant.

Part of the power of humour as a politeness device comes from its ambiguity. It can often be quite difficult to know how serious someone is being if they convey a message using humour. Humour can be used strategically to disguise the power behind a leadership message. Leaders can always deny that they were being serious if their humour doesn't land well. For instance, consider the following example from Amy, whom we met previously, taken from a weekly meeting of all the sales teams across the business.

Amy is chairing a meeting and is talking to her status equal, James. James had been missing from many of the previous meetings when his team had suffered drops in their sales figures. He has not sent apologies, or provided any reasons why he did not come, thus breaking the expected politeness rules. On this occasion, his team's sales figures have gone up and he has just finished detailing how his team have had the most successful week for sales across the business. Amy comes in and uses banter to criticise him for not attending in the previous weeks.

Amy: Is that why you came to the meeting today?

James: Hey, I'm sitting here next to three latecomers and business is dealt with too quickly, thank you very much.

Amy: You don't come all these weeks when it's down and when it's up, he's here!

[Laughter from meeting participants, apart from James, who glares at Amy.]

James: But I've been quite stretched.

Amy: I know you have; I'm only pulling your leg, James.[136]

Amy's banter caused a great deal of laughter from the rest of the meeting participants, half of whom were James's subordinates. The rather sudden shift in pronouns when Amy moves from 'you' to 'he' showed a powerful shift from talking *to* James to talking *about* him, effectively distancing and challenging him while he is still sitting right in front of everyone. Amy was damaging his reputation by deflating his ego and it quickly became clear that James was resistant to the negative way in which Amy was representing him, particularly as this was taking place in front of members of his team. He countered her criticism and Amy eventually backtracked with the idiom 'I'm only pulling your leg'. The criticism, however, remained implicit due to the ambiguity of humour in general. Amy had previously expressed her annoyance to me about James's repeated non-attendance and his failure to be accountable to the broader sales group when things didn't go to plan for his team, so clearly there was some truth to the leg-pulling.

In an interview with Amy, she described how, in her previous workplace, banter was frequently used and accepted as it was a competitive environment where sales staff were pitted against each other. Banter is defined as a 'jocular insult',[137] where people insult each other but under the guise that it is not to be taken seriously. Banter has also been referred to as belonging to the 'dark' side[138] of humour, as it is a more socially risky form of humour that involves attacking someone and there is potential for banter to be misinterpreted or offence to be taken. Banter, as a more threatening form of humour, is not common in this workplace. This is another example of where Amy's leadership style doesn't fit in with the workplace culture where she found herself. Banter as a form of humour is also seen as more of a stereotypically masculine speech style, which again distances Amy from the expected gendered norms for her as a female manager.[139]

In a study of the use of banter in IT industries in New Zealand, Barbara Plester and Janet Sayers[140] found that, in contrast to Amy's workplace, banter was very common. It was most frequent between those in more junior positions and between those who have equal status. Although leaders may sometimes take part in banter, they were found to initiate banter far less than their junior colleagues. The stakes are very high for leaders if they initiate banter and get it wrong, and senior staff reported being very wary of risking causing offence. Banter was only really used by leaders in cases where there was already a well-established relationship of trust and mutual respect between themselves and another member of staff.

The boundaries between banter and offence can be difficult to ascertain and, in worst-case scenarios, it can leave leaders and their organisations open to litigation cases if the comments are interpreted as harassing or prejudicial. This has become even more important in recent years as equity, diversity and inclusion policies are becoming much more firmly integrated into workplaces, and changes in employment law and industry regulation are being implemented as part of a broader cultural shift to address bias, harassment and prejudice in workplaces. And so leaders need to be very careful with banter, and ideally ensure that they only use it when they can confidently predict how it is going to land with the target.

Leaders also need to keep track, where possible, of how their subordinates are using banter towards each other and intervene in cases where politeness boundaries are crossed. However, as Plester and Sayers have observed, often colleagues will use banter to 'take the piss' out of each other when leaders are deliberately out of earshot. So, it may well be that leaders are not even party to a good deal of banter that takes place, and so there will be a limit as to how much they can monitor it in these circumstances. However, they will be called upon to pick up the pieces if something insulting, offensive or prejudicial is articulated that breaks the law and/or breaks the dignity policy of a workplace.

In the UK alone, workplace litigation cases which cite banter have reached a record high, with 2022 statistics reporting a 45 per cent increase in labelling behaviour as 'banter' as a form of defence from the previous year.[141] When workplace banter oversteps the mark and offence is caused, it can be classified as unlawful discrimination if remarks have been made about one or more of the protected characteristics covered under the Equality Act 2010: age, gender reassignment, being married or in a civil partnership, being pregnant or on maternity leave, disability, race including colour, nationality, ethnic or national origin, religion or belief, sex or sexual orientation.

Plester and Sayers[142] found that a good deal of banter focused on the personal identity features of colleagues including physical appearance, sex, race and ethnicity. This can result in expensive and costly grievances and employment tribunals. Solicitor Tom Clarke, at UK-based law firm Hay & Kilner,[143] draws attention to the overarching importance of workplace norms for banter in such cases. He cites a landmark case in which an employee had been called a 'fat, ginger pikey'. The complainant lost because their workplace culture normalised banter, and the claimant had often engaged in very similar banter himself. So, in the eyes of the law, it couldn't be reasonably established that such a comment was unwarranted.

It is part of a successful leader's responsibility to ensure that members of their workforce are not subject to abuse or harassment at work. And so, for best practice, it is advisable for leaders to carefully consider and review where the boundaries of politeness and acceptable behaviour are as far as banter is concerned. Ideally, leaders should be able to clarify the often blurry lines between banter and harassment for their teams. It is very helpful if workforce members can understand where the boundaries are between politeness and offence, as well as how the law works. Basically, it's important to realise that the established politeness norms for banter in any workplace *will* be drawn upon as evidence and can directly affect the outcomes of grievance hearings and tribunals.

Coming back to somewhat cheerier matters now, though, leaders can use humour in less risky ways, and one of the most creative methods to do this is through humorous storytelling, which enhances social bonds. Storytelling can also be a very effective way of giving orders more indirectly and so can be an important part of a leader's repertoire in some workplace cultures. To illustrate, here's an excellent example from meeting data collected by Stephanie Schnurr and colleagues[144] from another Māori organisation. The leader, chairperson and instigator of humour in this meeting is Rangi, who is well respected within his firm. There has been a complaint made about the state the microwave is being left in, and so Rangi needs to ensure that this impolite behaviour stops. To deliver the order that 'you must clean up the microwave immediately if you make a mess in it' to colleagues at different status levels from across the organisation, Rangi decides to tell a long, humorous story. It involves a series of fantasy sequences, with Rangi putting on the voices of different characters from the workplace, as well as pretending to be the messy microwave culprit. As Schnurr and colleagues point out, he delivers his order as a very lengthy humorous 'skit'. As part of this, he even brings along a prop, a cardboard box.

The skit starts as follows, and Rangi laughs throughout his speech: '*Kia ora koutou* ['hello everyone'], but before we start this is my magic box.' The magic box (Rangi's cardboard box) is

146

the workplace microwave. The research team classify this as an example of 'fantasy' humour, where the leader makes up imaginary sequences of workplace communication. He uses role play and word play to add to the humour and he frequently switches between Māori and English – all audience members are fluent in both languages. He makes it clear that the official start of the meeting hasn't yet come, but this is something he is going to talk about before the formal business begins. He pretends to be the dirty microwave 'culprit'. He tells a story of how he goes to make his lunch in the microwave, turns it on, but then his phone rings and so he goes to answer it. On his way back to the microwave, he then gets sidetracked again by talking to a colleague. He uses word play here to describe the informal, humorous phrase 'yackety yack':

> yackety yack yackety yack yackety yack
> ooh my [in Māori] kai [a meal]. I'll race down to the kitchen
> open the door bugger me days
> the damn thing's exploded
> doesn't matter I'll clean it later [sings] I kai away I go
> poor old Yvonne comes down the stairs opens the microwave
> and someone's spewed inside so (in funny voice)
> please team when it happens clean it out straight away.[145]

Rangi's fantasy performance results in much laughter. He manages to successfully deliver the order, whilst not being threatening towards or critical of any one person. Schnurr and colleagues point out that it would have been deeply humiliating and inappropriate in Māori workplace culture to pick out any one person as being responsible for his problem. Instead, the humorous storytelling preserves the reputations of everyone present, whilst simultaneously gaining their compliance, with this rather memorable delivery of a message – it is an ethnically appropriate way of delivering orders. It is not uncommon in

Māori workplaces for humour to be extensive. It also shows that, as a leader, Rangi has a good sense of humour and that he does not take himself too seriously.

Humour can also be used by leaders to build solidarity and collegiality through using insults or verbal aggressiveness towards people who aren't present. With leaders who favour a command-and-control style of leadership, they often present themselves as being the one person who will stand up for what is right by being outspoken. This is frequently accompanied by demonstrating some form of heroism, where the individual leader has succeeded in the face of adversity. In one manufacturing company where I spent time researching with different departments, sales and marketing leader Keith adopted this style of humour. He used verbal aggressiveness and insults as a form of humour to criticise others in the business who were not part of his sales team. Here is a typical example where he criticises the senior managers in the business who are responsible for ordering new product design forms:

> **Keith:** A form is a bloody form at the end of the day. For God's sake why do they keep on bloody changing it all the time? I just don't understand. It pisses me off it really does.
> [Laughter from many]

Keith also frequently tells stories in meetings of how he deals with difficult clients by using his direct communication style. In this example, company director Craig instigates humour by suggesting that Keith should be sent in to 'sort out' a difficult customer who has not paid his account. Keith continues the humour in response:

> **Craig:** We should send you in, Del, sort him out. [Laughs]
> **David:** Well, Del was ready, I've asked him.

Keith: I'm coming to the meeting.

David: Del was due to sit in on the meeting tomorrow.

Keith: Yeah, I polished me jackboots last night.

[Laughter from many]

. . .

Keith: They're wide boys at the end of the day and you have to treat them with the contempt that they deserve.

[Laughter from many]

Craig: I'm sure you're good at that, Keith.

[Laughter from many]

Keith: I am. They're sharks some of them and they'll shaft you soon as look at you, do you know what I mean, and you have to tackle them in a certain way.

[Laughter from many][146]

Craig shifts his term of address for Keith here, using the nickname 'Del', a shortened version of Keith's surname, which David then also adopts. This is the only point in the three-hour meeting where Keith is referred to as Del. It is very similar to how nicknames are used in all-male sports teams to strengthen group bonds (see chapter six). It is particularly effective here as Craig is drawing on metaphors of war and battle when he suggests that Del should go in and 'sort him out', a phrase with connotations of confrontation and violence. Keith continues this topic and extends the humour by bringing in a fantasy about polishing his 'jackboots'.

As a senior leader, Craig has instigated the humour and it works to build a sense of solidarity amongst his team at the expense of the difficult customers who are not paying their bills. He simultaneously praises Keith for being able to deal with people who are withholding money from the firm. It also acts to release tension – the business needs its customers to start paying their bills, which is a source of concern for many at the meeting who are worried about cash flow. We would assume that the insults 'wide boys' and 'sharks' would not be used face to face with these customers (unless something had gone seriously wrong with the relationship), but the humour from using these terms releases the tension and 'Del' is presented as the workplace hero who will go and sort them out on behalf of everyone with his direct and confrontational style. Keith's communication style in this company-wide meeting is very different from the other meeting participants', but it is similar to the rest of the sales team in this business who favour competitive, direct and confrontational communication styles. Whether he is acting as Keith or Del, these stereotypically masculine speech styles that Keith adopts are positively evaluated by his colleagues. He is not reprimanded by the leader of this meeting. Instead, Craig actively encourages this competitive style and it is seen as appropriate for the topic and the circumstances of the meeting, where the team are identifying themselves in opposition to their difficult customers.

Another effective way in which humour can be used is by subordinates to challenge their leaders. Humour again works as a protective guise in these cases and subordinates can hide behind the humour if the message doesn't land well with their leadership critique. The next example is from a workplace where I conducted research and observation. This workplace had missed its annual sales targets and no one had received their annual bonuses so morale was low. One of the reasons for this was that too much stock was ordered. Here, junior staff member Julie challenges her leaders for not listening to her:

Carl: I didn't realise we had fifteen pallets' worth.
[Julie exhales loudly and looks angry]
David: It's not true to say but—
Julie: [Interrupting] And I can't believe you're saying that!
    I told you lot about it. [laughs]
David: Oh, right.
[Laughter from many]

Julie does well here to use humour to successfully challenge her leaders. Their failure to listen to her has cost the company money. Challenging bosses in any way can be very risky, but Julie shows how a critical message can be delivered without any repercussions to her by using humour as a veil for the challenge. And, hopefully, for the sake of this company's success, they will remember this and look out for junior members of staff sounding alarm bells about excess stock at an earlier point in the sales cycle in future. Because humour is seen as something that does not officially count as 'real' business talk, junior staff can get away with criticisms that would be too impolite to deliver without the cushion of humour.

A final example of humour is also taken from the same firm. Simon has already been told by Sharon that the meeting that he is in charge of is running over schedule. Despite this, Simon opens up another topic under any other business, much to the dismay of those present. He then decides to go into great detail on this topic. At this point in the meeting, the other participants are fidgeting, getting their papers together and starting to put their coats on to signal their desire to finish. Simon picks up on the hostility towards him and responds to it by saying, 'I realise I'm boring you, but there's an important point to all this,' to try to hold their attention. Instead of taking Simon's remarks as an occasion to repair the relationship, the group continues their critique and increases their level of impoliteness towards Simon. Carol comes in and uses humour by laughing and issuing the direct order 'Yes, yes, come on then.' Becky interrupts him and then goes on to repeatedly bang her coffee cup on the table. This paralinguistic act is viewed by Simon as rude and disruptive, and he calls her out on this, giving her a direct order to 'stop hassling me'. Becky immediately responds, but not by stopping. Instead, she escalates the impoliteness, albeit under the guise of humour. She denies that she was hassling him and instead states, 'I wasn't, I was giving you a drum roll.' Simon does not know how to react to this. He hesitates, then says, 'Oh, right.' Julie and Becky then both use sarcasm to keep the humour going. They come in and say 'important, exciting bit' and 'important', respectively. Then Becky and Sharon start banging their coffee cups together in an even louder supposed 'drum roll'.

Becky, Carol and Julie have crossed a politeness boundary here and deliberately attacked Simon and his ability to chair the meeting, albeit under the guise of humour. They are frustrated with his inability to chair a meeting effectively and to be concise in his verbal style. Simon eventually regains the floor and makes his point, but at this stage, it appears that very few people are listening and the force of his message does not come through as he has lost his audience by bringing up the topic too late in a meeting that is already running over and by not being concise in making his point. If leaders wish to have a maximum impact when making serious points, then they should make sure that they are concise, and if a topic is that important, then it should go on an official agenda. If there genuinely is not time to do this, then the importance of the topic needs to be signalled a lot sooner, so meeting participants are prepared that they will be in the meeting longer.

The team have jointly engaged with one another in this episode of impoliteness to collectively attack Simon and his inability to chair meetings effectively. However, they do still use impoliteness under the protection of humour. As humour is such a powerful and ambiguous linguistic device, it enables them to get around Simon's direct accusations of inappropriateness by claiming that they are not being serious. The humorous guises they adopt make it very difficult for Simon to challenge their impolite actions.

In an interview with me following the meeting, Becky directly commented on Simon's ineffective chairing style and negatively evaluated how he dominates talking time in meetings. She said that 'he'd go on all day if we'd let him'. This, combined with the team's overall frustration that their sector director, the official meeting chair, had not prioritised coming to the meeting, added to the overall sense of frustration and arguably contributed to the impoliteness that took place.

Small talk

In a similar vein to humour, small talk has only recently been recognised as an integral part of leadership communication. It has been too frequently dismissed as something that is periph- eral and dispensable to workplace talk 'proper'. However, when real-life workplace talk is recorded and linguistically analysed, small talk has been found to be an essential part of workplace communication. Effective small talk is a key part of emotional intelligence. It enhances harmony and rapport between speakers, and it can also be used to minimise power and status differ- ences, as well as to release tension. By engaging in small talk in the workplace, leaders can actively demonstrate that they have an interest in the lives of the people with whom they are working. Failure to acknowledge the importance of small talk as a powerful tool of successful workplace communication and a key form of emotional intelligence means that it too often gets overlooked in training and professional development, with too much emphasis given to 'transactional' talk, the talk that gets work done.

Sociolinguistic politeness research has consistently demon- strated that transactional and relational categories blend into one another in effective leadership communication; any efforts to separate them out is unhelpful as the two elements are fundamen- tally interconnected. Leaders with strong emotional intelligence blend together good interpersonal communication with how they give orders, and effectively deliver all the messages and guidance that they need to disseminate in interactions with others.

Small talk also has some other essential uses in different lines of work. Dawn Archer and colleagues[147] draw attention to how security and military personnel working undercover have for many years used small talk as a core part of their job role to test someone's character. Effective use of small talk can enable undercover security agents working in airports and on board flights to make assessments about a person's credibility without the person who is of interest even realising. To illustrate, Archer and her colleagues drew on their expertise to work collaboratively with aviation authorities to create 'small talk' training packages for leaders working as behaviour detection officers, whose role is to spot whether people are behaving suspiciously in airports. Small talk works as an effective strategy that keeps the public safe with the added advantage of not alarming anyone – the undercover officers are in plain clothes and just blend in as they pretend to be fellow passengers.

Archer and colleagues created a series of mnemonics, one of which is termed 'FORCED', which stands for engaging in conversation on the following topics: family/friends, occupation/skills, recreation, current events, education/qualifications, dreams/plans.[148] These topics have been identified in English language teaching materials as being very typical conversational starters with strangers in aviation settings and therefore should not attract suspicion. Detection officers were advised to make sure that there was variation in terms for the time period that the FORCED topics referred to. They were trained to make sure that some of their questions focused on events from the past, whilst others focused on what was going to happen in future (in terms of arrival at destination, reason for travel, future goals etc.), to test the legitimacy of the identity being presented by the passenger.

Another of the team's mnemonics is the acronym PERFECT – this one is designed to help behavioural detection leaders focus on exactly how they can elicit responses and information from the passenger. PERFECT stands for: making provocative state-ments, encouraging complaining, using repetition, engaging in flattery, using erroneous statements/naivete, and criticising and testing perceived/reported reality, including feigning disbelief.[149] Archer and colleagues advised officers not to exceed a few min-utes of engaging in small talk to avoid suspicion, which means they need to be able to make decisions quickly. Officers are taught to look out for features including inconsistencies in facial expressions during small talk, inconsistent/anomalous body lan-guage or gestures, muscular tension, changes in skin colour and breathing patterns, along with not referring to the self (using 'I', 'me' or 'my') very often. All of these factors can throw up potential suspicion that the person in question may not be who they are claiming to be on their flight documents.

What is crystal clear from the work of Archer and her team is that small talk is far more than a device for maintaining good interpersonal relationships. It can also be used as a key strategic tool to attempt to thwart terrorist attacks (in this case, as part of the aviation industry), as well as being used in undercover police, military and security operations, where trained professionals also try and engage with people who are potentially behaving sus-piciously.

So far in this chapter, we have concentrated on leaders who work in larger organisations. I now want to diversify our leadership focus somewhat to also include those working in much smaller, more entrepreneurial industries, to see how small talk can present different issues for them and be used in different ways. Linguist Michael McCarthy[150] examined two professions where individ-uals were leaders in small businesses, as hairdressers and driving instructors. He was interested in working out the role that small talk plays when people are trapped in 'mutually captive' audi-ences: places where the professional and their client need to stay physically close to one another due to the nature of the service provision that is offered, like cutting someone's hair and teaching someone how to drive. These can be socially awkward situations, so politeness needs to come into its own in these environments to help ease awkwardness and potential tension. McCarthy argues that, whilst small talk may be regarded as banal or trivial by some, and technically it is non-obligatory, without it, the alternative is sitting in silence, which would be much more culturally threatening in UK contexts. In hairdressing and driving lessons, small talk is often well integrated with transactional talk and so plays important roles for both interpersonal relationships and for conveying important information.

McCarthy draws attention to a distinction between what he calls long-term relationships versus relationships with strangers, which will affect the amount and type of small talk that is used. The interactions McCarthy examines are long-term – it is common for people to keep the same hairdresser over a period of time and it is also expected that the same person will teach you how to drive until you pass your test. And so there was already an established set of politeness norms between speakers in these encounters, as they already know each other. Some of the main conversational topics that are focused on in the hairdressers are: the weather, holidays, the family of the stylist, family birthdays, a customer who suffered hair loss, and the issue of men versus women wearing wigs.

Here's an example of the client engaging in humour and small talk at the same time:

Stylist: There's some armholes in the gown.
Client: Oh, is there? [laughs] A bit like Batman otherwise [laughs].[151]

The 'Batman' part of the comment is not necessary in terms of the transaction of putting on the gown to protect one's clothing while haircutting takes place. But it is valuable as it does an effective job of enhancing the social relationships between the hairdresser and their client and likely helps with the client's potential embarrassment for not finding the armholes on the gown quicker.

In driving lessons, the main communication focus needs to be on instruction, for rather obvious safety reasons. McCarthy observes that when traffic slows down or there are periods of less intensity, the instructor and student will both move towards small talk. Here's an example of where they talk about the weather when the car is travelling at a steady speed and there are no obvious distractions:

Instructor: It's a nice day now, actually, isn't it?
Learner: Oh, it's beautiful, yeah.
Instructor: Makes you full of the joys of spring, doesn't it?
Learner: It does, yeah.[152]

The learner driver goes on to talk about a walk he does and the different flowers he sees on his walk. The instructor then brings the small talk to a close and immediately moves back to transactional talk: from 'It's a nice time of the year' to 'Back down to third again'.[153] The driving instruction is delivered directly, but this is fully in line with politeness expectations here, as there is a big power difference between the instructor and student. We saw this earlier on in the chapter with the firefighter on duty comment as the context demands urgency and efficiency of information exchange to ensure that everyone's safety is preserved.

In summary, when leaders demonstrate that they have an interest in the lives of the people with whom they are talking, they can use small talk to strengthen collegial relationships in workplace environments, as well as a strategy for networking. Small talk can be successfully used as a means of creating a sense of community, whilst maintaining and enhancing collegiality and solidarity in workplace teams, and simultaneously reinforcing a boss's leadership role. Other functions of conversations on personal or social topics include providing smooth introductions to work-related or core business topics. Also, social talk can be used to effectively mark out the beginning or the end of an encounter; leaders can control how much is said on a specific subject or they can simply move on to a different topic through small talk. Small talk can also help achieve or contest the transactional goals of the business.

Demonstrating emotional intelligence is a primary way for leaders to use politeness strategies to monitor the productivity and the well-being of their teams. One of the key ways to promote workplace inclusion is to engage team members in appropriate small talk so that they ideally feel fully integrated and not like their opinions and lives are being neglected, compromised or ignored. Whilst asking questions relating to how others have spent their weekend or enquiring about particular hobbies could be viewed as irrelevant or peripheral in workplace environments, extensive linguistic evidence and analysis shows that social talk is not only very common, but also crucial in business settings to ensure that strong interpersonal relationships are fostered, and that trust and empathy are present.

How to run a successful meeting: A model

Meetings have figured heavily in this chapter, precisely because they are so commonplace in everyday workplace communication. Whatever types of workplaces you have worked in or may currently be working in, the chances are that you will have spent time communicating in meetings. Meetings are frequently described as the lifeblood of organisations[154] and they have been seen as a microcosm for organisations as a whole. Meetings have been studied extensively in politeness research because of this, which has led to a significant amount of authentic, real-life workplace communication to draw on. The ways in which leaders communicate in meetings matters a great deal to their leadership success. A good proportion of the research and consultancy work that I have conducted has focused on meetings, particularly on troubleshooting how ineffective meetings can be improved and made to be more effective.

To bring together everything that we have learnt so far about effective leadership and politeness in meetings, I will now present a mnemonic for how to run a good meeting, based on my politeness research analysis of very effective meetings all the way through to completely ineffective and dysfunctional meetings over the past quarter of a decade. The model goes by the acronym AGENDAS and I have designed it as a planning tool for leaders, though it canbe used by any meeting participants who may want to use it for preparation or for reflection once meetings are over. It applies across industries and sectors. It can be equally applicable to informal meetings of community leaders in local village halls as it is to large, formal meetings which take place in the swanky boardrooms of large multinational organisations. The model brings together the various politeness considerations that need to be taken into account by leaders in order to hold a successful meeting. The mnemonic is broken down as follows:

Audience
Goals
Environment
Norms
Distance
Actions
Speakers

Audience refers to the people who are taking part in the meeting. There will be active and passive audience members, and audience roles will shift between being active and passive during meetings, as individuals are called upon to actively participate and then become passive again once their turn has passed. The meeting chair, usually the most senior workplace leader present, will likely be the most active participant. The chair needs to ensure that everyone who should have been invited to the meeting has been to avoid causing offence. Leaders also need to check if anyone in the audience has been invited by mistake. It is important for all audience members to know what their own role is so that they can be clear on the politeness rules right from the beginning. Who is chairperson? Who is taking the minutes, if there are any?

With hybrid meetings and online meetings, it is common for the politeness and etiquette rules to be formally written down and dropped into the meeting chat. This can include: how will audience members gain the floor? Do speakers have pre-allocated turns? If you want to have an opportunity to take the conversational floor, how will you do this appropriately, whilst still abiding by politeness norms?

Goals refers to what the leader wants the overall outcome to be. Leaders should be clear about what they aim to get out of the meeting and make sure that everyone else who is present is aware of this at the start of the meeting or even before, via email or written documents. Setting an end time and sticking to this is part of the goal setting. The purpose of a meeting may be to hold discussions, to make decisions, to disseminate information or it may be something else. Overall, it's important for leaders to make sure that their meetings stay focused and that the goals stay intact. As we have seen in this chapter, complaints about those who allow meetings to run over or to drift on to topics that were not originally supposed to be discussed are rife and it can often be a sign of poor chairing and planning.

Environment refers to where and when a meeting takes place. Leaders and any others who are assisting them with meeting planning need to make sure that they have an appropriate venue for the meeting that directly aligns with the level of formality that is required. Thinking back to the work of Spencer-Oatey and Xing[155] and the problems that were created by the perceptions of impoliteness that stemmed from the seating arrangements decided by a British company when hosting Chinese guests, it is important for any culture-based politeness expectations for the venue and the room layout to be carefully considered, including deciding beforehand if seating plans are needed.

The consideration of environment also needs to take into account any eating and dietary requirements if food is being laid on to ensure that everyone is appropriately catered for. There have been many meetings that our research team have observed where impoliteness has taken place due to individuals feeling that their needs have not been fairly considered. The time of the meeting should also be carefully planned to ensure that those with caring responsibilities who may work flexible hours are fully able to participate.

In some workplaces, it may be completely acceptable for meetings to take place in more informal environments, such as shop floors, on hospital wards, in garages or on the street, as well as in the more obvious and more traditional meeting room spaces in white-collar businesses. Sometimes meetings can be spontaneous and unplanned. They may take place in corridors, for example, when people just bump into one another, or in private offices when people pop in for a chat about one thing and then end up having a conversation that then turns into something more structured. However, in other settings, formal meetings will be required to take place in boardrooms with carefully planned, pre-circulated agendas. In more formal meeting contexts, we would expect more formal language, including more formal terms of address, to be the norm, along with detailed sets of minutes which track who was present, who said what and when. If any of these aspects are missing from formal meetings when they would be expected, then this can be problematic. Most often in formal meetings, participants will be asked if the minutes are a true and accurate record of what happened in the previous meeting encounter, which gives the chance to correct any inaccuracies that may have crept in.

Environment also includes the channel(s) of communication that will be used for the meeting – what format will the meeting take and what difference could this decision make? Is the meeting face to face, digital or a hybrid? If hybrid, then it is up to the leader to ensure that everyone has equal access to the floor and that clear mechanisms are in place to allow participants to signal they have something to say. It's important to ensure full participation for those online so that they are not having a reduced experience of taking part. It is also key to consider how written texts are used as part of the meeting environment. Most commonly in meetings, you will have a combination of spoken and written communication channels, with written language of minutes, documents for circulation and agendas providing one channel of communication, which then integrates with verbal and non-verbal communication. If a meeting is formal and minuted for organisational records, then it will be essential for all documents to be written in accordance with the workplace's rules for official documents, particularly if these are formal minutes that need to be kept on file and distributed to wider audiences, other than those in the physical or virtual meeting room.

Norms refers to the politeness and etiquette norms that are expected to be in place for any workplace meeting. If we review what we have seen in this chapter, this will include expectations for meeting openings and closings, including how much pre-amble a meeting needs to officially open. This may be short or long, depending upon workplace and community expectation. It also includes the amount of humour and small talk that the group will tolerate, the topics that it is acceptable to talk about, and the levels of directness and indirectness that are expected as group politeness norms during the meeting.

Distance refers to the amount of social distance that exists between audience members in any meeting and how this relates to politeness and power in the workplace in question. What is the hierarchy between people? Who is chairing the meeting? Why have they been selected and who has selected them? Are they the leader of all present or is there another reason why they are chairing? Is a meeting being co-chaired? Why? Or is the chair at the same status level as everyone else? How will these factors affect the chair's ability to control the meeting, if at all? Also, there will be points in meetings at which audience members will have more expert power than the meeting chair because they have more knowledge and authority on a particular workplace topic. At these points, the chair will need to cede the floor to the person(s) with expert power. This means that power should be viewed as something that is fluid in any meeting encounter. In some meetings, social distance will be strong and, in these cases, meetings will tend to be more formal. In other meetings there may be a much greater sense of solidarity between colleagues than social distance, particularly if audience members are status equals, and so this may result in a more informal meeting style.

Actions refers to any of the communicative actions that take place. It includes speech, writing and any non-verbal features of communication. For example, how direct are the conversational strategies used? What can this tell us about politeness and culture in this workplace? What turn-taking system is used? What is the manner or the tone in which something is said? What verbal and non-verbal cues can you use to decide this? What facial expressions and body language are being used?

Leaders will use gaze, including length and frequency, as clues to the emotional state and attitude of their meeting audience, including interest and engagement in the topic. Leaders can also use their own gaze strategically, such as when allocating turns or saying something that they think is directly relevant to particular individuals. For neurodiverse colleagues, this may prove more challenging. In terms of other non-verbal cues, touch will most likely take place as part of ritual openings and closings of meetings, including shaking hands, bowing or giving hugs, depending on intimacy, which again provides cues of emotional state and attitude.

Speakers and silence refer to who speaks when, how speakers change and how silence occurs. Meeting chairs will control the type of conversational floor of the meeting, along with the number and length of turns people take. Linguists have developed turn-taking systems to explain the complexities of how speaker change happens in more structured situations such as meetings, from a politeness and impoliteness perspective. In meetings, for example, speakers may cross the boundaries of acceptable politeness if they interrupt.

There are two main types of conversational floor in meetings and workplace talk more generally speaking. The first is a one-at-a-time floor, where just one person will speak at a time. Bosses allocate the floor carefully and grant turns to different individuals through verbal and non-verbal prompts, often based on meeting agendas. If there is a pause or a gap then the next person who wants to talk can select themselves, often by signalling this to the meeting chair first. The second type of conversational floor is more collaborative and refers to when more than one speaker speaks at the same time. Speakers may finish each other's sentences in a supportive way or they may say similar but slightly different things at the same or similar times, or it may be where two (or more) people say exactly the same thing at the same or slightly different times. This happens most in collaborative, facilitative workplaces in which speakers show support for each other's ideas.

The type of conversational floor adopted by the meeting chair will depend upon a range of factors, including their favoured communicative style, the workplace and broader culture, the task at hand, the context of talk and the personal and social identities of those involved. The conversational floor may shift at strategic points. If companies have flatter structures and favour collaborative, communicative styles, then collaborative floors are more likely to occur.

One common complaint in workplace meetings is that speakers have been interrupted before they have finished their point. Whether or not individuals succeed in gaining the conversational floor in meetings will depend upon whether their boss and/or other colleagues let them carry on or whether they are cut off. The use of these strategies will also be culturally dependent. The cost of using some strategies may outweigh a perceived benefit, depending on politeness norms and expectations.

Dealing with conflict at work

Even in the most harmonious of workplaces, there will be periods of disagreement, argument and conflict that leaders must navigate. Inevitably, there will be times when difficult decisions need to be made and relationships will come under pressure. The key to resolution is how quickly and efficiently leaders can repair such issues, and this will depend upon whether and to what extent politeness norms have been broken and how quickly and efficiently leaders handle workplace conflict.

Business communication research has shown how dis-agreement is an inevitable and important part of workplace communication. When managed properly, it can form an essen-tial part in helping businesses grow and develop. Constructive disagreement, when facilitated by a strong, well-respected leader, can result in pushing businesses forward with creativity and innovation. If there is a foundation of respect and strong social bonds between colleagues, then good rapport can be quickly re-established and harmony can be restored. However, if the boundaries of politeness are crossed, then conflict can become disruptive and negative. In worst-case scenarios, relationships can break down and leaders may not always be able to resolve things. Here we will look at what happens when conflict takes place and politeness boundaries are crossed.

I will start by examining a complex relationship between Sharon and Simon, whom I observed during a workplace con-sultancy project. They both worked for a large multinational manufacturing company and I spent six months observing this organisation at its UK headquarters, including analysing meetings, examining different leadership styles and conducting interviews with leaders and managers as the firm went through a period of structural change following profit losses.

Sharon and Simon were status equals who occupied exactly the same leadership position. They had very similar levels of experience, although Simon had been with this company for three years longer. Sharon and Simon had a very tense working relationship and in interview with me, Simon informed me that he believed Sharon had been hired to do exactly the job that he was already doing. In his view, there was no need for her to have been appointed. There was no formal job advertised; instead, she had come into the business with a new company director who had brought her with him from a competitor organisation. Simon saw far too much crossover in their roles and he felt that Sharon's presence in the business was negatively impacting his career. When I interviewed Sharon, she focused on Simon's personal leadership style and how that created problems for her and for everyone else in the business. She made disparaging comments about his ability to lead, blaming his ineffectiveness on his tendency to pay too much attention to incidental details that she saw as unimportant and his inter-related habit of talking far too much. The following is a typical example of impoliteness taking place between them. This is taken from a company-wide meeting. Sharon and Simon have been asked to report back on yearly sales figures – a task that they had been jointly allocated:

> **Simon:** So that's gone up from three something up on the autumn side [he pauses and looks confused]
>
> [Sharon repeatedly whistles at Simon and then waves a piece of paper at him. She throws this across the room to him rather aggressively]
>
> **Simon:** I'm SOOO sorry [he pauses and picks up a different sheet to the one Sharon had thrown at him]. On page five of the autumn winter one.

Sharon has realised that Simon is reading out the wrong sales figures. However, instead of attracting his attention politely through speech, she instead chooses to try to get one up on him by whistling at him aggressively, which at least ensures that she gets his attention, as well as everyone else's who is at the meeting as part of the audience. It is a communication method that is more commonly associated with pet owners trying to attract the attention of their animals and not something that would be expected in a white-collar boardroom. If we consider alternative ways in which Sharon could have got Simon's attention here, she could have verbalised an utterance such as: 'Simon, I'm really sorry to interrupt but you've got the wrong sheet – here's the right one.' This would at least have been seen as an attempt to mitigate the damage. But by drawing attention to Simon having the wrong sales figures, Sharon simultaneously highlights her own competency in contrast – she is the one who has the correct figures, not Simon.

Sharon's impoliteness towards Simon, expressed by interrupting him and whistling at him like he is a naughty pet, means that the conflict and tension in their relationship is clear to see for all present at the meeting. Sharon's behaviour is interpreted as intentionally impolite by Simon, as an attempt to belittle him. He replies to her sarcastically by performing an apology that is obviously insincere, the sarcasm signalled by shouting 'SOOO' loudly, to act as an intensifier. Simon refuses to use the sheet that Sharon has thrown at him and instead finds the correct sheet in his own bundle of papers, signalling that he does not need Sharon's help. This extract is a typical illustration of how Sharon and Simon try to undermine each other in front of their colleagues. The struggle for power and status between them causes a great deal of tension not just for them, but for those who work with them.

We can conclude from this that leaders are at their most effective when they have a clear remit for their own leadership role. If two people are appointed to effectively do the same role, without being told they are co-leading, and they have no clear role delineation between them, then chances are that they will get in each other's way and conflict and tension will occur. This can negatively affect them and everyone else that they work with.

Shortly after this meeting was recorded, Sharon left the company for a new role in a different organisation where she had more autonomy and more room to develop her career. She expressed in interview that her relationship with Simon was at breaking point. The competitiveness between the two of them had resulted in impoliteness taking place regularly in meetings and this was no good for anyone. Sharon had therefore decided to apply for more senior roles with other organisations so that she could move on and make a fresh start. She was promoted to one of these posts and made the decision to leave the firm, much to Simon's delight.

In another study of workplace conflict, impoliteness and leadership, Carolin Debray[156] investigated a team of six professionals who were part of a cohort of Master's students studying for an MBA (Master of Business Administration) at a UK university. They had been placed in this team as part of their MBA qualification with people whom they didn't previously know. Their collective task was to complete four business projects together in eight months, which involved them working as a team of consultants with external organisations. Outside the university setting, they all had established, high-profile leadership positions as their day jobs.

While the group tried to work together, it quickly became dysfunctional. One problem was that one team member, Alden, was far too silent, which all other members found problematic. They decided to get around this by ignoring Alden and carrying on as if he wasn't there. Not an ideal solution, of course, and not one that I would advocate, but it did mean that the group could carry on with their projects. But a much more disruptive problem emerged from another group member, David. David's communication style was repeatedly seen as impolite as he was too direct and too disrespectful to the rest of the team. Different group members had the chance to lead the different projects during the eight-month period. The following example is taken from when David was selected as group leader. His impolite leadership style is epitomised in the following:

David: Everyone understands that we need to have work on the table by 11 February? . . . If people haven't done it then they're really letting the entire team down because we're really up against it here, so please make sure that stuff is done . . . I'm literally going to go fucking crazy if people don't get their shit done.[157]

None of the other team members resorted to direct, explicit threats or the use of expletives that David uses when it was their turn to lead. David presumably adopts these strategies because he thinks they will work as motivational tools, but without reflecting on the difference in styles or taking time to consider whether his style negatively impacts the group.

In an interview with members of the team, Bev explains why she believes David to be the most problematic group member: 'I feel like the rest of us . . . we respect each other's opinions, we feel comfortable, but once he is in the room there's this pressure to do something different.'[158]

Debray observes how Bev and others back down quickly when talking with David. They do not question his decisions and they show him extra consideration, but this doesn't bring positive results. In fact, there is only one team member, Akshya, who feels able to challenge David. However, their interactions often descend into unproductive conflict and damaging arguments, which side-tracks the group and stops them from progressing. In the following example, David and Akshya have already been arguing for at least fifty turns already. They are disagreeing about some text on their presentation slides. At this point, David uses metacommunication to bluntly and directly deliver his point of view:

David: I can't explain it more clearly.
[loud laughter]
Bev: We knew that the both of you would never agree.
Bruno: It was just a matter of time, to be honest.
David: Can anyone else see my point of view? I don't understand—
Akshya: I understand what he SAID, I'm just SAYING SOMETHING ELSE.

Bev: It's okay for both of you to just, no you can't drive us in. We've been doing this for all of twenty years. This is just one tiny thing in all our slides. Can we just move on?

Jay: Yes! it's just one line.

Bruno: Yes, right, okay.

David: I think it is important.[159]

Despite Bev, Bruno and other team members trying to resolve the argument and get David and Akshya to move on, this topic never gets resolved. In the end, they decide to entirely leave out this controversial part of their presentation from their final report, despite it being central to their project. They therefore put the avoidance of conflict before their project's success and end up compromising their academic achievements.

After the MBA projects had been completed, some of the group expressed regret for not standing up to David. For example, Bev said, 'Right now, I kick myself. There are many times I should have told him off and said my piece . . . maybe we would be in a different place.'

The group also realised that because they didn't confront David about how they felt, they never gave him the opportunity to try to change his leadership style. In his interview, David spoke positively about his colleagues. Of course, we cannot know that he was being genuine here, but because there was no direct confrontation, it is difficult to assess how much awareness David had about how unpopular he was.

The difficulties with politeness that arise when you want to be critical of someone's leadership style are one of the reasons why many organisations employ what's called 360-degree feedback, where workplace teams can anonymously assess their leaders in questionnaire form, without the threat of having these comments attributed to them and without having to do this face to face. Whilst the method of 360-degree feedback is not perfect and is not without its critics, it is one way of attempting to get around the problem of the socio-cultural politeness norm of wanting to maintain rapport at all costs, which can make it difficult for people to criticise, especially if they do not feel comfortable with the person whose style they do not like.

In Debray's study, these participants have not known each other for long and they show that breaking politeness norms is not something that they find easy, even if they are frustrated and disagree with someone who is being difficult. With the exception of David and Akshya, members of the team are very reluctant to break rapport, particularly with someone quite hostile, like David. It is not uncommon for people at work to decide that it is easier to keep the peace short term by abiding by politeness norms than it is to have open conflict, particularly if that person has a direct, aggressive communication style.

Also, the group in Debray's study knew that their time with David would come to an end as they were only together for the eight-month duration of the projects that they needed to complete for their MBA studies. As it was, the other group members couldn't wait for the project stage of the MBA to be over and they never made contact with David again (despite the group otherwise all staying in touch with each other).

However, in many workplaces, there is no end date in sight for people in dysfunctional teams with leaders that they find to be rude and inappropriate – this was the case with Simon and Sharon. If there is too much emotional cost to individuals and/or if people feel that they are being treated unfairly or inappropriately, then their relationships may well break down to the point that they can no longer be functional on a day-to-day basis. Sharon and Simon did not show respect for each other and strong social bonds were clearly not in place. Their relationship had deteriorated over time, taking them to a place where the conflict between them had become damaging and unproductive. In such cases, individuals may well decide to leave an organisation. Sharon had certainly had enough of the conflict between her and Simon and this prompted her to find a new job with a different company so that she could move on with her career.

Summary

What does everything that we have encountered in this chapter tell us about politeness, impoliteness and leadership success at work? How can what we have learnt here be used to improve leadership performance? I would argue that successful leaders are those who can respond appropriately in any situation, even in the most challenging and demanding of circumstances, with the most difficult of people. Learning how the unwritten rules of politeness and impoliteness work in any business or organisation and being able to shift and adapt quickly in response to ever-changing contexts and situations are critical for effective leadership. Knowing your audience and ensuring the clarity of the message being delivered, whilst still maintaining strong interpersonal relationships are key.

I would also argue that an effective leader is one who has the ability to reflect upon their own communication styles, without needing to be told to do so or without being forced to do so by colleagues or workplace processes. Leaders should be doing this as a matter of course. Good leaders need to be emotionally intelligent. They need to be able to form strong interpersonal relationships with others. Paying very careful attention to politeness norms is key to ensuring that emotional intelligence is not lost. Good leaders will continually assess their interpersonal relationships and review how their communication strategies are being received and understood by their audience. They are able to consider whether they need to adjust their communication to get the outcomes they want, and they will change their behaviours accordingly if required. It may include using non-traditional leadership tools such as humour and small talk to one's advantage. If leaders can ensure that trust, respect and strong social bonds are in place between themselves and their audience, whether this is their subordinates, customers or clients, then they will be prepared for any conflict that may come their way. Ideally, they will be set up to manage disagreement in productive ways. Relationships can be quickly repaired if leaders can adeptly handle difficult conversations and so, ideally, conflict can be contained within the boundaries of politeness. If it can be turned into a productive and creative discussion, that can then move the business forward in a positive direction.

It is worth remembering at this point that the leadership politeness strategies in this book are not presented as guarantees that workplace leaders will get certain results. Rather, hopefully it is clear by now that language is unpredictable and messy, and that, as speakers and hearers, you may not get what you originally intended. Rather, I am giving you access to different styles to reflect on, with the aim of raising your conscious awareness of a variety of strategies which have been used successfully by leaders in real-life workplace communication, so that informed and strategic decisions can be made.

It is also worth recalling that, quite often, different teams and departments develop distinctive subcultures and they may use very different communication patterns and norms as part of these subcultures. Some subcultures may compete with one another and some may be resistant to the norms and values of the organisational culture as a whole. For instance, in one multinational organisation where I conducted research, the communicative strategies of leaders varied greatly depending upon the type of department – the organisation's sales and marketing director favoured a very competitive, assertive style, whereas the design department's leader preferred a very co-operative, collaborative style. When they came together in larger meetings where both departments needed to be represented, they frequently clashed and impoliteness would occur. There was a good deal of rivalry between the two departments. The sales department frequently complained that the designers were letting them down by being too 'airy fairy' and taking too long to finish new product designs. So, the type of role responsibility that each team has, particularly in larger organisations, can differ and different subcultures can emerge. This can play an influential role in the communication strategies that are favoured by leaders and other members of these teams.

The important overall message here is that, whether you are communicating as a leader in a monolingual environment where everyone is from the same town, or in a multilingual environment with people from numerous countries, if you are experiencing miscommunication problems, then culture could be playing a role. However, it is essential not to fall back on cultural stereotypes when trying to unpick this just because they provide easy explanations. There are various facets to all of our personal, social and professional identities which could be affecting politeness and rapport.

We have focused on assessing how successful leaders use politeness strategies to get workplace tasks successfully achieved, whilst also maintaining strong interpersonal relationships, ensuring that mutual respect and rapport is maintained. This has included dispelling some ingrained myths about politeness and leadership, including those around politeness and gender stereotypes, and around politeness and national cultural stereo-types. We have also seen how the levels of clarity with which some orders and demands need to be delivered in workplace cultures can literally turn into matters of life and death, as with the earlier fire service example.

This chapter has focused on how leaders communicate to ensure tasks are being achieved, and how good leaders are able to shift and adapt quickly in response to ever-changing contexts and situations. Competence and abilities of leaders will change over time with increased experience and expertise, further qualifications, promotions and the length of time that a leader has been with an organisation. Whilst we have seen patterns around different workplace cultures depending upon whether a command-and-control or more egalitarian set of communication principles are dominant, the best leaders will be able to use a wide repertoire of styles to suit their particular circumstances.

As workplaces continue to become more diverse, global and technologically advanced in future, and politeness norms continue to shift, the most successful leaders will be those who are able to adapt and blend together different communication styles in response to the context and whom they are interacting with. The ability to be flexible and adaptable is critical for any successful leader. Being able to successfully maintain rapport, trust and respect is the foundation to building solid and long-lasting workplace relationships with colleagues, clients and customers, whatever the industry or sector.

6

Using Politeness to Win: Effective Dynamics in Sport

earning about politeness and etiquette in sport can teach us a great deal about success, teamwork and competition. As well as being of interest and practical use to those engaging in all kinds of different sports activities, the knowledge in this chapter can also be applied beyond sporting contexts, to workplaces, community groups and other settings where effective teamwork, good leadership and developing individual skills, belief and confidence matters. Additionally, we will also see how having a deeper understanding of the importance of politeness rules and etiquette codes in sport can be useful when dealing with competition, rivalry and high-pressure situations wherever they occur. Overall, I will argue that being able to abide by politeness rules and etiquette codes can increase chances of success and make us better people, both inside and outside of sport. So, let's kick off and see how integral politeness can be to bringing sporting success.

Politeness rules and sporting values

Every sport has its own set of rules of play. These rules draw on politeness principles which govern how to participate in sports appropriately and fairly. They will have been created, recorded and endorsed over time by different sporting bodies, societies or federations, such as FIFA in football (soccer) and World Rugby for rugby union. Sporting rules are in place to pinpoint exactly when codes of conduct have been broken. Breaking sporting rules, and their accompanying politeness and etiquette codes, often results in conflict and a breakdown in relationships; sanctions may also be implemented which can include fines and bans. As well as written rules, there are also unwritten rules of politeness and etiquette that are learnt by participants as they engage in sporting activities over a period of time. With any community, the longer you are a part of it, the more you will learn about acceptable and unacceptable behaviour, and sport is no different.

Being successful in many sports, particularly at professional levels, also relies on talent, skills and a serious dedication to training. However, I would argue that politeness plays a key role in approaches to training and learning skills, including how talent is focused and how skills are taught. We are going to examine a range of sports and levels here, from grassroots through to elite sport, but let's start at the top, with the Olympics.

One of the cornerstones of the games is the International Olympic Committee's Olympic Charter,[160] made up of three core sporting values: respect, friendship and excellence. These values act as principles that need to be followed in all Olympic sports. As we've already seen throughout this book, showing respect is a fundamental part of negative politeness. The charter states how Olympic participants must show 'respect in many different manners: respect towards yourself, the rules, your opponents, the environment, the public'. Showing respect in sports includes a commitment to playing fairly and to being a good sport in all public spaces, including when communicating with the media. To maintain respect, if defeated, others should not be blamed, even if controversy has taken place. And so decisions made by referees, umpires and other officials should be respected. If victorious, bragging or being conceited should be avoided, as this fails to show respect to others and the sport.[161]

Politeness in the form of building rapport and solidarity can be seen in the two Olympic values of 'friendship' and 'excellence', which, according to the charter, should be displayed by 'encouraging people to be the best they can be'. This can be achieved by using strategies of positive politeness to enhance athletes' reputations.

There are a number of communication strategies which simultaneously demonstrate respect and friendship. A key part of this is participating in politeness rituals, such as shaking hands with opponents and officials before and/or after competitions, regardless of who wins. Some sports also have polite, ritualistic phrases, such as 'well played' or 'good game' (for example, in football or tennis) when an event ends, regardless of the reality of who has played well or who has won. The meaning of these utterances matters less than the ritual of saying them to each other. They can be delivered with a handshake, a bow or another paralinguistic feature, such as a brief embrace, depending on the sport and how well the athletes and coaches know each other.

Whilst the speech that takes place between athletes on the field of play is difficult for anyone other than themselves to hear, if gestures are missing, such as athletes not shaking hands when expected, then this is very noticeable for their fellow athletes who have been snubbed, as well as spectators, and umpires or referees who enforce the politeness rules, and global audiences watching on television or via online video. The handshaking gesture (or an equivalent) works to reaffirm respect and friendship towards each other as athletes and coaches, as well as respect for the sport and its rules, so it is a significant and important ritual to fulfil if athletes are to abide by etiquette codes. If politeness rituals are missing or refused, then this can have serious consequences for those who are in breach, due to the overarching importance that is placed on compliance with politeness norms in sport in many different societies.

For example, in one of the judo events at the Rio de Janeiro Summer Olympics in 2016, Egyptian judoka Islam El Shehaby refused to shake hands with his Israeli opponent, Or Sasson, at the end of their contest, on political grounds. Such is the importance placed on the Olympic values that El Shehaby was sent home by the Olympics Disciplinary Commission for breaking the Olympic values of respect and friendship. He tried to fight his dismissal by arguing that judo does not have the handshake as an official part of its written sporting rules. However, it is expected of all judoka and so the committee argued that the handshake is an expected etiquette norm and every other judo athlete had participated in the handshaking ritual. The harsh consequences imposed for failing to abide by this unwritten rule illustrates the importance that the International Olympic Committee places on etiquette. The disciplinary commission reported that they had given a 'severe reprimand' for 'inappropriate behaviour'. They ordered the Egyptian coaching team to ensure that all their athletes were given what they termed a 'proper education' on the importance of abiding by Olympic values.[162]

This case emphasises how the Olympic values of friendship and respect take precedence for the governing body over any political considerations. It shows us that, for the Olympics, politeness rituals which encode respect and friendship must supersede any attempts to make political points. If athletes are unable to abide by the rules then their ability to compete and the positive identity and status that comes along with being an Olympic competitor is immediately removed. This example shows us the power of politeness and etiquette norms in upholding the rules and values of the Games. Engaging appropriately in politeness rituals is seen as an important signifier of compliance in sporting practice and if its norms are broken then the negative consequences are swift and serious, presumably to act as a deterrent to any other athletes who may be thinking of using similar means of deliberately breaking etiquette norms to make a political statement or to draw attention to a political cause.

These principles go way beyond the Games and can be equally applied to many other amateur and professional sports, and so are worth looking at in more detail. It is fascinating to consider how athletes and coaches use politeness rules and strategies to encourage excellence in team sports and individual sports.

Politeness rules in sports interviews

As well as playing by the rules when participating in sporting events, professional sports figures and their coaches also have the additional task of showing respect and coming across as good sports in broadcast media settings, even when they have lost. In addition to sports rules on the field of play, many professional sports also have separate codes of conduct for their members to abide by to ensure that politeness rules are not broken when representing their sport and making comments to the media. Professional sports stars in elite sports are almost constantly under the media spotlight and maintaining a polite professional identity can sometimes be very challenging. Some of the most difficult environments for professional athletes and coaches to navigate are post-match interviews and press conferences if teams have lost or under-performed.

Post-match interviews are frequently recorded live and often take place immediately after an event has finished, with journalists trying to gain access to instant reactions when emotions may still be running high. An additional part of the pressure comes from the fact that audience reach can very quickly become global, with interview and press conference clips being rapidly distributed via social media platforms, as well as through more traditional media channels. The stakes are high. Media interviews therefore present tricky contexts for sports stars to maintain a positive identity, especially as journalists will frequently try to deliberately provoke interviewees to talk on emotive topics, often involving controversial decisions or behaviour, designed to provoke impoliteness. Seeing how interviewees manage to resist this provocation tells us a great deal about how we can sidestep confrontation by avoiding answering questions head on and also how we can look out for people who are trying to draw us into conflict when it is not necessary. The strategies that are used in these interviews are very similar to those that we may find elsewhere in settings when our resolve is tested, such as in formal interviews or courtrooms, or in informal contexts when someone tries to provoke a reaction or start a disagreement.

One of my colleagues at the University of Warwick in the UK, Kieran File, is a sports language specialist. He has worked extensively on the language that players and coaches use to display their sporting identities in post-match broadcast interviews. In one of his projects,[163] he analysed 160 media interviews of professional footballers and rugby players from Europe and Oceania. He chose two different sports being played on two different continents to see if there was any noticeable difference in how sporting identities are displayed between the type of sport and the geographical location where it was played. He found various ways in which players communicate successful, professional sporting identities which were consistent, regardless of whether they played football or rugby, or their geographical location.

File demonstrates that players who are good sports reject an interviewer's attempts to draw them into conflict about match officials. He gives the following example of Australian footballer Matt Simon, who is asked a provocative question by a post-match interviewer about whether his team should have been awarded a penalty. He replies:

'They're all pens, aren't they, for me in our eyes, but, you know, the referee's there and he's made his decisions so we're not gonna make any excuses about anything.'[164]

Despite the attempts of the interviewer to draw him into controversy, Simon resists and instead displays that he is a good sport by showing respect for the referee, even when pushed to criticise. File points out that Simon does this by constructing his response as his own view (stating 'for me' and 'in our eyes'), taking care that this comes across as a difference in personal opinion, as opposed to open criticism or a challenge to the professional status and decision-making of the referee. As making excuses for defeat is a prime sign of being a bad sport, File argues that Simon carefully resists this identity and instead shows himself to be respectful of decisions made and therefore a good sport.

When on the winning team, praising the opposition helps in not coming across as conceited or big-headed. File gives an example of Australian footballer Matt McKay, who expressed this view when asked about the strength of his team's victory:

'We haven't got on top of them throughout the whole ninety minutes only at periods so they're a great side and they were very unlucky today.'[165]

McKay manages to positively evaluate the opposition whilst also commiserating with them for losing, evaluating their performance as 'unlucky'. He is being a good sport here by engaging in appropriate behaviour which fits the sport's politeness rules. The opposition has not been derided or undermined and so there is mutual respect and the interview remains a polite and uncontroversial encounter. This ensures that positive relationships between the two teams will remain, and McKay comes across as professional and gracious, which enhances his professional status.

Another part of being a good sport is being modest. When

185

players receive credit and praise from interviewers, File argues that there is an unspoken need for them to be humble in response to avoid coming across as big-headed. In another of File's examples, the interviewing journalist gives an individual compliment to Australian footballer James Meyer: 'You're the one who basically single-handedly salvaged the point.' Meyer instantly dismisses this and instead shares the compliment with his fellow teammates: 'I wouldn't say single-handedly, all the boys played well.'[166] He very swiftly reframes the praise from himself to 'all' of the team.

File argues that the team-based nature of football and rugby places constraints on interviewees' replies. In the example of McKay, there is evidence of him addressing the status and reputation of the opposing team. Meyer disagrees with the interviewer and risks damaging his interpersonal relationship with him to prioritise praising all his teammates to strengthen the team's belief in themselves. Players need to think about the feelings of the team as a whole, not just their own responses, as would be the case in individual sports. Evidence from both sporting and workplace contexts shows the importance of not neglecting a team's collective identity if group dynamics are going to be successful.

So far, we have looked at what players have said in the media, but it is also useful to get access to players' personal accounts of how they feel and react when they are taking part in media interviews. To assess this, File conducted twenty-two hours of interviews with current and retired rugby players and footballers in Oceania and Europe, outside of the glare of the media spotlight. He asked them about their motivations and attitudes towards media interviews and how they deal with the challenges that such interviews pose to them and their reputations. This gives a rare opportunity to access the inner thoughts of sports professionals when engaging with the media. File extracted this rather brilliant illustrative quote from New Zealand footballer Tim Brown:

'You don't wanna go around pissing people off . . . you've got to get on with people in the same way you've got to get on with people in your office . . . no one likes a dickhead and media is a great way to make yourself unpopular . . . you want to be a good guy to have around and that's probably a big part of being a successful athlete.'[167]

Brown explicitly highlights the similarity with other workplaces, drawing a direct comparison between his sporting world and the world of office-based work which File occupies – being able to get along with colleagues is fundamentally important to the day-to-day positive functioning of any office or workplace. For Tim Brown and other elite athletes, media interviews are a core part of their workplace environment, and so it is vital within these settings not to say 'something stupid' which can negatively affect your relationships with your colleagues, especially in a very public space with large audiences.

To be successful, there's a need to be a 'good guy'. It turns out that Brown is speaking from bitter experience here as he went on to tell a story of when he'd said something controversial about his teammates in a media interview. He came into the dressing room the next day and the newspaper cutting was hanging above his locker – the players made their feelings that he had overstepped the mark very clear to him. This tells us that teammates in sport (as well as members of other groups we all belong to at home or at work) will monitor the boundaries of impolite behaviour displayed through too much ego, self-aggrandisement and/or threatening the status and reputation of others by disparaging them or insulting them. For the rest of us, it can also happen if we have engaged in gossip, or written something disparaging or potentially offensive that may upset or annoy colleagues on email, social media or in a work report, for example. If a team member oversteps the mark, then others are likely to make them aware of this, through subtle or not so subtle communication.

Actions such as these send very clear messages that a boundary has been overstepped and that this should not happen again.

As we have seen in all these examples, showing respect for each other by displaying a positive public persona is very important to come across as a good sport. Good sports are positively evaluated as professional, level-headed and accomplished. To avoid negative evaluation, fines or bans for breaking the rules, there is a need to resist external pressure from journalists when professional identities are on display in the media for all to judge. Those who are able to stay calm and strategically navigate the boundaries of rules for public comments in these highly pressurised settings avoid sanctions for rule-breaking. Of course, in safe backstage environments, where there is no overhearing public audience, then things can be different. But frontstage, in public, reputations need to be upheld. And even in backstage settings, relationships will need to be appropriately repaired for teams to recover from bouts of impoliteness and insults which may result from team losses and bad performances, if the team members are going to continue playing together.

Solidarity building in teams

In team sports, there are a variety of ways in which linguistic politeness can help build successful athletes and teams. Sports linguist Nick Wilson[168] has investigated solidarity-building language in team talk in men's amateur rugby teams in New Zealand. Wilson highlights the importance of nicknames and shared terms of address for building successful teams, including the familiarisers 'bro', 'guys', 'mate', 'boys', 'fellas', 'cuzzy' and 'lads', in his data. These terms were used as positive identity markers by players, captains and coaches to encourage success by building a sense of togetherness and connectivity. Wilson also analysed how the rugby players engaged in player huddles before, during and after matches. These huddles included collective chants, and the team captain would always shout 'brothers on three – one, two, three'[169] at the end of their huddle. The players count together and then all put their arms in the air simultaneously. Many teams across different sports have very similar solidarity-building rituals. As public displays, in full view of the opposition and any spectators, they can simultaneously operate as tactics of power and intimidation towards the opposition.

The pre-match haka performed by New Zealand's All Blacks rugby union side is arguably the most famous global example of a sporting ritual. It is performed on the pitch, using foot-stamping and many other powerful gestures, as a combined dance and chant by the whole team. It acts as both a solidarity-building device and as a challenge to the opposition. The All Blacks home page[170] reports that the haka is performed with 'precision, respect and passion', and as its performance is based on respect, it falls within the politeness rules of the sport. The haka has a long tradition and it has been performed before the start of international rugby matches since 1888. It stems from Māori culture as a war dance to bond tribes before they went into combat. It is also used as a ritualistic way 'to celebrate, entertain, welcome and challenge'[171] others. It is traditionally led by a player of Māori heritage on the field of play and the most common haka performed is 'Te Mate', written in the 1800s as a celebration of life.

The Black Ferns, the New Zealand women's rugby team, have also regularly performed a haka since the first women's Rugby World Cup was held in 1991. In 2006, the Black Ferns had their own haka written for them, called 'Ko Uhia Mai' (translated as 'Let It Be Known'), which they have used ever since. The importance of the haka as a bonding ritual in rugby culture and for New Zealand's cultural heritage is clear here, with its instant adoption in the first major sporting event of the women's professional game.

Whilst the haka is being performed by the All Blacks or

the Black Ferns, there are specific politeness rules that need to be followed by both teams to avoid etiquette breaches. The teams need to be separated by at least ten metres on the field of play and the halfway line should not be crossed. For opponents facing the haka, the politeness rules that it should be received with respect as part of the heritage and tradition of the game. Opposing teams in the men's game have responded in different ways. The Tongan and Fijian rugby teams have immediately followed the haka with equivalent ritualistic performances of their own battle dances, called the Sipi Tau and the Cibi respectively. Some opponents have controversially tried to ignore the haka, turning their back on its performance, instead participating in their own warm-up exercises. The Australian national side did this in 1996 and they were subject to much criticism. This was not helped by the fact that Australia also lost the game by a considerable margin, 43–6, so it was clear that ignoring the haka did not bring victory – far from it. Also, opposition to the haka is not just restricted to players. Both Welsh and South African spectators were criticised for being disrespectful to the haka in 2019 when they sang their own national anthems very loudly whilst the haka was being performed.

Whilst none of these occasions resulted in formal sanctions, there have been other times in men's rugby where the opposition is judged to have gone too far and breached rugby's etiquette surrounding the haka. The French national team were fined in 2011 for getting too close to the haka performance. All players in the French team put their arms around each other's shoulders and advanced towards the All Blacks in silence, overstepping the ten-metre rule whilst glaring at all the players. The England team were also fined in 2019 when they lined up in a reverse V shape and crossed the halfway line, again getting too close to the haka.

Sports scientists have investigated whether the solidarity-building power of the haka gives a performance advantage to the All Blacks. A study carried out by Vince Kelly[172] at the

190

University of Queensland in Australia used heart rate monitors on the All Blacks players when performing the haka, as well as testing the heart rates of the listening opposition. He found that the haka performance increased the heart rate of the All Blacks players to over 90 per cent of its maximum in some cases.[173] So, if the opposition stands still while the haka is being performed, then they may well be less physically ready to start the game, as their heart rates will be lower. However, Kelly advises against teams ignoring the haka in order to perform their own warm-up instead. He argues that 'potentially disrespecting the haka by not watching it or warming up while it is performed would just upset the players who did the haka more ... And then [the All Blacks] would probably be more pumped up to do well.'[174]

So, actively performing solidarity-building rituals that are physically and emotionally intense can give teams an advantage – they will be more physically ready to play and will have a psychological advantage if the other side feels intimidated or their sense of solidarity as a team is weaker. The fantastic win rate of the All Blacks indicates that this solidarity-building ritual performance could well be a contributing factor to their long-term sporting success. The All Blacks are one of the greatest global sporting teams of all time, having won 76 per cent of their 619 international matches.[175] Kelly's heart rate study provides evidence that collective, solidarity-building rituals that involve a good deal of physical movement can bring a competitive advantage in performance; this is why they have endured the test of time.

Linguistics researcher and amateur hurling player Fergus O'Dwyer[176] has explored the ways in which humour and jokes, including funny stories, play an important part of solidarity-building politeness in a men's hurling team in Dublin, known by the pseudonym Club Fingal. He observed his team over a period of four years, tracking the development and retelling of jokes and funny stories over time. One of the stories that was retold the most by the team is about a snowball fight. One of O'Dwyer's fellow team members, whom he nicknames 'Free' in his study (a pseudonym), burst into the dressing room completely naked on a snowy night after training and challenged O'Dwyer and another teammate to a snowball fight outside. Free instigates the snowball fight by shouting, 'Come on ye bastards, I'll take the two of youse on.'[177] They go outside and during the snowball fight, O'Dwyer's friend jokingly asks Free if he is right in the head. Free replies by howling at the moon, which results in much laughter.

This naked snowballing story about Free howling at the moon has since become quite legendary at the club; it is told over and over again as a running joke and so the telling of the story has become a ritual in its own right. The original humour instigated by Free and its various retellings as a story shared by others shows how its topic successfully conveys social bonding and solidarity for the team. O'Dwyer points out that telling funny stories works effectively to reify solidarity and engaging in such humour (known as 'the craic' in Ireland) provides a release of tension from the stresses of the outside world, including high unemployment, which directly affects members of the hurling team. The group's social bonding through humour is used as a successful device to regain status in the world of sport when it has been lost in the outside world. O'Dwyer's friend draws attention to the importance of humour and being able to relax as a key part of friendship and bonding in the hurling team: 'It's a combination of being with people you enjoy the company of, having the craic, but above all, it's the humour and just being able to drop your guard . . . it's just letting things go and having a laugh that is the most important thing for me at the end of the day.'[178] Here then, shared humour, including retelling funny stories, are key ways that sports teams can build solidarity and strengthen group bonds.

*   *   *

192

To summarise so far, to effectively build solidarity in team sports, a series of positive politeness techniques can be used to strengthen social bonds, build team spirit and increase the chance of winning. This includes using nicknames and familiar-isers to address each other, as well as participating in sporting rituals, and engaging in jokes and humour. But all of this takes place within the rules of the games being played, or in dressing rooms once matches have officially finished.

However, in our next example, a group of amateur volleyball players develop solidarity and social bonds with each other in a way that is similar to what we've seen already with one crucial difference – instead of playing by the rules, they do this by com-pletely dismissing the established politeness and etiquette rules and make up their own version of the game. The team, studied by linguist Koenraad Kuiper,[179] was made up of male players who know each other first and foremost because they work together for a large company based in New Zealand. The players come from all over the firm and some of them are in positions of authority over other players in their day jobs.

Kuiper observed how this group formed bonds by collec-tively breaking several important politeness rules and etiquette codes for the game. Volleyball rules specify no talking when playing – it is impolite and distracting, and so breaks the rules of fair play. However, this set of players consistently talked away to each other when playing, blatantly breaching the rule of silence. Because they all broke the etiquette rule and talked whenever they liked, they did not negatively evaluate one another as disrespectful or as bad sports. Instead, they collectively dismissed the no talking rule, deeming it to be unimportant to their group. They also went a stage further by developing their very own politeness norms and rules, which were often directly opposite to the proper rules. The talk included extensive conversations, running commentaries on all stages of play, and giving compliments to each other, even though none could play that well and some of them were really unskilled.

Instead of trying to win, the group gave preference to keeping fit and wanting to socialise with one another. They came up with an agreed set of unwritten rules, which were often directly opposite to the real rules. Some of their behaviours also completely defied the general etiquette rules for organised team sport. For instance, they did not care what the real score was and, quite often, they would just make it up. They also decided not to have set teams and so some players would drift around and change sides as a match was taking place. Whilst all of these rule-breaking behaviours would be completely inappropriate for anyone who wanted to play volleyball properly, this group had a strong sense of solidarity and togetherness because they did not value winning or playing by the rules. Although there was ample opportunity for players to be humiliated, given their complete lack of volleyball talent, this never happened because being good at volleyball was never the intention of the group. Instead, they used sport as a way to get together and strengthen social bonds in an unconventional yet successful way.

Any player who joined the group who wished to play volleyball properly, or who was competitive, rapidly left. Kuiper describes how the members of this community were very committed to the new politeness principles they had devised together and successfully built solidarity, collegiality and camaraderie through their own rules. This team operates as a reminder that success for those who take part in sport is not always defined by winning – sometimes it is enough to belong to a group and use a sport as a reason to get together socially, with the desire for friendship and group bonding far outweighing the desire to play according to the rules.

Coming back to professional sport, it's important for players and coaches to strengthen group bonds and show solidarity externally too, in front of public audiences, not just to each other.

The media give professional athletes ample opportunities to do this in interviews. In the following, taken from a national radio interview, England footballer Jill Scott provides a great example of giving encouragement to a fellow player, building solidarity and rapport with one of her England and club teammates, Keira Walsh. This interview was broadcast a few days after the England women's football team had just won its first major tournament, and so the backdrop for the interview was one of celebration on the back of significant sporting success. Scott has been asked by the interviewer for her evaluation of Walsh's footballing ability and what it's like to play alongside her:

> **Scott:** Awww, she's amazing, I think I've played with her now at City for eight years and her coming in as a kid she went straight into the starting line-up. She's so talented, like I can't say enough good things about her. Going into this tournament I was so excited cos I was like the world's going to see what Keira Walsh can do. But in training, the amount of times we're training and people will just stop and clap sometimes. The phrase turning on a sixpence – honestly, I've never seen someone turn so quick on that ball. So yeah, I'm so happy for her, the tournament that she's had and yeah, as a person . . . she's very funny, down to earth and so humble as well.[180]

Scott uses a series of positive politeness strategies in the form of compliments and expressions of approval to show publicly how much she values and admires Walsh's footballing skills and abilities, as well as her personality traits. Scott positions herself as a very supportive senior player, giving status to her younger teammate through her expressions of approval. It is important for teammates to praise one another in public, and the status and kudos of this is even greater if it is well-respected, senior professionals who are doing the praising, to show how much they admire and value their junior teammates. Using positive politeness to express praise and approval of each other via the media (including radio, TV and social media), where the audience reach can be large and potentially global, is an excellent way to show solidarity. This demonstrates how powerful positive politeness strategies can be in building team confidence, strengthening bonds and promoting camaraderie. When public praise enhances team bonding, player confidence and belief, then it helps to improve the chances of winning.

Politeness and impoliteness in professional football coaching

Journalists have explicitly used the terms polite and impolite/rude as terms to evaluate English Premier League football managers' different leadership styles and behaviours. When Unai Emery returned to the Premier League to take charge as head coach of Aston Villa men's team in November 2022 (he had previously managed Arsenal's men's team three years before), members of the broadcast media positively evaluated his return because of his politeness. On Twitter, the @BBCFootball account posted the following comment after Emery's first game:

> The politest man in football is back in the Premier League [folded hands emoji] Unai Emery enjoyed a dream start to life at Aston Villa with a 3–1 win over Manchester United. [flexed biceps emoji][181]

The tweet was accompanied by a video clip of Emery from his first post-match interview, to provide evidence for BBC Sport's evaluation of him as the 'politest man' in football:

Emery: 'So thankful with everybody here, Aston Villa club and the supporters today, they were amazing supporting us . . . I am a privileged man to achieve it with Aston Villa.

Interviewer: We wish you well.

Emery: Thank you, thank you. [shakes the interviewer's hand]

Interviewer: Thank you have a good day, cheers, thanks a lot.

Emery: Thank you.[182]

Here, Emery uses a succession of strategies which give positive politeness to Aston Villa as a club and to the club's supporters, showing himself to be respectful, humble and grateful for his new job. The interview took place after his team had just beaten Manchester United at home for the first time in nearly thirty years, so his respect and modesty demonstrates that coming across as a good sport is more important to him than bragging or being big-headed about the success that he has just achieved. He shows deference, describing himself as a 'privileged man'. To thank the interviewer and to shake their hand is an unusual action for a coach or manager in a post-match interview, and again shows Emery using conventionalised politeness to demonstrate respect and appreciation towards the interviewer. The interviewer seemed somewhat taken aback, like he is not used to this level of respect from a high-profile interviewee. The interviewer responds in a way that would be more expected at the end of an informal, friendly conversation, rather than a formal interview, telling Emery to have a good day.[183]

Unai Emery is the only Premier League manager to say 'good afternoon' or 'good evening' at the start of his post-match interviews and press conferences – it is a key part of his unique style and approach. In doing so, he shows that he is being respectful to the person interviewing him and also to the wider audience.

He does this no matter what question he is asked and regardless of whether his team has won, lost or drawn. He thus emphasises that he is framing these interviews through politeness and respect and that he is not approaching them as hostile encounters.

Another mainstream UK TV football channel, TNT Sports (previously BT Sport), similarly labelled Emery as 'one of the politest men in football'[184] on their Twitter account. The tweet was accompanied with a greeting, 'Good evening Mr Emery!' and contained a video montage of several different clips from post-match interviews in which Emery has used 'good evening' to open the interview. The video provides a light-hearted, humorous take on why Emery is evaluated as one of the politest men in football and how this manifests itself linguistically in the post-match interview space.

TNT Sports showed mutual respect by choosing the honorific 'Mr Emery' to signal respect, status and deference to him in their tweet. Similarly, Aston Villa fans have given Unai Emery the nickname 'Mister' as a term of endearment derived from the formality and respect that he shows towards them and to everyone else in media interviews. Emery often uses the metaphor of family, which can be classified as a positive politeness device, to enhance the depth of solidarity and togetherness between himself, the fans and his players. In an Instagram post directly after a game when Aston Villa had beaten Chelsea 2–0 away, he posted: 'Proud of this team, proud of the whole Villa family. Thanks for your support from the stands in London or from home.'[185]

In a media interview with Ezri Konsa, one of Emery's players, Konsa reported on Emery's use of instilling family bonds from when he first took over and the positive impact that this has had on the club ever since: 'Everyone is enjoying coming to training every day. We are all close. When the boss came in, he wanted us to be like a family, a small family. I would say that ever since he has come in that is what we have been. I feel that on the pitch. We trust each other more and we are getting results from it.'[186]

198

Here, we can see how Emery's use of the family metaphor has worked as a solidarity-building device to enhance trust and closeness with his players. Successful families have genuine care and respect for each other, and Konsa reports on how Emery has managed to achieve this with his group of players. He has instilled belief, confidence and a strong team spirit in his team and supporters. Using family as a metaphor is a convincing way to instil strong bonds in teams if it is backed up with a genuine sense of caring, respecting and trusting one another on and off the field of play.

After sustaining a long-term injury, one of Emery's players, Emiliano Buendía, reports in a local news interview how Emery 'told me to be calm, that it was time for me to recover in the best possible way and to enjoy family. That if I needed anything that I would tell him. Almost every day he asks about my evolution. How I feel and how I am psychologically.'[187] Emery's close attention to his player's psychological needs are clear here. In Buendía's comments, we can see how Emery attempts to keep up Buendía's morale, as well as consistently attending to his needs on an almost daily basis, using positive politeness to come across as an available, approachable and caring leader.

When players are not performing to their full capacity, Emery encourages them by expressing his belief in them frontstage. When Ollie Watkins, one of his strikers, wasn't scoring goals, Emery reported the following interaction in a public media interview: 'I said, "Ollie the goal is coming. Calm. You have my respect but not just that, you have the respect of the team and why? Because even when you're not scoring you're doing your work."'[188] He shows that he is not afraid to directly articulate his respect for his players, which amplifies the belief he has in them and provides his players with a very public confidence boost in front of a mass audience. These communication strategies are a successful part of Unai Emery's coaching style and it clearly works. He has won several trophies at the clubs he has managed across Europe. In his first year in charge of Aston Villa, they qualified for Europe for the first time in thirteen years and they went on to break a number of records for the most wins in any calendar year in the club's 150-year history.

When awarded the prestigious Premier League Manager of the Month award for the second time in January 2024, he instantly said in the media that the award was not for him but instead for everyone associated with the club: 'It's for everybody, the players, the coaches, the workers here. I am thankful for our players, coaches, supporters, owners, for everybody. Of course, it's not for me. It's for our work.'[189] Emery uses a series of positive politeness strategies, including giving thanks to everyone for their collective work and expressing his appreciation and approval of his players, colleagues, the club's supporters, his bosses and everyone else associated with the club.

By refusing to take credit for individual awards, leaders such as Emery display a collaborative approach to leadership. Instead of being egotistical and presenting themselves as individual heroes who have achieved a great deal on their own merit, they show humbleness and gratitude towards others. Positive politeness techniques work to give recognition and appreciation to the roles of many others in achieving a team goal, to emphasise how it is a collective effort. Negative politeness techniques are also used to show respect and acknowledgement of others. Taken together, these communicative approaches can enhance the sense of a successful family, with everyone working together towards the same goal; everybody is included in a collective identity and takes responsibility to care for each other. And so, sports coaches and managers (as well as workplace leaders beyond sporting contexts) can instil a great sense of belief, confidence and collectiveness in their teams by engaging in such collaborative communication styles which enhance solidarity and give everyone a sense of value, belief and purpose.

In every post-match interview, Emery thanks the club's

supporters. He often describes the fans as the twelfth man[190] (in a sport where teams consist of eleven players on the pitch), which is a very effective strategy for sports leaders to use to directly include all fans in a collective identity label as a recognised part of the team. Villa Park is famous for its banner 'Holte End The 12th Man' on its Holte End stand. Whilst this was in place before Emery took over, Emery's reference to and endorsement of this shows how he has acknowledged and embraced the fans' unifying identity label and that he too believes that the fans in the Holte End stand are the twelfth man of the team.

Additionally, he also uses heart as a powerful metaphor, describing the fans as 'the real heart of the club', and he goes on to state that 'we are trying to connect with them and play for them, trying to enjoy together. They are the heart of us.'[191] The choice of heart is a powerful visual metaphor, representing the fundamental importance of the fans to the club, and how they provide energy to the players by metaphorically becoming their heart. This use of metaphor is a very successful way of building solidarity and strengthening social bonding between the head coach, the fans and the players. Emery delivers all of these messages in interviews and press conferences with sincerity and authenticity, which ensures that fans genuinely feel that they are a critical part of the Villa family he creates. This instils belief in him, his team and in the club's ability to achieve their ambitions.

When Emery joined Aston Villa in November 2022, he inherited a football team that was just above the relegation zone and he was tasked with keeping them in the Premier League. Within four months, the same team was in the top half of the table, challenging for a place in prestigious European football competitions. 'Part of the pride' is one of the club's mottos (the emblem on Villa's club badge is a lion) and the politeness strategies that Emery uses in his leadership style epitomises this sense of belonging, with pride as part of a group as well as having pride in the team.

Emery's style is a combination of politeness to build solidarity, inclusiveness and belonging (positive politeness) and politeness in terms of showing respect, humility and deference towards others (negative politeness). Of course, behind closed doors, in the privacy of dressing rooms, Emery's communication styles are likely to be very different, but his public persona expressed in his interactions with supporters and the press, and his players' evaluations of him in public interviews are very consistent; it is clear to see how he maintains his reputation as the politest man in football.

For any coach, manager or leader who wants to instil solidarity, belief and togetherness to enhance the performance of their team, successful ways of doing this include using family and heart metaphors, using collective terms of address (the twelfth man), issuing compliments, giving praise and expressing approval – all of these strategies work together to create something which feels special and unique, and allow many people to feel part of a movement. This creates a sense of belief and confidence which, in turn, helps players excel and succeed. Leaders and coaches who follow collaborative styles like Emery's will also tend to present themselves as self-effacing, humble and gracious when they succeed. They show respect and appreciation for everyone who has helped them succeed and they also pay tribute to the abilities and achievements of other teams and coaches, as we have seen with players earlier in this chapter in Kieran File's work.

If we view the politeness of Unai Emery's leadership style of football management at one end of the coaching scale, José Mourinho could be said to be at the other, as he has been consistently evaluated by the media as one of the most impolite and disrespectful football managers in professional football. *Guardian* journalist Jamie Jackson pointed out that 'his abrupt manner told many that this was a man who could be rude and disrespectful'.[192]

His impoliteness has also been called out by other footballing professionals, including fellow managers.[193] He has received fines and bans at every club he has managed for his persistent rule-breaking and inappropriate behaviour, including several yellow and red cards pitchside for outbursts at referees, other match officials, and the managers and players from the opposing teams.[194] He has also been fined for his comments in post-match interviews for improper conduct and bringing the game into disrepute.[195] Most recently he was sent off for mocking the opposition's manager just before he got sacked at Roma, for making gestures of fake crying when his team Roma scored late on in a match.[196]

Mourinho has even directly evaluated himself as rude.[197] In a post-match interview after Chelsea (Mourinho's team at the time) played Southampton in the English Premier League, Mourinho was given a red card by the fourth official for verbally abusing Southampton's goalkeeping coach in their dugout. When the interviewer asked: 'What happened when you received a red card?' The exchange went as follows:

Mourinho: I received it because I was rude, but I was rude with an idiot, so I clearly deserved a red card. I was rude.
Interviewer: Can you expand? What was said?
Mourinho: No. I was rude.[198]

As well as evaluating his own talk as 'rude' four times in very short succession, he then adds in more rudeness – this time in a very frontstage, public setting to a mass audience – when he brands Southampton's goalkeeping coach an 'idiot'. There is no sign of any apology here or any contrition, and Mourinho refuses to elaborate on his answer when the interviewer asks him to expand. He breaks the rules of being a good sport by being disrespectful, insulting and aggressive towards a fellow professional, despite the fact that, on this rare occasion, he agrees that the official was right to reprimand him.

Despite his persistent rule-breaking, Mourinho has been undeniably successful. This seems to somewhat go against one of our arguments in this chapter, that abiding by politeness rules leads to success. Mourinho has won major competitions in every country where he has managed (Portugal, Spain, England and Italy), including league titles and the most prestigious prize in European football, the Champions League. This tells us that there is not just one route to coaching success where politeness is concerned – that would be over-simplistic. Different coaching styles can lead to success. However, despite his career achievements, Mourinho has also been sacked from his last five managerial roles, all with top-flight clubs. And although he has been very successful, Mourinho's rude and impolite antics have also made him a highly controversial figure. He has been involved in several altercations and controversies over the years. He frequently attacks fellow managers, players or match officials using a series of impoliteness strategies including scorn, derision, insults and ridicule.

He created a term of address for himself, 'a special one' in his very first press conference when appointed manager of Chelsea, preceded by his own evaluation of himself as arrogant: 'I am a bit arrogant, but we have a top manager . . . I think I am a special one'[199] in a display of ego and self-aggrandisement.

Mourinho is also infamous for the insults he has given to fellow managers – he once called the then Arsenal manager Arsène Wenger a 'voyeur' and a 'specialist in failure';[200] he evaluated Frank de Boer's time as manager at Crystal Palace as evidence of him being the 'worst manager in Premier League history'[201] and he described Pep Guardiola's success at Manchester City as a 'scandal'.[202] He is the opposite of the modest professional who is a good sport – Mourinho is often impolite towards journalists, and displays bad sportsmanship. The following exchange happened when he was manager of Manchester United and they had just lost 3-0 to Tottenham Hotspur. Mourinho felt they were being unfairly criticised by the journalists present. He addressed the following rebuke to them and then physically demonstrated his disgust by walking out of the press conference, thus bringing it to a very abrupt, unplanned end:

Do you know what was the result? [holding up three fingers]. Three nil. Three nil. Do you know what this means? Three nil. It also means three Premierships and I won more Premierships alone than the other nineteen managers together [he stands up and starts to leave]. Three for me [pointing at his chest] and two for them [moving his hand up and down at waist level and shouting as he walks out of the press room]. Respect, respect, respect, man, respect.[203]

Despite being very impolite himself, using scorn and derision to chastise the journalists in the audience, rather ironically, Mourinho then demands respect from them. He inflates his own ego by stating that he is much better than all the other nineteen managers in the league as part of his comment on why he should have respect – a classic example of self-aggrandisement. As he gets up and leaves the room, his continued repetition of 'respect' demonstrates how he feels that the journalists do not respect him for all that he has achieved, that they are therefore being so disrespectful he can no longer stay in the press room with them, and so the conference must come to an end.

In 2004, the BBC quoted Volker Roth, head of UEFA, (the European footballing body),[204] who had commented that 'people like Mourinho are the enemy of football'. His comment came in response to a situation in a post-match interview where Mourinho had criticised referee Anders Frisk for decisions he had made in a Champions League match when Mourinho was the manager of Chelsea, including accusing Frisk of colluding with the opposition's manager at half-time.

The BBC reported that, after this match, Frisk and his family received death threats from irate fans and Frisk decided to leave refereeing immediately.[205] Although Mourinho cannot be held personally responsible for what happened to Frisk or his decision to resign, which UEFA itself acknowledged,[206] Sepp Blatter, head of FIFA at the time (the global footballing body), made the following comment: 'I am appalled by the verbal attacks directed at referees . . . It is often such extreme behaviour that sparks off trouble among supporters. I strongly urge everyone concerned to show respect towards referees and demonstrate fair play. Anyone who attacks a referee, attacks the football environment in which he lives.'[207]

Mourinho has also had some very public spats with players, including Ricardo Carvalho at Chelsea. In a press interview, he insulted him by accusing him of being unintelligent or mentally ill, stating that: 'He seems to have problems understanding things; maybe he should have an IQ test, or go to a mental hospital or something.' Insults are clearly part of his leadership style and sometimes they would cost him his job if he lost the respect of the dressing room.[208]

What we can see from the contrasts between Mourinho and Emery is that there are different leadership models that can bring sporting success in terms of winning trophies. However, Mourinho's success comes at quite a hefty price. His professionalism and sportsmanship have been questioned due to his rude and arrogant behaviour in public towards match officials, other managers and players – sometimes including his own players. His disparaging remarks about fellow managers show that he does not have mutual respect with his colleagues.

When Arsène Wenger was asked to reflect on his exchanges with Mourinho, he looked back on these much less fondly than those with other managers. He evaluated his rivalry with Mourinho as 'very personal' and sometimes 'out of control'. He described how he would 'already have resentment because of what has been said in press conferences, so nine times out of ten you hate the guy on the other bench'.[209] In one game, in October 2014, things got out of control when they ended up pushing each other on the touchline.

And so, if we think back to the Olympic values, in the examples we have seen, Mourinho does not appear to value respect or friendship very highly in public. There have been damning comments made about Mourinho's behaviour by both the European and global footballing bodies, as well as criticism from fellow managers and players.

Mourinho is a classic 'hero' leader, in the sense that he places himself at the centre of the successes he has and wants to take the plaudits for these achievements. The creation of his own egotistical term of address for himself as 'a special one' epitomises this – he views himself as better than everyone else and he has no issue putting someone down and disparaging their abilities if it makes him look good. Since he declared himself to be 'a special one' back in 2013, journalists and sports commentators have continued using this term of address for him for many years, tweaking it slightly so he became the one and only, 'the special one'.

Mourinho's success tells us that impolite and rude leaders can succeed if they are talented tacticians. Clearly Mourinho can motivate teams in the cases where he has had great success, but his relationships with clubs and players can change very quickly, and there are many damaged interpersonal relationships along the way. And so this is not a model of leadership sporting success that can be placed on a pedestal as far as upholding the values of politeness, respect and friendship in sport is concerned. There are different levels of coaching success and different ways of succeeding. Arguably, Emery and Mourinho represent two opposite ends of a politeness–impoliteness continuum, and other coaches and managers sit at various points in between. I would argue that success that is based on mutual respect and on restoring harmony after a well-fought competition, regardless of any controversies that may have taken place, is the best example for younger generations to follow and we'll come back to this point a little later.

We'll now look at two more cases, this time to see what happens when coaches have failed to win and the role that impoliteness has played in negative evaluations of them from journalists, commentators and supporters. We'll see how their struggles can be related to impoliteness and evaluations of what constitutes appropriate and inappropriate behaviour, and the role played by social media.

If managers and leaders struggle to gain respect and trust as new appointments, then chances are that they will struggle to get good results. Having respect for a new boss and feeling like they are on your side is crucial for getting a team to work together to build a collective sense of responsibility, solidarity and belief. If new coaches cannot get teams to respect them from the beginning, then it is likely that they will struggle to win games.

To illustrate, a rather unusual situation took place at Birmingham City men's football club in the English Championship during the 2023–24 season. Nine matches into the season, Birmingham had been enjoying a good campaign so far, occupying a play-off position, in sixth place. However, a new owner came in and he unexpectedly decided to fire manager John Eustace, despite his good results. He brought in Wayne Rooney instead, and whilst Rooney is one of England's most decorated and successful footballers, he had yet to prove himself as a manager.

During his tenure, there was much made of a comment of Rooney's in the very public setting of a post-match interview, when he stated that 'some players in there need to grow a pair of balls',[210] after his team had played out a goalless draw. A common slang phrase in British English, it means that some of his players lacked bravery and courage, traits stereotypically associated with having balls and being a 'real' man. In choosing this phrase, Rooney arguably insulted his players in public by calling their masculinity into question, as well as their professional abilities as footballers.

This public insult was evaluated by some social media commentators as an error, which would have lost the respect of the dressing room as he had not taken any blame or responsibility himself for the bad result, instead making the players solely to blame. One football media hub's Instagram account showed a photo of Rooney with the quote 'grow a pair', alongside its own evaluation of Rooney's outburst: 'dressing room = lost!!'[211] These social media memes increase the negative evaluations of supporters and the morale of players; this incident and Rooney's choice of language was discussed extensively. After only fifteen games in charge, Rooney was fired. The team had lost nine of these matches and only won two. They conceded thirty goals in the process, more than any other team in their league during Rooney's period in charge.

Of course, this unsuccessful record cannot just be attributed to Rooney's press conference comments, but criticising team members in public arguably meant that it was going to be difficult to regain players' respect, particularly because they'd had success with their previous manager. It is unusual for a new manager to be brought in when things are going well, so this already meant that Rooney was coming into a very difficult situation, with players likely still feeling loyal to their old boss who was unexpectedly sacked. In his departure statement, Eustace stated that he left with a 'heavy heart' and that his players 'went out on to the pitch every week and fought for each other with a togetherness and spirit'.[212]

Also during the 2023–24 season, Erik Ten Hag had been struggling to get consistent results as manager of Manchester United. The team was consistently outside of the top four in the Premier League and were knocked out of the Champions League before Christmas. There were accusations that Ten Hag had lost control of the players and no longer had the respect of the dressing room.[213] In September 2023, the sports media reported on conflict within Manchester United's men's team. Impoliteness in a social media post from player Jadon Sancho had resulted in a breakdown of the interpersonal relationship between him and Ten Hag. Sancho had taken the rather unusual and highly risky step of taking to social media to criticise his boss. He wanted the right to reply in public to Ten Hag to challenge a comment that he made in a post-match interview, that he had left Sancho out of the squad because of poor conduct in training that week. Sancho took to the platform X to counter this accusation. He stated that he had been a scapegoat for too long and that this was unfair.

This public post triggered a long-term, irresolvable conflict. Ten Hag banned Sancho from training with the first team and prevented him from having access to any of the first team facilities for attacking his managerial authority, accusing him of not telling the truth in public.[214] Although Sancho wrote that he had 'respect' for all the coaching decisions, this was not enough to counter the personal accusations he had made in his tweet, in reference to Ten Hag's interview comment: 'Jadon, on his performances in training we did not select him. You have to reach a level every day at Manchester United and we can make choices in the front line. So for this game he was not selected.'[215]

Media sources reported that the relationship had reached an impasse as Sancho had refused to apologise.[216] Sancho deleted the tweet but only after it had been up for two days.[217] He then made no further comment. The relationship could not be repaired and, after Sancho had been training with the youth players for almost five months as a punishment, Sancho moved to another club in Germany as soon as the transfer window opened and he was able to leave.

During the time of this conflict, there were also media reports of dressing room 'bust-ups'[218] between other high-profile players. At the time, the team was still doing poorly and there is likely a strong connection between these reports of behind-closed-doors impoliteness and conflict and the bad results that Manchester United were suffering. The team had been underperforming all season and the media were partly attributing this to a lack of leadership and team spirit[219] – individually, they were very talented players, but the sports media criticised them for lacking togetherness, belief and respect for one other. Supporters repeatedly called for Ten Hag to be sacked, alongside a long-standing call for the club's owners to sell.[220]

There are some important takeaways here in terms of what we can all learn about impoliteness and conflict in sport, which can also be applied more broadly to any team and leadership situation. The very public nature of attacking one's head coach frontstage, on social media, can be seen as unprofessional and as a breach of discipline through breaking politeness rules. By taking to such a public platform and challenging his boss's integrity in public, in front of the whole sporting world and media, the risks for Sancho were very high. The tweet had been read by over 60 million people prior to its deletion.[221] However, it is also important to acknowledge that Ten Hag decided to make negative comments about Sancho's abilities and commitment to his job in public first, which threatened Sancho's status and reputation as an accomplished, professional sportsperson.

Leaders need to be very careful how much backstage, personal information they decide to put into the public domain about their evaluations of individuals' performances. In this case, Sancho felt that his boss had overstepped the mark and so he retaliated, making it clear that there was a long-standing problem between them. Apologies can go some way towards repairing relationships. No public apology was made from Sancho and he then left the club.

In any situation like this that has resulted in conflict, relationships ideally need to be repaired very quickly to avoid long-term impact on the overall performance and morale of the team. But this can only happen if there is a genuine desire on both sides to heal the rift. When teams or individuals stop playing for their leader and/or for each other, team solidarity starts to fragment. Relationships can unravel very quickly, particularly in professional sport if results start to suffer and teams start to lose. If underlying conflictual issues are not resolved, then negative performances may well continue until there is a change of personnel or some other form of intervention from either senior leaders or club owners. Most often, a change of leadership and/or players is required to change a negative situation and mindset.

A wider lesson that can be learnt from this is that it is very risky to change leaders if a current leader is doing a good job, even if you can bring someone else in who is more famous or prestigious. As a leader, it is not advisable to insult team members in public. This runs the risk of damaging their confidence and self-belief, as well as likely causing more long-term damage to your interpersonal relationships. It's also advisable to avoid the use of stereotypical gendered insults to attack players' abilities in public, as this will likely cause anger and/or damage self-esteem. Gaining the respect and trust of team members and being able to bond with them is critical to success. Even when frustrated with results, if leaders use impolite language about their team in public, then this may well end up damaging morale further and can also cause more resentment. Eventually, someone has to go, and the likely result is that coaches and managers will be sacked or players will be forced to move on.

Respect campaigns in grassroots sport

In an ideal world, there would be no need for respect campaigns in professional or grassroots sport, as players, spectators and coaches would treat each other well and there would be no rule-breaking in terms of inappropriate language or behaviour. However, just as we've seen above in some of the examples from professional football, respect is not always shown and impoliteness which causes repuataional damage in public can be common in conflictual situations. The very existence of respect campaigns shows how difficult it can be to take part in sport.

Respect campaigns have been created in many different parts of the world by various sporting bodies to attempt to change undesirable behaviours and attitudes. The Olympic values of respect, friendship and excellence are clearly lost in some sporting situations and these campaigns have been designed to change hostile environments into more supportive and encouraging arenas for players, coaches, match officials, spectators and anyone else involved in organised sport.

To illustrate, I will focus on the English Football Association's large-scale Respect[222] campaign, which has a core focus on bringing positivity into every aspect of the game. The mission is described as follows: 'With a focus on positivity, through the "We Only Do Positive" campaign, The FA and Football Foundation aim to ensure that all grassroots footballers are able to play in a safe, fun and inclusive environment.'[223] The campaign has been designed to make everyone involved in grassroots football stop and think about how they may be breaking the rules of appropriate conduct when playing, coaching or spectating. It also focuses on how everyone should have the confidence to call each other out if someone is being impolite, rude or insulting.

The campaign was created to address the findings of research the FA conducted which revealed the negative experiences of young people, including being derided, ridiculed and shamed on touchlines by spectating adults, including coaches and care-givers. It found that 90 per cent of young footballers play much better in environments that give positive encouragement.[224] And so the campaign focuses on the importance of using features that we have identified as belonging to positive politeness – the solidarity-building strategies which build strong team bonds, such as complimenting players and avoiding criticism at all costs (for instance, coaches and spectators using phrases such as 'good effort', 'unlucky', 'keep going!' as words of encouragement instead of criticising a player for a mistake). It also aims to eradi-cate negative behaviours on social media platforms, in response to reports of parents abusing and insulting referees on WhatsApp groups[225] after children's football matches.

As part of the campaign, teams take a 'pledge of positivity',[226] based on the principle of showing mutual respect through use of positive language that is supportive and rapport-building for the players, coaches, match officials, parents, spectators and anyone else involved in the game.

The FA reports that there have been too many negative experiences for some children learning football, which can have serious adverse effects on their abilities and their overall enjoyment of sport.[227] The campaign is based on attempting to eradicate any form of impoliteness, including inappropriate behaviour on social media. If positive behaviour replaces criti-cism and aggression, children's grassroots football can become a much more supportive place for individuals to grow their talents and hone their skills. It's essential for children's sport to embrace respect agendas so that as many children as pos-sible feel able to continue in the chosen sport. As they become adults, these politeness principles will be firmly ingrained in their understanding and practices, improving adult sports in the future.

*　　*　　*

Many sports, including hockey, basketball, baseball, athletics, soccer, American football and Australian Rules football, have recently reported problems both recruiting and retaining referees, umpires and other officiating staff.[228] Being subject to rudeness and abuse is frequently cited as a factor that causes match officials in professional and grassroots sports to quit, as well as putting people off in the first place. Competitive sports, from children's grassroots clubs right through to fully professional adult sports, simply cannot take place without officials there to enforce the rules. This is a significant problem that many sporting bodies are trying to urgently address, by bringing in initiatives such as Respect campaigns to try to change behaviours.

The following quote is from an interviewee who used to be a high school athletics official in the US, and it neatly summarises the perspectives of many officials: 'The hassle of dealing with arguing players, coaches and parents – and the growing level of disrespect for officials. It starts to wear on you.'[229] In a study of basketball in the US, Jacob Tingle and colleagues researched why experienced women working as basketball officials had left their roles. They found that workplace 'incivility' was to blame. This included a lack of mutual respect from male colleagues, being the victim of gender-based abuse, inequity of policies, including how top games were allocated, and a lack of role models and mentoring. One former official, Jill, summarises her experience of verbal abuse which echoes the rest of the data findings:

A lot of times I was just the first one yelled at, because I was the young girl on the floor. I would walk out on to the court and I could see people looking at me, like, 'Oh God, we have a woman officiating our game.' I mean, it's tough, especially working men's games; there's a lot of things that have been said to me when I'm either handing the ball in or they're [the players] standing right next to me making inappropriate comments. It's hard to have thick skin and deal with the criticism especially when it's being yelled right in your ear while you're trying to 'work'. It's especially hard knowing that you're more experienced than your partners out there, but you're the one getting yelled at, because of your gender.[230]

They argue that such incivility prevents a community of officials from developing because the attrition rate of female officials is so high – strong workplace communities and bonds are critical in keeping people in any profession, and if there is a high turnover of staff then establishing bonds becomes very difficult.

Sports researchers Pamm Kellett and David Shilbury[231] reviewed multiple studies from different continents and found that verbal and physical abuse of sporting officials is an accepted and expected part of the professional role responsibility of officials globally, across multiple cultures. Historically, referees and umpires have been consistently portrayed in popular culture as villains or figures of derision, and so abuse and a lack of respect remains accepted, with the roles still negatively evaluated in wider society. This history makes such views deeply ingrained and very difficult to shift. Clearly, these embedded cultural attitudes need to change if respect is to be brought more comprehensively into competitive, elite sport, and if campaigns such as the FA's Respect campaign are ever to succeed. The rules to protect officials are in place in multiple sports but they are not being adhered to.

Campaigns to bring more respect and harmony into sport at the very least shows an acknowledgement of the problem at a grassroots level and a desire to bring social change by the governing bodies. Even if nothing else changes, at a minimum, these campaigns play a role in awareness raising. Talking about abusive behaviour puts it on the table as a problematic issue that warrants our attention, with the need for rude and abusive behaviour in sport to be called out and addressed by everyone who participates. It is going to take time to change deeply ingrained cultural norms in sports such as football, but it will be worth it if it means that children can gain a much greater enjoyment out of playing sport and not feel under threat or fearful of experiencing abuse from other players, coaches or spectators when they play. If coaches, parents, caregivers, other spectators and match officials can work towards eradicating impolite, abusive behaviours on the touchline, then hopefully there will be a much greater chance that children will carry on playing sport in future, into their adult lives, taking with them better practices for playing fairly, with respect for one another and an emphasis on being a good sport at the centre of what they do.

Respect and etiquette in martial arts

In contrast to these negative experiences of rude and impolite behaviour, which are present in many sports, I now want to examine sport from more traditional Eastern practices and cultures by focusing on martial arts. Martial arts developed from Chinese, Japanese and Korean culture. At first glance, the practice of martial arts may seem like an unconventional place to discuss the importance of politeness and etiquette in sport. Dictionary definitions rightly focus on martial arts as forms of combat, where participants fight each other to win. In feudal times, training in martial arts literally meant the art of learning how to kill an opponent, whilst avoiding being killed in the process. All of this may lead us to think about martial arts as more relevant in discussions of conflict, aggressiveness and impoliteness. However, in reality, politeness rules and etiquette codes are so fundamentally integrated into martial arts practice that they are included as an essential part of the practice itself. Whilst martial artists practise their sport by engaging in combat until one person overpowers their attacker, politeness is

217

still incredibly important. Being able to follow politeness rules and codes is essential if a student is to be seen as a successful martial artist, due to an inter-reliance on politeness, etiquette and sporting practice.

In some martial arts, including the Japanese martial art of aikido, politeness and etiquette are completely integral to taking part – rather than optional, as in some of the other sports that we have examined so far. Failure to comply with etiquette in martial arts can lead to interpersonal conflict between instructors and students and/or between students themselves; if left unresolved, this can result in a rejection of individuals as 'authentic' and 'legitimate' members, and most often, non-compliant individuals leave.

And so, despite its focus on overpowering one's opponent in a form of combat, martial arts also aim to create better people, in terms of producing students who wish to improve themselves and their relationships with others. Learning about the integrated importance of politeness rules and etiquette principles in martial arts can help a great deal with interpersonal relationships inside and outside of sporting contexts. Whilst martial arts has got to be effective as a form of self-defence and as a tool of fighting in combat, it also most importantly aims to enhance the lives of its practitioners and those around them. And this is what the principles of politeness and etiquette, so embedded in martial arts, enable practitioners to do.

Japanese martial arts are based on *budo* – 'the martial way', a spiritual path leading to harmony. The importance of striving for harmony to add value to the interpersonal relationships in our lives is a fundamental principle that lies at the heart of aikido, but it also echoes elements of the sociolinguistic descriptions of the importance of politeness to human interaction. As we saw in chapter two, without politeness, there is no human co-operation, and so maintaining harmony and avoiding disharmony through politeness is identified as critical to the development of successful interpersonal human relationships. There is a philosophical connection here. *Budo* is the martial arts path that leads to harmony and thus results in bettering oneself and one's social and interpersonal relationships with others. And as a communicative set of tools, politeness is an important vehicle for bringing harmony to human relationships, and it can therefore be seen as a key part of why humans co-operate with one another, resulting in the strengthening of social bonds, which add value to people's lives.

Learning the principles of *budo* helps martial arts practitioners become better people who can lead better lives, by being more resilient, more considerate and calmer in the face of conflict and hostility. The practice of learning martial arts focuses on developing an all-round awareness, the need to be alert and calm in conflictual situations, as well as acknowledging that timing is of critical importance.

Strict politeness rules and etiquette codes focusing on respect, civility and courtesy feature heavily as a core part of martial arts practice, and without these rules and codes, there is no sport. For instance, the International Judo Federation[232] cites politeness as one of the most fundamental principles of martial arts. It argues that, without politeness, the sport would cease to exist as it would just become fighting.

As we saw in chapter three, different types of martial arts have successfully spread around the world since the end of the Second World War. Martial arts and their accompanying politeness norms and etiquette codes have evolved into different styles and paths, depending on which tradition is followed. We will focus on the Japanese martial art of aikido in particular, as the connection between politeness and harmony in aikido is particularly clear – the first part of the word aikido (*ai-*) translates from Japanese as 'harmony' (along with 'spirit', *ki*, and 'way', *do*). Aikido is also a martial arts tradition that I have trained in over a number of years, and so I have practical knowledge of the deeper connections between politeness, etiquette and harmony, and how this relates to the art of combat. I have gained much insight from senior practitioners, including those who travel the world teaching aikido. One of these instructors, Joe Thambu Shihan, has been interviewed for this book.[233] He has been practising aikido for over fifty years, and was the first person to take aikido to Australia, where it has grown significantly under his leadership.

Aikido is based on conflict avoidance, non-aggression and harmony as a broader part of the learning process around principles of self-defence. Aikido should only be used if a person is attacked first. I will illustrate the fundamental links between politeness and etiquette in aikido by drawing on real-life examples from interactions within *dojos*.

More than just a sport?
Redefining politeness and success

Because of the overarching focus on improving oneself, one's relationships with others and striving for unity, many practitioners argue that martial arts are far more than just sports. The etiquette that is present when practising combat stretches beyond a sporting context and becomes an integrated part of practitioners' everyday lives, regardless of age, sex, gender, race, ethnicity or geographical location.

Some practitioners dedicate themselves to martial arts as part of a broader, often lifelong journey of self-discovery and improvement, and politeness and etiquette lie at the core of their journey of morality and reflection.[234] Although this chapter has the title of using politeness to win, successful engagement in sports is not *always* about winning. Whilst judo, karate and taekwondo have medal-based sports competitions and are included in the Olympics, not all schools compete in this way. Some schools of aikido have student belt gradings and demonstrations, but they do not have competitions, as winning is not believed to be the most important part of the art.

The founder of aikido, Morihei Ueshiba, believed that competitions are driven by ego and therefore go against the harmonious aims of aikido, where you need to use your opponent's energy harmoniously first of all to take them off balance. He argued that a true form of victory was 'victory over oneself',[235] so martial arts practitioners should be striving towards achieving a greater sense of self-awareness and control, ideally resulting in conflict avoidance and resolution, and not, therefore, based on rewarding individual egos with medals and trophies for winning a battle. He famously argued that 'Aikido isn't a way to defeat your enemy, rather it is a way to unite human beings.'[236]

Learning about etiquette codes and how they work in martial arts can reveal much about how to be a more aware, resilient and reflexive individual in sporting contexts and beyond. I'm not suggesting that you have to practise martial arts to be able to benefit (though if you've never tried it and you are able, I would strongly recommend giving it a go). However, by understanding how martial arts operates, the aim is to show how the basic principles that lie behind aikido practices, so deeply steeped in politeness and etiquette, can be adapted into everyday settings to provide conflict resolution and strategies to avoid conflict in the first place, all with the aim of striving towards more harmonious relationships. The overall aim is to help us make better, more self-aware decisions when under pressure in a range of contexts and communities, including at home, at work and in other public spaces.

Modern-day aikido classes originating in Eastern cultures are delivered to millions all over the world.[237] Abiding by politeness and etiquette in aikido (and any martial arts for that matter) will only work if students collectively understand, believe and respect the historical traditions of politeness principles from Japanese culture and appreciate why they are important to learn. This tells us that, in order to join different communities and groups, individuals may need to put the politeness principles of their own culture to one side and instead embrace the principles associated with another for a concentrated period of time. This may be initially challenging, but it provides an excellent experience of cultural immersion through seeing how politeness and etiquette are enacted in different cultures and traditions, to gain more authentic training experiences.

In aikido, the traditions of the art were created in the 1920s (though its origins can be traced much further back, to samurai times). As we've seen already in this book, in Japanese culture, hierarchies are emphasised – expressed by showing respect, deference and explicitly signalling differences in status through different forms of verbal and non-verbal communication, including partaking in prescribed rituals. In aikido *dojos* around the world, participants draw on principles emphasising formality, status differences and social distance to show respect, civility and courtesy to instructors (as we've seen in chapter three through the use of the terms of address *sensei* and *shihan*), to fellow students, to the *dojo* building and to the history and tradition of the art.

For aikido instructors and students, participating in a martial arts community brings a strong sense of tradition, history and gravitas to the practice, as well as a sense of belonging to something much bigger historically and culturally, which is a significant way of building group identity and solidarity amongst its students.

Unlike with social etiquette codes, where access is most often based on social-class privilege, (for example, as discussed in our considerations of dinner-table etiquette), in aikido and other martial arts, access to etiquette codes is equal to all who enter the *dojo*. As students leave their identities from the outside world behind, anyone who has the desire and commitment to learn has the same access to knowledge of *dojo* etiquette. Although martial arts are technically individual sporting activities, students and instructors work together to create a martial arts community for successful training. And in aikido this is a particularly important principle.

In aikido, most training takes place in pairs or small groups and students need to work with each other co-operatively, otherwise they cannot practise combat etiquette or self-defence techniques. The importance of co-operation is always present. The *dojo* should be a safe space to practise. If a training partner is trying to hurt a student by applying a technique too strongly or being too physical when the student is trying to learn how a technique works, then they are breaking *dojo* etiquette by not showing enough respect to their partner. Students also need to learn to harmonise their movements with each other so that they can practise the importance of timing and how this enables them to take their partner's balance to overpower them.

Instructors and students work to co-create a world where politeness rules and identities apply that differ from the 'outside' world, based on a ranking system of belt levels and experience. In some *dojos*, instructors tell their students to leave their egos at the door, so that they enter the building with a different sense of self. Entry into the *dojo* space symbolises a process whereby aspects of identities that are prominent in the outside world become unimportant. This includes age, profession and social status. On occasions, special classes known as *gasshuku* will be held, which loosely translates as 'intensive training together', and at the start of these events it is common for *dojo* doors to be locked at least fifteen minutes before classes start, so that latecomers who have failed to plan properly and therefore not shown enough respect to the event and its teachers, will not be admitted. Time offences in these contexts are not tolerated and so there is no option to turn up late with an apology as the offence caused by the etiquette breach cannot be rectified.

223

Thambu Sensei explains the interconnection between etiquette and martial arts and how the two cannot be separated: 'Martial arts for me is steeped in etiquette, and for me, if *budo* is a way of being, then etiquette is learning how to be, it's the guidelines on how to be.'[238] Etiquette is exemplified by self-awareness and should be a 'moral compass' for conducting oneself in all areas of life, not just in martial arts, hence its broader applicability outside of the sporting world. The overall aim of aikido and other martial arts is to build good human beings. Thambu Sensei states his view that 'rude people churn my stomach'[239] and therefore he only wants to have people around him who have good etiquette. Furthermore, he explains that etiquette used to mean even more than this: 'In the old days, etiquette was not just a way of being, but it was a way of not being killed, because if you walked into the wrong setting or offended the wrong person, you'd lose your life, so it was a way of how to not die.'[240]

And so historically, etiquette was essential for survival. It was a way of demarcating who was a threat (as an insider) and a way of avoiding being seen as a threat (as an outsider), and so etiquette and combat are deeply intertwined. To be an effective martial artist, then, you need to be able to use your etiquette skills to have good all-round awareness to appropriately assess different situations, including those that may be conflictual. As aikido is an art of self-defence, not attack, if you go into the wrong place, then you should have the skills to recognise this and get out without being attacked. You should be humble and respectful enough to be able to leave a potentially hostile situation without causing offence or being attacked. Aikido teaches students to defuse situations and, ideally, how to walk away without getting into combat at all. However, if this is not possible, then it is important never to attack or deliberately hurt someone; it is only in self-defence that you should incapacitate your partner so that you can escape, using an attacker's energy against them and making them fall by taking them off balance.

Before, during and at the end of training, there are a series of etiquette rituals that need to be observed, including correct bowing, and sitting correctly. When training, it is considered a breach of etiquette and a sign of disrespect to the *sensei* to talk unless you have been instructed to do so. Whilst the no-talking rule may slip occasionally, Thambu Sensei argues that if this happens it's important to regain focus quickly. It is fine not to be serious 100 per cent of the time but being casual is not acceptable.[241] It is also bad etiquette to teach another student, as this undermines the *sensei*'s authority. Knowing one's position and role within a *dojo* hierarchy is important and this demands continual observation and an awareness that develops and deepens over time as a student progresses.

It is impolite to question or challenge a *sensei* in any way on the mats, either verbally or physically, or to express one's own views, unless invited to do so. One of the rudest things a student can do is to reject or question a teaching point given by their *sensei*. It is essential for students to work on what they have been told to so as to abide by the hierarchical model of power. Thambu Sensei points out that students only tend to challenge him on the mats once. If they challenge him physically, he will likely respond physically, by throwing them very hard to make a point. The person in question will then either learn to comply very quickly with *dojo* etiquette or they will leave.

Although talk is frowned upon, one verbalisation that is encouraged is the Japanese term *osu*, spoken as a short, firm utterance. Students should use *osu* in response to instructions, questions or comments from the *sensei*, regardless of the language in which the martial art is being taught. *Osu* is imbued with respect, deference and solidarity. It carries many different meanings and fulfils different linguistic functions. It can be used as a greeting, as a way of closing conversation, a way to express thanks (in place of using conventionalised politeness forms, such as 'thank you'), as well as meaning 'yes', 'I agree' 'I'm ready', 'I'm listening', 'I understand', 'I hear you'. It also means 'I will train harder', 'I will persevere', 'I will endure'.

Thambu Sensei argues that the ability to endure, to be pushed and not to give up, is the one thing that people who no longer train remember more than anything else about aikido, and they take this skill with them into workplaces and other contexts. He comments: 'Students who have left my *dojo* after training five or ten years, these are people who have worked in IT, the tax department, in accounting, in law, in a lot of different walks of life. They have said, essentially, that their biggest takeaway was to never give up.'[242] Finally, *osu* can also mean 'be patient with me', as a direct message to a training partner or instructor. As Thambu Sensei points out, 'You cannot have manners and etiquette without patience.'[243] A good training partner will display patience as a crucial part of *dojo* etiquette.

The fact that such a short utterance can have multiple meanings emphasises the importance of brevity and students ideally not speaking more than one word when training. *Osu* can be spoken individually or collectively. Collective *osu* acts simultaneously as a solidarity-building device and as a sign of respect and compliance with an instructor's commands. These communication practices are all ways for martial artists to verbally mark out their membership of a close-knit group, using authentic Japanese terms to create solidarity and group bonding, as well as to show respect and compliance. In addition to *osu*, students learn a range of different Japanese words and phrases describing the self-defence movements and other politeness and etiquette terms, all of which brings a sense of history, tradition and belonging to a much larger, global community.

The principles of aikido can also help to enhance leadership, management and team-building skills in the workplace, including in the business world and education to improve concentration, focus and performance, and in job roles such as law enforcement, the military and security work, where employing conflict resolution and physical self-defence techniques is an expected part of the job. In aikido, when learning self-defence techniques, students are taught to stay calm in conflictual situations and avoid knee-jerk responses. You also learn how to redirect your partner's energy effectively, and so you can consider how someone's impoliteness or inappropriateness can be deflected straight back at them to gain you an advantage. You are taught how to adapt instinctively to changing circumstances, such as the need to adapt politeness strategies for different people in ever-changing situations. Plus, students are taught to harmonise with their partners in training exercises and how to learn about the vital importance of timing – harmony and good timing can be crucial to the successful delivery of politeness strategies, and the strengthening of collaborative interpersonal relationships and co-operation across sport and other workplaces of all shapes and sizes.

One other key issue that Thambu Sensei raises relates to politeness, etiquette and identity on social media. Because of the disembodied nature of communicating online, the seniority of instructors is frequently unknown, as they do not appear on social media platforms with visible honorifics. There are various aikido discussion forums on social media, and these can present opportunities for building communities, sharing practices and making connections. However, as we have seen already with digital media, these spaces can quickly become hostile and confrontational, particularly if disrespect is shown, intentionally or unintentionally.

Thambu Sensei reports witnessing junior students being impolite and disrespectful to very senior instructors on social media because they did not know who they were. This is a significant breach of martial arts etiquette. He makes the point that, when interacting online, students need to think very carefully when they do not have knowledge of who their interlocutor is: 'You need to know whom you are talking to, find out whom you are talking with and then speak appropriately. I've had friends of mine who are really, really prominent martial artists, really good, and they've been disparaged by people who don't know what they're talking about and have no right to question. And these guys are just like, "No, it's not important, it's okay." It says more about the person that's slinging the mud than the person that's wearing it.'[244]

Thambu Sensei draws attention to the impolite, conflictual side of social media, whilst also pointing out that those senior instructors who have been spoken to inappropriately choose not to retaliate and favour conflict avoidance instead. The advice given by Thambu Sensei for any online media where individuals do not know exactly with whom they are communicating operates as good advice for all social media interactions – make sure you know whom you are talking to so that you can address them appropriately, and always be respectful. If you can't be respectful, then refrain from participating altogether.[245]

Teaching children politeness rules

Many *dojos* around the world teach children martial arts from an early age. As part of learning self-defence moves, children are also taught social norms for appropriate communication and behaviour, through learning and practising *dojo* rules of politeness and etiquette. This provides an excellent way for them to learn about the social value of politeness and begin to see how their developing knowledge can be applied both within the *dojo* and in the wider world. Showing deference and respect to instructors, to each other and to the *dojo* is an integral part of children's training.

At the Aikido Eagle Dojo in Nottingham[246] where I am one of the children's instructors, one of the first rituals that all students aged four to eleven learn is called the 'Student Creed',[247] put together by Sensei Phil Musson. This is a set of principles for how they should behave in the *dojo*, but it is also clear that these principles apply equally to the world outside the *dojo*. The children memorise this creed and they receive a badge when they can recite it fully. Part of the way that they practise it is to join in when it is ritualistically recited by all children at the start of every class. It has been written as a set of intentions for children's future behaviour, based on the politeness and etiquette rules of aikido, but also interweaving wider societal expectations of polite and appropriate behaviour, for children to take with them into their lives outside of training. The Student Creed is as follows:

> *I intend to develop myself in a positive manner, and to avoid anything that will reduce my physical health and mental growth. I intend to develop my self-discipline, to bring out the best in myself and others. I intend to use what I learn in class constructively and positively to help myself and others and to never be abusive or offensive.*

When the Student Creed is collectively performed, it fosters a sense of bonding and belonging between students. It lets children verbally articulate their intentions to be positive and to do their best. This shows us the uniform nature of politeness principles both inside and outside the *dojo* in terms of the importance of abiding by society's politeness norms for children. It also shows that collectively reciting a set of intentions can help draw attention to politeness rules and codes that often exist at a subconscious level. Having a creed that needs to be regularly spoken into being at the start of each class as a ritual helps children to remember and reinforces politeness in their daily practices wherever they are. The last line, 'to never be abusive or offensive', makes clear how such impolite behaviours have no place in the *dojo* or in children's behaviour in the world outside.

The Student Creed does not explicitly mention the self-defence aspects of aikido, partly because it is designed to prompt students to consider the broader value of what they are learning through *dojo* etiquette and how to apply it to their everyday lives. Also, in aikido, children are also taught conflict avoidance and conflict resolution techniques, with self-defence being the last resort; children are given skills to enhance their relationships with others through etiquette principles, including their peers, parents, caregivers, teachers and family members. Aikido aims to improve children's self-awareness, focus and concentration, along with their self-confidence, discipline and resilience.

Aikido training also helps children to learn the rules of conversation in more formal settings. They are taught not to interrupt or shout out, and encouraged to recognise and practise when it is appropriate for them to talk and when it isn't. This also aids the development of their listening skills so that they can respond quickly and appropriately to instructions and advice – especially to keep them safe when training.

The British Aikido Board has developed a set of rules not just for children but also for parents and caregivers when bringing their children into *dojos*, to ensure that etiquette codes are also visible to other adults entering the *dojo* space who are not students. Similar to the FA's Respect campaign, this is useful as it enables adults to reflect on their behaviour in the *dojo* and how it influences others, as well as modelling good behaviour for their children. Key parent/carer etiquette rules are as follows:

As a responsible parent/carer attending any aikido training/coaching sessions and other events you will:
   Act with dignity and display courtesy and good manners towards others
   Avoid swearing and abusive language and irresponsible behaviour including behaviour that is dangerous to yourself or others

Be aware that your attitude and behaviour directly affects the behaviour of your child and other young aikidoka

Avoid destructive behaviour and leave dojo venues as you find them[248]

Many *dojos* that offer children's classes in a range of different martial arts operate as important community hubs where different politeness rules and etiquette codes are formally taught. In a study of a children's karate club in London in 2019, linguistics researchers Zhu Hua and colleagues[249] found that this *dojo* fulfilled an important social role as a community space for a Polish immigrant community in a deprived area of inner-city London. Their *sensei* had never been to Japan but that didn't matter. He taught a version of karate that had all the traditional Japanese language features, which enabled students to build an imagined karate world. It was a space in which families, instructors and students felt mutual respect, ownership and pride, providing an environment where strong community bonds developed through a shared interest in karate and its politeness and etiquette rules. The authors pointed out that many *dojos* around the world are located in deprived areas and fulfil similar social functions in terms of bringing a sense of community.

This highlights the importance of community groups having access to physical sporting spaces to provide opportunities for children to learn sporting skills, as well as about the importance of showing politeness and etiquette at the same time. Sport enables children to develop different identities and take on different responsibilities, which can help with their continuing acquisition of interpersonal politeness skills, in a supportive environment that will feel different to being in school.

Building sports communities

In addition to teaching respect and deference through etiquette, aikido *dojos* function as important social spaces for all participants to build a strong sense of solidarity and community. Learning a set of shared physical and verbal practices, and working together to create a safe training environment, can result in very strong bonds forming within *dojos* for children and adults alike – particularly because *dojos* encapsulate very specific norms and language practices that are not shared with anyone else outside of a *dojo* setting. Solidarity and community membership are fostered during training when students collectively participate in shared language practices and take part in formal training rituals following sets of traditional Japanese commands. Being able to understand key Japanese words and phrases is essential to being able to participate properly in training. Once class is formally over, then students will talk socially, engaging in jokes, humour, shared stories and other, more informal forms of communication – but only after *dojo* mat cleaning rituals have been completed.

Successful *dojos* in aikido work by establishing a strong sense of community, where a martial arts world is co-created, which is heavily underpinned by respect and adherence to politeness rules and etiquette codes. Those who share these etiquette practices can form very strong social bonds. Those who do not share in etiquette practices tend to leave. Like Unai Emery in professional football, some *senseis* use family metaphors to describe the bonds between *dojo* members.

Overall then, because politeness is so fundamentally important to building social relationships, even in situations of combat, it is essential to draw on politeness and etiquette to try and build effective relationships, based on tradition and adherence to politeness practices which stem from strong historical traditions.

232

The development of shared communication practices that we have covered here provides an excellent foundation for the successful running of grassroots sports groups and community hubs for people of all ages. These principles can be adapted and transferred into workplaces and a number of other public and private settings.

The final whistle: Summary

In this chapter, we have looked in detail at team sports and sports where the main influence of modern-day politeness rules and etiquette codes have emerged from both Western and Eastern practices, which have been exported around the world. We have uncovered different approaches to politeness and etiquette codes, which can enhance our understanding of the integral roles that politeness plays in the sporting world and the world beyond.

Sport and leisure activities are important in societies as they give opportunities for people to gain status and to take on different identity roles for the good of others in ways that may not be open to them elsewhere. Sport often plays a pivotal role in social cohesiveness in communities and societies for children and adults alike. There are many ways in which individuals can be a part of sporting activities. It can be through participating as a team player, athlete or student; it may be through officiating, coaching, instructing or by watching someone we are close to play sport in our roles as caregivers, family members or friends. It could be as a spectator attending elite sporting events, such as the Olympics, World Cups or various leagues and competitions live in stadiums; or it may be by watching sport on TV, keeping up to date online or listening in on the radio/via mobile apps. Not everyone chooses to participate in sport, but what we have seen in this chapter is that we can learn a great deal about human behaviour through sport, particularly when politeness

233

and etiquette rules are broken and in contexts where they are prioritised as part of the sporting practice.

This chapter has focused on politeness and impoliteness across a wide range of sporting activities. We will now bring this together by consolidating our learning as a set of tools, to try to bring success to our own lives and to the teams to which we belong.

We have seen how abiding by politeness rules and etiquette codes can lead to success in competitive and non-competitive sports such as aikido, when success is measured not by medals but by working on self-defence and personal control through Eastern-influenced etiquette, to become a better all-round person. Success in sports at grassroots and amateur levels can also be measured by enjoying being part of a friendship group and socialising with one another, not necessarily by winning games. Individuals and teams who are successful and who are also highly regarded by their peers and the public in their respective fields tend to abide by politeness rules and etiquette codes, even if they have rewritten these codes themselves, as in the rather unusual example of Koenraad Kuiper's volleyball players in New Zealand.

In sport, successful team dynamics can be created and strengthened through a wide range of different communication strategies, including: formal or informal terms of address that give specific status to individuals, such as formal titles which show respect and deference, as well as nicknames and familiar-isers that show solidarity and collegiality; taking part in rituals and developing shared language practices, including humour, jokes and the retelling of stories that become part of a team's history and sense of togetherness. Team members and leaders can enhance performance and belief by giving encouragement to one another by issuing compliments, praise and expressing approval, and through inclusive language devices such as family and heart metaphors to build a sense of collective identity. Showing respect is essential for the smooth running of teams. Individuals can communicate respect by being modest about their own skills and abilities, as well as being humble, grateful and recognising one's own privilege, if relevant. They will avoid impoliteness by not criticising or blaming others; they avoid disagreement, arguments and conflict, and do not engage in insults or derision. They will not be big-headed, conceited or self-aggrandising – they will share out praise by downplaying their own roles and being self-deprecating. They will also avoid acting like lone heroes whom everyone else needs to admire and revere, because success will be shared.

We have learnt about how being as self-aware as possible and keeping in control of a situation is integral to success. Practising patience and resilience can give better outcomes so that we can be more positively regarded by our peers. Respect and a professional and appropriate atmosphere can be created and upheld by being punctual, dressing appropriately and having a good demeanour that is appropriate for the context. In addition, respecting rules that apply to buildings and physical training spaces also play a key role in fostering team spirit, as does being positively evaluated for behaving appropriately in frontstage public settings.

Our consideration of politeness rules and etiquette codes around spoken communication has also emphasised the overall importance of knowing the rules and boundaries of conversations in formal spaces, integral to any setting. Knowing how and when it is appropriate to mix and shift between different languages, and learning different politeness rituals, such as whether to bow or shake hands, is vital in being able to participate fully and appropriately. Offence can be quickly caused if we do not respect sporting rituals or we do not participate in a culturally appropriate manner when it is expected. If there is a lack of cultural knowledge or if these rituals are delivered inaccurately or inappropriately, then negative perceptions will be given and relationships can become damaged or even break down as a result. Acquiring cultural knowledge of rituals as quickly as possible is essential to team integration and to having successful professional relationships. It's also important to know what topics are appropriate to talk about, as well as what questions are appropriate to ask in different contexts. We should make sure that we do not talk on inappropriate topics if we wish to maintain harmonious relationships.

On a more positive note, we have also seen how politeness rules can be actively taught to children during their engagement in sporting activities. As part of this, they take what they have learnt with them in sports settings into different contexts in the rest of their lives – at school, at home, with friends and family, etc. This can be an important and effective way of encouraging children to be thoughtful, caring and responsible citizens who see the importance of politeness rules and respect in sports contexts as well as in school, when talking with parents, caregivers, teachers, within friendship groups and with other family members. Furthermore, politeness rules and etiquette codes are important for parents and caregivers to abide by in order to model good behaviour in front of children as a key part of their children's learning. The FA's Respect campaign is targeted at parents and caregivers as well as players, as this is also the case with the British Aikido Board's prescribed rules for parents and caregivers.

This helps us to highlight the importance of how demonstrating good behaviour when watching sport can have a very positive impact on children around us who will be moulded by how the adults in their lives react to situations where children are performing and they are spectating. This includes situations where their children are being taught how to deal with and perform under pressure in order to properly partake in a sport. In football, this will be during competitive matches and in aikido, this will be during belt gradings.

As we can see with international events like the Olympics, politeness rules in sport stretch across geographical boundaries and common practices are formed with people all over the world, who will share the same politeness rules and etiquette codes which transcend cultural differences. However, refusing to take part in established politeness rituals, such as handshakes across country boundaries, can become part of deliberate political acts, especially in international events with a good deal of media coverage, as we have seen in the Olympic judo example. Breaching politeness rules can be a powerful way of making a political point, as it is clear to all who are watching that there is non-compliance with the etiquette norms and that the activity has become about something more than just the sport itself. In professional sport, deviation from politeness norms can very quickly result in a great deal of media attention, particularly in the age of social media, where information circulates so quickly, as well as gaining attention from sports' governing bodies if broader political statements are being made. Such governing bodies then decide on what action will be taken to restore the politeness equilibrium.

With other sports, certain language practices may be shared with the tradition of the sport across geographical boundaries. Only some of the 50 million people who regularly practise Japanese martial arts all over the world will speak fluent Japanese. However, all practitioners will have learnt the Japanese terms and phrases they need to show politeness and etiquette in their sporting participation, even if they cannot speak or recognise any other Japanese terms. By sharing language practices, etiquette and rituals with different people who practise the same martial arts all over the world, a global community exists. Many instructors and students frequently travel to participate in international events, regardless of their native language (sometimes with translators), due to a shared understanding of politeness, etiquette and respect, combined with a shared knowledge of a sporting practice and its Japanese communication rituals.

It is hoped that this knowledge of the essential roles that politeness rules and etiquette codes play in sport can be of

237

practical use to anyone who actively participates in any sport, as either athletes, spectators or supporters. If you do not participate in sports, even as a spectator, what you have learnt here in terms of the importance of politeness and respect can still be directly applied to many other contexts and settings, including professional and business contexts, and any within other community-based groups and teams of which you are part. Politeness rules and etiquette codes in sport enable us to see the boundaries for acceptable behaviour. Individuals can become better people and teams can operate far more effectively if we become more aware of our own politeness behaviours and how these affect individuals, teams and wider organisations inside and outside of sport.

7

Is Bad Language Really That Bad? Swearing and Taboo

This chapter will unpick language myths about swearing and go beyond the classic stereotypes of swearing as a form of 'bad' language. Even if you do encounter language that you find offensive in here, please try to approach the chapter with an open mind. The intention is not to try to make everyone more sweary – far from it. Instead, this chapter is designed to make us think carefully and critically about why people swear, how they swear and the crucial role that politeness plays in all of this.

Let's begin by saying we form strong evaluations and judgements about people based on their use of swearing, so it is a very emotive and powerful form of language. The more we know and understand about politeness, impoliteness and swearing, the better our understanding will be about how we use and judge this linguistic choice.

There is a commonly held view that the more polite someone is, the less they will swear. Stereotypically speaking, swearing is seen as impolite behaviour, and deemed to be uncivilised, distasteful and offensive. Part of this negative evaluation of swearing stems from a persistent myth that those who swear do so because they lack the intelligence to have acquired a bigger vocabulary. Such speakers allegedly resort to swearing because they are unable to express themselves properly. Basically, because they are lazy and not smart enough to know any better. This view has come to be known in sociolinguistics as 'poverty of vocabulary', and it offers simplistic and inaccurate explanations of why people swear.

However, swearing on account of language poverty is a powerful stereotype, and one that frequently appears as a form of classism and intellectual snobbery in popular media. It is most often used as a form of prejudice to denigrate and dismiss lower-class speakers, particularly working-class men. However, when we look at the scientific research and evidence, there is no data to support this argument whatsoever. Instead, what we find is a much more complex picture of swearing, taboo and politeness.

US psychologists Kristin Jay and Timothy Jay[250] found that speakers with the greatest language fluency tend to swear more, with a wider range of vocabulary, as swearing acts as a useful form of self-expression. Those people who did not score highly on language fluency also scored poorly on their ability to swear. In an earlier, single-authored study, Timothy Jay[251] had found that, instead of reaching for swear words to cover a lack of vocabulary, speakers with lower levels of fluency would instead use verbal fillers such as 'erm' or 'err' if they could not find the words they needed. There was no evidence that swearing was used when speakers were struggling to find words.

At Lancaster University in the UK, linguistics researcher Robbie Love[252] conducted a large-scale study of conversational British English. He investigated the connections between swearing and speakers' identities, including social class and educational levels. He measured the amount of swearing that took place by calculating how many swear words were spoken per 10,000 words uttered in all conversations. Love found that swearing was used almost equally by middle-class and working-class speakers: for every 10,000 words spoken by middle-class speakers, 11.53 words were swear words. For working-class speakers, swearing was at 11.81 per 10,000 words. In contrast to these similarities, the group who swore the most in Love's conversational data was university students, who are required to have high educational achievement levels to enter a university setting in the first place. The university student data showed students swearing every 25.27 words per 10,000, considerably higher than the other two social class groupings.

Twenty years earlier, Love's predecessors at Lancaster, Anthony McEnery and Zhonghua Xiao,[253] found that there was an increase in swearing fluency at the very top end of the social grading system in Britain. Those belonging to the highest socio-economic group, defined by the Office for National Statistics as 'higher and intermediate managerial, administrative and professional occupations', were swearing more than those in the group below. This group has high educational levels and strong verbal fluency, showing again that swearing can and is being used by those with very high attainment levels. After twenty-five years in academia, I can say with complete confidence that many academics who have extensive vocabularies and lists of educational qualifications as long as your arm, including PhDs, Masters and undergraduate degrees, can be frequently heard swearing in certain backstage, private contexts.

Broadcaster, actor, author and well-known language commentator Stephen Fry also dismisses the swearing as a lack of vocabulary argument in a particularly memorable way. Fry comments that 'the sort of twee person who thinks swearing is in any way a sign of a lack of education or a lack of verbal interest is just a fucking lunatic'.[254] So, the research evidence shows us that the commonly held view that working-class, uneducated people are society's swearers is a complete myth. People who swear come from a wide range of educational and social class backgrounds. Swearers have extensive vocabularies and often multiple educational qualifications. The relationship between swearing and politeness is much more complex than a simple 'swearing equals impoliteness'. Whilst swearing is an undeniable part of impoliteness when it is used aggressively to insult or abuse, it also fulfils a wide range of different communication functions. Simply viewing swearing as something that is impolite, uncivilised and rude is to miss out many of its other important and highly effective communication functions.

Studies from multiple academic disciplines including linguistics, psychology, neurology and sociology have proven how swearing can have very positive effects in many contexts. Swearing can be used as a device to show positive politeness through signalling solidarity in groups, including amongst friends, sports teams, work colleagues or in other close-knit community groups, as in 'fucking brilliant goal'. When it is socially accepted by a group, swearing can be a highly effective way of showing intimacy and camaraderie. Its use can strengthen social bonds and be very cathartic, particularly if the swearing is mutual.

Swearing can also be an effective way of demonstrating trust and intimacy with one another. Acceptance of swearing shows shared values – speakers feel comfortable enough to swear around one another and there is no fear of sanction or negativity, because people know and trust each other's reactions. Features of positive politeness include expressions of joy, excitement and exuberance, which can all be intensified by swearing ('This is fucking amazing!' 'Hell, yeah!' or just 'Fuck!!'). Swearing can also be used to create humour and entertainment in conversation – for example, in joke-telling or recounting funny stories, where swearing adds to the humorous impact of the story. Many people will enjoy swearing with friends and colleagues whom they know well.

Keith Allan and Kate Burridge[255] argue that swearing plays an indispensable role in our social and emotional well-being. In addition to its positive effects as a form of politeness, swearing has also been proven to help alleviate feelings of pain, anger and frustration. I do not think I will be alone in saying that swearing can often be heard in my household when DIY projects take place, as fingers or toes are accidentally damaged. Expletives are also given in frustration when screws, bolts or other crucial pieces are missing. For many households, flat-pack furniture could justifiably come with a warning label on its packaging that 'construction may generate expletives'.

Allan and Burridge points out that, whilst the left-hand side of our brains controls most of our language production, swearing is actually controlled by the right-hand side. This is the area of the brain that provides us with strong, instinctual responses to our environments. The language functions on the left-hand side of the brain act as a gauge, but the instinct to swear comes from the right-hand side, which is why we swear when experiencing pain and other high emotions. Even those who profess to hate swearing or who claim they never swear may do so instinctively when in pain or in a sudden moment of anger. Because of the right-sided location of swearing, some speakers, such as sufferers of strokes or Alzheimer's disease, can still swear, even though many other cognitive functions of language have been lost.

A number of experimental studies have consistently shown how swearing can help with relieving pain. Richard Stephens[256] and his colleagues have conducted experiments in which they asked participants to place their hands in freezing cold ice water. On one occasion, the participants were allowed to swear. On a separate occasion, the same participants held their hands in ice water but this time they were only permitted to utter a neutral word. The experiment showed that those who were allowed to swear showed a significant increase in their pain tolerance. Their perceptions of pain were lowered and they could keep their hands in the freezing water for forty seconds longer than when they used the neutral word whilst fulfilling the task. From the study, the researchers deduced that swearing increases the body's emotional response, which leads to an increase in heart rate and skin conductivity. This then stimulates activity in the sympathetic nervous system, which releases an analgesic so that pain perceptions were lowered.

Stephens designed this research after observing his wife swearing vociferously whilst experiencing agonising contractions during the birth of their daughter – with such swearing being a very normal and regular occurrence from women in labour, according to midwives. Swearing at times of physical pain is not a sign of boorish uncivilised rudeness but instead should be viewed as a strategic verbal response that helps our bodies create and release painkilling analgesics.

In a similar study, Stephens and his colleagues investigated whether swearing could improve physical performance in sports. They found that swearing increased muscular power and strength in both cycling and resistance tests. These findings were consistent for both men and women. In the first instance, they asked their participants to use a swear word that they would use if they accidentally banged their head. Then, on a separate day, participants completed the same cycling and resistance test but used a neutral word to describe a table. During the tests, the participants repeated their word every three seconds while cycling on a static bike in controlled conditions. Their strength was tested by pulling on a muscular hand grip. They found that 81 per cent of participants applied greater force and got better results when they were swearing. Similar to the ice-water study, Stephens and his colleagues concluded that swearing out loud increases physical performance as it increases tolerance to pain and discomfort. So there is clearly much more to swearing than meets the eye. Arguably, some speakers may be denying themselves the opportunity to defuse situations and engage in stress relief based on restrictions imposed by the conservative norms of polite speech.

Another politeness myth is that swearing is part of a modern-day plague of impoliteness that is currently blighting and corrupting the English language. However, swearing is far from being a modern phenomenon. Language historians have consistently found that swear words in English can be traced back at least 1,000 years,[257] as can the accompanying arguments about how swearing is corrupting the English language. The persistence and longevity of swearing tells us that it has clearly played an important part in how we communicate with each other for many centuries, but the fact that people resist and protest its use demonstrates that its controversy is also unlikely to go away any time soon.

One thing that is undisputed about swearing is that it is a very powerful language device. Its power stems from the fact that it draws on topics that are socially and culturally taboo, which is what gives it the power to shock and evoke strong emotional reactions. This power is critically tied to politeness and impoliteness norms, which vary across different cultures, geographical settings and time periods. These taboos include words relating to sexual acts, sexual body parts, religion and bodily functions and fluids. Let's talk more about that.

Politeness and swearing scales

As we all probably know, there are differences in the strength and force of swear words. This affects how they are used and how strongly they are evaluated in society as forms of impoliteness and politeness. People who are tolerant of swearing and enjoy using it in their communication may still find some words inappropriate and highly offensive, so it is useful to think about swear words on a swearing scale, with mild words at one end and the most offensive words at the other end. This scale is fluid, and words tend to change places along it at different points in history and in different contexts.

To give a prime example, whilst 'cunt' is now seen as highly offensive by the majority of speakers, and is often voted as the most offensive word of all in the English language, this has not always been the case. It was first used as a descriptive term for female genitalia and was not considered rude or offensive. It appears in Chaucer and Shakespeare without the offensive connotations. But over time, it became a derogatory term. As its meaning changed, its offensiveness increased and it became taboo. Gender plays a role in the strength of the social stigma surrounding cunt, and we will come back to this word a bit later in the chapter when we consider swearing in relation to gender and politeness in detail.

Another good illustration of how the strength of swear words can change over time can be seen if we consider religious terms and blasphemy. As the number of people who identify as Christian has decreased significantly in countries such as the UK, so too has the force of impoliteness and offence associated with words regarded as profane and blasphemous ('God', 'for God's sake', 'bloody hell', 'Jesus Christ'). For many, these would now be classified as mild swear words and they are frequently heard in many different formal and informal contexts.

However, in different cultures and for those who are religious, blasphemous words still retain the power to shock and cause offence, even in informal conversations, as they will still be ranked as strong, deeply impolite expletives. Robbie Love reports that 'fuck' has now overtaken 'bloody' as the most popular swear word in casual, informal conversations in Britain, when compared to the data of McEnery and colleagues collected twenty years before, in 1994. In addition to where the offensive word sits within a broader history, the ways in which swearing will be judged also depend on the setting, time and place. There is nothing contained within any word in isolation which makes it inherently offensive or impolite. Rather, it is the context in which it is uttered and the meaning that is then attributed to the word in context by those who hear it that make it taboo.

248

As with all aspects of linguistic politeness, cultural context is everything and it's important now to look at this in more detail.

Whether swearing will be viewed as impolite or not will depend on a number of contextual and cultural factors. Firstly, the identities of the people who are communicating with each other and the relationships between them are important considerations when trying to predict how swearing may land. This can include any age gaps, differences or similarities in gender, race, ethnicity, religion and sexuality. It also includes any power disparity and solidarity or social distance that exist between people, which is influenced by different social roles that individuals occupy. These roles can be unequal, as in doctor–patient, teacher–student, boss–subordinate, parent–child, etc. Or they may be more or less equal, such as friends of a similar age or workplace colleagues at the same level as one another. Evaluations and judgements about swearing will also depend on the setting and culture where the communication is taking place, the topic and purpose of the conversation and how emotive the topic may be to all who are present. Whether there are any overhearers or eavesdroppers present who may hear the swearing can also play a role in evaluations, judgements and repercussions. And finally, of course, the strength of any swear word used is critical, bearing in mind the different positions that words can occupy on a swearing scale.

Imagine that you are frontstage, in a workplace office, where you are being interviewed for a job by a panel of interviewers whom you have never met before. In this scenario, they have a significant amount of power over you (you really want the job). Job interviews are a setting in which swearing is always high risk. Even if an interviewer swears, it would be inadvisable to respond in kind – in such a formal situation, you are constantly being judged and evaluated, and the group politeness norms and boundaries will not be known to you. You do not yet have a legitimate membership of this group. Even if you currently work in exactly the same profession and swearing at work is a norm in your current workplace, it would still be high risk to do this in a job interview, particularly with complete strangers.

If we go further up the formality scale and consider the frontstage setting of a courtroom, individuals who swear in this context can face a contempt of court action, resulting in a criminal sentence. The only real exception to this is if individuals are reporting on swearing that they heard and have been asked to present this as reported speech to the court as a form of evidence. Even if emotions are running very high, swearing in a courtroom is highly likely to have serious negative consequences. In the UK, such politeness breaches are punishable by a fine and up to two years in prison, with similar punishments given in other countries.

In some countries and cultures, swearing in public spaces is illegal and punishable by imprisonment and fines. If you are prone to public outbursts that include expletives, it is very important to be aware of differences in laws if travelling to such countries. In the United Arab Emirates, swearing and rude gestures are considered obscene acts and offenders can be jailed or deported. This also applies to online communication, where swearing contravenes cyber laws. Crucially, in the UAE online communication does not have to be public; it can be in private conversations between individuals.

In 2019, the UK news media reported on the case of a British woman who worked as an HR manager in Dubai.[258] She faced jail time and deportation due to an ex-flatmate reporting her for using a swear word in a private WhatsApp conversation just between the two of them. The British woman had written 'fuck you' to her flatmate during an argument in lockdown about who got to work at the dining room table. The WhatsApp chat was then submitted as evidence to the police by her flatmate as the woman was on her way to the airport to return to the UK. She was arrested at the airport and had her phone and passport seized. She faced two years in prison and a fine of up to £52,000. Eventually, she was let off with a £600 fine and allowed to travel home, but only following intervention from the UK diplomatic service.

In terms of the wording of the law in the UAE, the use of fuck is a specific offence as it 'disgraces the honour or the modesty' of a person (article 373 of the UAE penal code).[259] Viewed through the lens of politeness, 'honour' and 'modesty' are traditionally associated with more formal politeness rules, and so under UAE law, the person who received the WhatsApp message had been disgraced by her former housemate. The newsworthiness of this case partly stemmed from the fact that the conversation had been backstage and that it had taken place online on an encrypted chat network, where no other audience members were included. This example serves as a strong reminder that swearing in writing, including on social media, creates a permanent record that can then be shown to different audiences, which can vary from the original, intended audience. Even if a message is deleted from an online chat at a later point, screenshots may still exist and be used as evidence that swearing had taken place.

The Caribbean island of St Kitts and Nevis was in the news in 2016 for arresting rapper 50 Cent, who swore on stage as he was performing his song lyrics during a concert. Despite the stereotype of Caribbean islands being very laid-back, St Kitts and Nevis has a strong religious culture of Christianity, and this influences very strict anti-swearing laws in public, which includes open-air concerts. And being famous and performing one's art does not exempt you from these rules.

Perhaps even more surprising in the list of countries that have anti-swearing laws in place is Australia, where swearing in public places is also illegal. Public places are defined as locations outside of the home (where swearing is not punishable by law) where people can gather. The list of these public places includes parks, pubs, restaurants, beaches, shopping centres and cinemas, as well as on the street. These laws date back to the 1800s, when swearing was thought to damage the sensibilities of women and young children. However, the law has not been changed and swearing is still punishable under the Summary Offences Act, where a definition of offensive language includes 'conduct which offends against the standards of good taste or good manners'. Politeness standards and appropriacy are again articulated here, as swearing is classified as being in direct opposition to good taste and manners and so this breach in politeness remains punishable by law. The law is still actively implemented and people are prosecuted each year.

To add to the complexities of this law, the legal wording and punishments in terms of the amount of time in jail and the cost of the fines varies between Australian states. Penalties can be issued by police officers as on-the-spot fines in some juris-dictions. In other states, cases may have to go to court and so costs increase. Prison sentences range from three to six months, though jail time is not a legal punishment in New South Wales or Western Australia. Fines can be as high as $1,250 where cases have to go to court, as is the case in South Australia. In Queensland, average fines are much smaller amounts, around $110, though jail time is an option there too.

There have been many calls to change or abolish Australia's offensive language laws, with prosecution statistics showing that both fines and prison sentences are being given disproportionately to First Nations people. For example, Australian law firm LY Lawyers[260] have drawn attention to double standards in how the law is being implemented, comparing the case of an intoxicated homeless Indigenous woman in Queensland sentenced to three weeks in prison with a group of footballers swearing in a pub, where no one bats an eye, as it is considered typical Australian banter, rather than a serious breach of offensive language laws.

Because of these inconsistencies and prejudices, the New South Wales Law Reform Commission recommended that the government consider abolishing offensive language offences. The commission argued that what was considered offensive was 'subjective and difficult' for any law enforcement officer to decide. Additionally, the commission concluded that offensive language caused 'relatively minimal harm' and fines were being implemented inconsistently. This commission report was published back in 2012 but nothing has yet changed – all of these offensive language laws with their state variations are still in place across Australia at the time of writing (2024).

The commission's observation about difficulties in making judgements draws attention to one of the key themes in this chapter, that the ways in which swearing is judged depends on subjective interpretations – what one person finds offensive another will not. This is a problem with legal definitions and implementation of laws that rely on politeness breaches, particularly those articulated in vague language about politeness, including breaches of 'good taste' and 'good manners'. These are subjective and judgements will inevitably be made inconsistently.

There are other public contexts in which official breaches of professional rules and standards may occur if swearing takes place, though sanctions may differ. Given the strictness of the laws about swearing in public in Australia, there tends not to be any swearing in Australian government chambers, where there are strict rules of politeness and appropriacy. Breaches of politeness through offensive language in these spaces are classified as 'unparliamentary language'. There are a number of examples of politicians swearing in government chambers in Australia, though instead of receiving fines or being arrested, politicians are asked to withdraw their remarks, either by the speaker of the house, as the official rule enforcer, or by other politicians, who may have overheard the expletive. If they comply in withdrawing the comment, it is like the swearing was never uttered in the first place. This ritualistic setting, with its own set of politeness rules, seems very different from the public world outside of parliament, where normal citizens are not given the option of withdrawing swear words.

In a recent example of swearing in the Australian parliament, Senator David Pocock uttered the expletive 'bullshit' in the Senate chamber during a heated debate on the climate crisis. He was asked to withdraw the remark. In response to this instance, the *Sydney Morning Herald*[261] conducted a search of Hansard and found thirty-nine instances of 'bullshit' recorded in Australian Senate chamber since 1979, with another twenty-one instances in the lower house. There were also another 263 instances of 'bullshit' found across all parliamentary proceedings and committees. Bullshit, it seems, was not just a one-off slip – there is a history of this expletive being used in the seat of Australia's government, despite the country's offensive language laws.

Technically, one could argue that parliament is not a public place, but there are clearly different interpretations of the rules at play here. Bullshit is defined as untrue talk or speaking nonsense to someone in an attempt to deceive. The choice of 'bullshit' is interesting as it is also strictly forbidden in a parliamentary setting to directly accuse anyone of being a liar. Bullshit, although clearly breaking politeness rules, enables an informal language alternative to calling someone a liar directly on record. He went a stage further on the swearing scale in parliament to intensify his criticism of the opposition's views on climate scepticism, making the accusatory argument: 'You fucked up the Pacific relationship when you were in government and now you're making it harder for us to fix it.'[262] He was asked to withdraw this remark by another politician who had overheard what he had said, which he did. He then faced no further sanctions.

It is not just in formal parliamentary chambers where politicians engage in swearing on official political topics. In May 2021, Teodoro Locsin Jr, then secretary of foreign affairs in the Philippines, made global news headlines[263] when he went on social media to address his views to China about a dispute between the two countries regarding territory in the South China Sea. From the Philippines' perspective, the country has a 200-mile exclusive economic zone surrounding their islands that is theirs alone. The area has many valuable resources – including fishing, oil and gas. China, however, believes it has a right to the area, despite the judgement of an arbitration panel in The Hague in 2016, which concluded that China's claims were based on an outdated map and contravened international law. China has continued to ignore the outcome of the arbitration panel at The Hague.

At the time of Locsin Jr's social media post, the Philippines' government had announced that there were currently hundreds of Chinese military ships and fishing fleets in these Filipino waters. Although social media inevitably introduces an element of informality to political communication, using 'get the fuck out' to another country was deemed to be offensive and unprofessional, and his tweet drew a great deal of criticism. The outburst, which was on Twitter, was seen as far from the style of language that would be expected of a diplomat, where polite, formal language is considered a professional global norm.

Locsin Jr's tweet was remarkable as he appeared to set the scene for a polite diplomatic exchange by explicitly mentioning politeness, asking, 'China, my friend, how politely can I put it?' So far so good. However, the next line made it very clear that his use of 'politely' was ironic. He replied to his own question, breaking all diplomatic politeness rules, by using a strong expletive, albeit using asterisks: 'Let me see . . . GET THE F*** OUT. What are you doing to our friendship? You. Not us. We're trying. You. You're like an ugly oaf forcing your attentions on a handsome guy who wants to be a friend.'[264]

The shock value of a diplomat using such a strong expletive conveys high emotion and frustration at China's actions, intensified by Locsin Jr's choice of shouty capital letters to

255

signal that he was delivering his sweary command loudly and aggressively. He follows up with a name-calling insult in his tweet, using a simile to describe China as acting 'like an ugly oaf', in opposition to the Philippines, who is 'a handsome guy'[265] who only wants friendship. Such as a shift in register and style, from an initially expected polite exchange, is highly unusual in public political communication from politicians, especially given the global reach of Twitter and the permanency of writing an expletive for all the world to see. This, arguably, was the goal of the tweet as it garnered media attention from all over the world, and so it did successfully shine a spotlight on China's illegal activities.

Locsin Jr openly defended his swearing by commenting that the 'usual suave diplomatic speak gets nothing done', drawing attention to the ineffectiveness of polite communication that is the expected diplomatic language norm. Prior to his tweet, the Philippines had made seventy-eight diplomatic protests about China's actions and nothing had changed. It had also been five years since the ruling in The Hague that China's actions were not recognised by international law. Although Locsin Jr was heavily criticised and his professional judgement as a diplomat was called into question for his use of such inappropriate language, by being deliberately impolite and offensive he at least drew global attention to a political problem.

During Donald Trump's tenure as the forty-fifth president of the United States, he frequently used swearing as a key part of his presidential identity when engaging in public speaking. Swearing in these official public contexts – at rallies, public debates and in formal political meetings – breaks all of the expected politeness rules for political talk and the language standards of elected politicians interacting frontstage and in public life. However, researchers have argued that swearing is not something that happens accidentally; it is one of his key strategies to appeal to voters.

Trump uses swearing to show how different he is from all other politicians. His swearing distances him from the polite standards of political language that define the establishment, as does how brazen he can be in flaunting these standards. Whilst on the campaign trail in Las Vegas in 2011, he infamously dropped the f-bomb repeatedly and said were he to be president, his first message to China would be, 'Listen you motherfuckers, we're going to tax you 25 per cent!'[266] After he had been successfully elected, he described Haiti, El Salvador and African nations as 'shithole countries'[267] in a formal meeting about immigration and changing the US visa system. The UN Human Rights Office condemned Trump's comments as racist, but no action was taken against him. He intentionally flaunted formal politeness boundaries on immigration with abusive, insulting, racist language. In 2019, *The New York Times* ran a story with a headline that named Trump the 'Profanity President'. The article noted that, in only one short speech earlier that week, he had used 'hell', 'ass' and a couple of 'bullshits'. In a rally earlier the same month, he had used ten 'hells', three 'damns' and a 'crap'.[268]

His supporters responded positively to his communication strategies. The critical observation here about Trump's language is that his audiences were not interpreting his behaviour as impolite, offensive or rude, but instead applauding his use of swearing and insults for breaking down traditional power barriers. US language researcher Melissa Mohr argues that Trump has used swearing to appeal to ordinary voters and a big part of this appeal is that swearing is related to a perception of authenticity. She writes: 'We tend to believe people when they swear, because we interpret these words as a sign of strong emotions. In his case, the emotion is often powerful anger, which his supporters seem to love.'

Instead of hiding behind the confines of politeness rules, diplomacy and etiquette, Trump has consistently used the idea of 'telling it like it really is' to develop a vote-winning identity for himself as a genuine man of the people, and swearing is a key part of that campaign. Trump rewrites expectations for politeness rules in mainstream politics by refusing to apologise in situations where they would be expected.

Outside of these very public-facing arenas, what about swearing at work in general? As with everything politeness-based, how swearing at work will be evaluated depends on context. Yehuda Baruch and colleagues[269] interviewed fifty-two professionals working either as business executives, doctors or lawyers in organisations based in the USA, UK and France. They found that males and females of all age groups reported that they swear at work, and that swearing was used for positive purposes that benefited both individuals and workplace teams, including stress relief and enjoyment in communicating with one another. They argue that this finding should lead to a reconsideration of what makes up uncivilised behaviour in these professional occupations.

In my own experience of conducting workplace consultancies and research in a range of industries, swearing is commonplace and fully accepted in some teams and organisations, but hardly used at all in others. Its use can depend on a number of factors, including the industry, the workplace culture and the strength of the social bonds and trust between the group. When new members enter a workplace, they need to observe and learn the rules of swearing very carefully before properly engaging.

Fly-on-the-wall workplace documentaries can also provide good evidence of when, how and why swearing at work takes place. Of course, these documentaries may well be heavily edited to maximise drama and storytelling, but in the field of impoliteness research they have been drawn upon to examine swearing and impoliteness in contexts that it would be very difficult and potentially dangerous for sociolinguists to gain access to. TV programmes such as *Police Interceptors* can provide data sources such as the communication strategies used in police car chases and arrests. In an examination of politeness and impoliteness in the documentary series *Ice Road Truckers*,[270] swearing was commonplace, with 'fuck' and all of its variations being the most favoured swear word. It was used positively as well as to display anger and frustration, and to issue threats and insults.

The work of Nicola Daly[271] and colleagues sheds important light on the use of swearing in blue-collar workplaces. Their long-term research focuses on 'fuck' and how it is used by workplace leader Ginette in a soap factory in New Zealand. They demonstrate how Ginette uses 'fuck' as part of her everyday leadership style to fulfil a range of functions, including giving orders and expressing disapproval and reprimands, but she also uses it as a team-building solidarity device and how its use is a norm in this workplace community.

Swearing and age

As has already been touched upon, age is an incredibly important factor when considering who swears, when and why. In Robbie Love's[272] study of university students who swear, he argues that the university student data shows the powerful significance of age and how swearing is interpreted. Love found a very similar pattern to an earlier study by McEnery, which revealed that swearing starts to increase in childhood, continues increasing through adolescence and then peaks when people are in their twenties, the age of our university student cohort. But swearing then declines in people's thirties and continues to decline with age. The most likely reason why swearing starts to drop off according to both Love, McEnery and colleagues is that it is at the age when people start to become parents and so they are likely to swear less so as not to influence their children to start swearing.

As we've seen in chapter four, when we looked at politeness with family and friends, parents and caregivers play a significant role in teaching their children politeness rules and norms, and part of trying to model polite behaviour for their offspring tends to include avoiding swear words. Although children are aware of swearing and may well hear swear words from an early age, it is not socially sanctioned for children, particularly younger children, to swear, and it is commonly seen as a parenting failure and a cause of much social embarrassment when they do.

In their psychology research, Timothy and Kristin Jay[273] found that children start to learn taboo words around the age of one or two. This correlates with potty training as they begin to learn the vocabulary of bodily functions, such as 'poo' and 'wee'. In a study of predominantly white middle-class children who started in school aged five in the US, Jay and Jay found that these children knew around forty-two mild taboo words at the point when they entered school. This may seem surprisingly high but it shows how knowledge of language taboos are an integral part of language acquisition. Law researcher Elyse Methven[274] argues that punishing children for swearing does not lead to a decrease in them doing it, but instead tends to have the opposite effect as it reinforces the strength of the taboo and gives them a button for when they want to test boundaries.

Arguably, part of a caregiver's role is to teach children and young people about how they will be treated if they swear, as well as the importance of context. This includes making children aware of the inappropriacy of swearing in many frontstage contexts, and the negative sanctions that they can face if they swear, including social disapproval and punishment in schools. As children progress through to adolescence, swearing often becomes an observable part of the speech patterns of many teenage friendship groups. At this age, teenagers are striving for their own identities and may often reject the rules of authority, including politeness rules, as part of this process.

Linguistic evidence from the everyday talk of teenagers can help us move away from the stereotype that young people use swearing to be verbally aggressive and to insult one another. In a study of swearing in teenagers in London, Palacios Martínez[275] investigated how teenagers used expletives as address terms to refer to each other. The three most popular terms were '(son of a) bitch', 'bastard', and 'dick(head)'. Whilst there is evidence of these words being used as offensive insults, there was also evidence of them being used to show affection towards one another and to strengthen social bonds. Palacios Martínez argues that addressing each other through expletives reinforces these teenagers' identities as unique, thereby establishing their own identities as different from others, which is important to them as they are at a stage of adolescence where they want to be different from everyone else and establish a unique and potentially social risky identity for themselves, as a marker of social status.

Some sociolinguists, including Robbie Love,[276] have argued that secondary schools should consider formally teaching students about the different functions that swearing can fulfil as part of the curriculum. This would enable schools to help promote responsible and informed language use. Love suggests that this would help teenagers learn about the swear words that they are likely to encounter or hear on films and other broadcasting channels, and to understand which ones are potentially the most offensive, so that they can be properly informed about their use. Whilst having an honest debate about this would be valuable, it feels unlikely to me to catch on, due to the strength of conservative thinking around verbal hygiene, politeness standards and language purity that dominate.

I would also argue that teaching young people the subtle differences between swearing when used for social bonding, humour or banter, and the same swear words when they are being used to deliberately cause offence, insult or harm could be a way of getting young people to recognise bullying and violence (towards themselves or others) quicker. Saying that swearing is bad language is overly simplistic and unrealistic, and we need young people learning how to distinguish the different functions of swearing and when it is being used to insult or abuse them.

Regardless of strict politeness rules and language standards, it is abundantly clear that we cannot prevent children from learning taboo language or hearing swear words – swearing is an inherent part of human communication. Expletives have been around for centuries and they are learnt from a very early age. Punishing children for swearing does not make swear words disappear from use. Classroom conversations which talk about societal politeness rules, where they come from and why they are in place could lead to a much more informed understanding of swearing and its consequences.

Whether swearing is formally taught in classrooms as a part of the curriculum or not, teachers will have to deal with swearing and taboo language on a regular basis. How to do this frequently comes up as a topic on teachers' advice-seeking forums online. In one forum in the US, where teachers share ideas and views on how to handle swearing in classrooms, many report that when they do make swearing the topic of discussion in the class, there are positives that result. Blog author Jill Staake[277] reports that when teachers kept a tally on the board of swear words used by individual students, the students consistently responded that they had no idea that they were swearing so much, and so it raised their awareness of how frequently they were using expletives. Teachers then used these findings to open up conversations about how, if swearing was being used so frequently and yet unconsciously by students, and it had become such a natural part of their conversations, then this could limit their job prospects

262

and/or get students fired in future, as many workplaces and employers would deem swearing to be inappropriate. And so the message of needing to be consciously aware of when one is swearing and how often was successfully delivered.

Staake makes the crucial point that children are more likely to change their behaviour if they can understand the value and benefits of doing so, and so it is important to have these conversations with them. Other teachers have asked students to show an awareness that a classroom is a different context to home, or to put on a language filter when they enter the classroom, which they can be sent out to reset. Or they may have swear jars or let students accrue swear-free points that result in a reward. Whatever strategy is chosen, it is clear that making swearing a topic of conversation opens up spaces for students to reflect and learn about how their ingrained swearing may affect future prospects.

Swearing and gender

Another dominant stereotype about swearing and politeness is that women and girls should not swear, as it is not 'ladylike' or 'proper' to do so. This is a particularly persistent and pernicious form of verbal hygiene along gender lines. As we have seen earlier in the book, whilst gender fluidity and equality movements have questioned such stereotypes, there is still a lasting myth that women and girls should be more polite than men and boys in order to be viewed as properly enacting societal gender roles. Research findings consistently show that negative consequences of swearing are far more marked for women and girls than they are for boys and men. As we have already seen in this chapter with the example of Australian swearing laws brought in to 'protect' women's delicate ears from public swearing, historically, swearing was thought to be too offensive for women to even hear, let alone utter.

Back in the 1970s, US linguist Robin Lakoff[278] drew attention to the stereotype of swearing being unladylike, impolite and uncouth for women. She argued that women were more likely to say 'oh dear' or 'fudge' instead of 'shit'. In later work, she drew attention to strict politeness standards of 'niceness' for women, where it is seen as normal for men to swear, but abnormal and politeness law-breaking for women, and not something that women should do if they want to be viewed as authentically feminine. Lakoff convincingly argues that women and girls experience much more social pressure and social stigma than boys to avoid swearing, and that rules around politeness mean they can be punished if they stray outside the boundaries of appropriate behaviour. Lakoff identifies these politeness rules as white middle-class norms which have come to be identified with what it means to be an authentic, 'proper' woman or girl. For non-white women and women from other social class backgrounds who operate outside of these politeness rules, they will often be viewed as deviant and stigmatised from the gendered norm of the white middle-class woman. Mareyliena Morgan[279] draws attention to the powerful stereotype of the loud, aggressive black woman, who is deemed to be boorish, sweary and rude. The angry black woman stereotype[280] is seen to play a key role in preventing gender equality in the world of work.

Tony McEnery and Robbie Love's research on British casual conversation, conducted twenty years apart, found a consistent pattern of men swearing more than women in both time periods. Another finding from both studies was that women and men were far more likely to swear in single-sex groups rather than in mixed-sex company, which again suggests the swearing is being used to build solidarity and strengthen social bonds. But I would argue that the most important thing when we consider gender, swearing and politeness is not trying to work out who swears the most; instead, it is the persistent negative stereotypes about women who swear, with women being more stigmatised than men for using expletives.

The mass media have long been obsessed with the topic of women swearing and how impolite and deviant it can be. Newspapers and magazines still regularly focus disproportionately on women's swearing, regarded through a male gaze, and how it may well damage women's chances of succeeding in heterosexual, romantic relationships. As one example amongst many, the *Metro* in the UK recently ran a story asking, 'Do men find women who swear unattractive?' Perhaps unsurprisingly, 'yes' was the answer, operating as part of the cultural stereotype that good girls do not swear and everyone is heterosexual so those that do should fear being left on the shelf.

There is a double standard at play here: the same level of obsessive discussion about men swearing simply does not take place. Some researchers have suggested that negative attitudes towards women using expletives are because swearing is traditionally seen as a normal part of men's talk. However, there is no real evidence to support this argument and it is dismissed in linguistic circles for being overly simplistic.

Earlier in my career, I gave a presentation at an international linguistics conference looking at storytelling around gender-based violence in Eve Ensler's *The Vagina Monologues*.[281] Despite the title of my talk including the name of the play and a description of how I would be analysing swearing and taboo language, one audience member complained afterwards about how awful it was that such 'a nice young lady' would utter such vulgarities in public, particularly first thing in the morning. You have to wonder if this would have been seen as less offensive by this person if I'd delivered the presentation at a different time of day, but academic conferences do not have a watershed rule like the broadcast media. There was a choice of four other talks running at exactly the same time in different rooms on the same corridor, so maybe the person complaining hadn't read the programme correctly and had accidentally found themselves in the wrong room, expecting someone else to speak on a much politer topic, more suitable for morning ears. Whatever the case, I could not help but be amused by the fact that this proved my point about swearing and taboo language being more stigmatised for some groups than others based on perceptions of gender and age.

Transgender author and comedian Amanda Kerri tells of her surprise and frustration when she experienced the much stricter gender-based swearing rules that are imposed on women and which seem not to exist for men after she transitioned. Her experiences present a really telling example of how her language is evaluated very differently:

> That language that I so freely tossed about as a guy, I wasn't really allowed to say any more. Apparently women, at least *feminine* women, aren't allowed to talk like that . . . Men don't react to a woman cursing and saying lewd things the same way they do with guys. Most recoil from it. Even other women seem to be averse to the sailor-tongued lady . . . Cursing is always an aggressive expression of frustration, anger or exasperation. Women aren't supposed to be angry. They're supposed to be the gentle sex and when they get upset, instead of calling someone a 'limp-dick motherfucker', they're supposed to just cry and eat a tiny morsel. As far as graphically describing sex, feminine women are supposed to just moan and gasp in bed and use children's words to describe sex.[282]

Robin Lakoff's[283] description of unladylike behaviour is alive and well here in Kerri's quote. Despite Kerri's decision to keep swearing as she did when she was a man, she reports that she soon realised there were strict limits on what society would tolerate. Also, when using swearing as a form of banter with men, as she had done so frequently when she was a man, Kerri was viewed as overly aggressive and 'a bitch' when engaging in exactly the same verbal behaviour as a woman.

The c-word: The most offensive word of all?

In our modern-day use of the English language, one of the most offensive swear words of all is that which refers to women's genitalia: the c-word, or, to name it properly without any euphemism: cunt. The use of the word 'cunt' is avoided in many contexts to preserve politeness rules. As well as being euphemistically referred to as 'the c-word', its use has also been termed 'dropping the c-bomb'. Or, if written down, it may appear with asterisks, as c**t or even ****. In a recent study in the UK conducted by Ofcom,[284] the communications regulator, the top 150 swear words were ranked in order of offensiveness by the British public. 'Cunt' was ranked as the strongest, most offensive word, closely followed by 'fuck' and 'motherfucker'. Using this research to inform future broadcasting standards, Ofcom argued that any words that came under the 'strong' category should only be shown or uttered after the 'watershed' (9pm in the UK). In the US, politeness rules and expectations are stronger than in the UK around the use of cunt, and it has been listed as a word that is unwise to broadcast on non-subscription channels.

Its use can cause shock, offence and silence, even if it is not aimed as an insult at anyone in particular. Lexicographer Susie Dent[285] points out that 'few of us would use "cunt" in polite company or any of its derivatives, which include use as a verb, as in being "cunted" (to be drunk), or as a noun, such as "cunt-face" (a supreme idiot), or "cuntsmith" (a gynaecologist).' Dent's description of 'polite company' here can be seen as aligning with a middle-class norm, that the majority of people would avoid the term as it is so socially stigmatised.

Dent tells us that the first time the c-word appeared in a dictionary was in 1785, in Francis Grose's *Classical Dictionary of the Vulgar Tongue*. The 'Vulgar Tongue' is a rather graphic description for the reader of the rude and impolite terms contained within its pages. Cunt was deemed to be so vulgar and obscene that it appeared only as four asterisks – presumably making it very difficult to check its spelling, despite the book being a dictionary, albeit a vulgar one. Cunt did not then reappear in dictionaries until obscenity laws began to be relaxed in the UK during the 1960s. Cunt is currently defined in the full version of the *Oxford English Dictionary* (OED) as an 'offensive and chiefly derogatory' term. Firstly, it is defined as 'a woman as a source of sexual gratification; a promiscuous woman; a slut' or as 'a general term of abuse for a woman'. The second entry as a derogatory term lists it as 'a term of abuse for a man'. The OED also gives a more descriptive, literal definition as 'the female genitals, the vulva or vagina'. It then charts the historical transition of the term. It was initially cited as a surname, place name or geographical feature as early as the 1200s. The OED lists the first known example as 'Gropecunte Lane' in Oxfordshire in 1230, thought to be an area frequented by prostitutes. As a geographical feature, it was used to describe a cleft in a hill. The OED then traces its development through to a term that became slang as it grew in offensiveness over the centuries.

There are no equivalent slang terms for men's genitalia that break politeness boundaries to the same extent as cunt does. The use of 'dick' or 'prick' are relatively mild expletives in comparison. They do not have anywhere near the same amount of force or ability to cause offence. Language and gender expert Deborah Cameron[286] argues that there has been a more recent transition from cunt being used as a term of abuse for women to it now being used as a term of offence to describe men.

There have been attempts to reclaim the word cunt by feminists, to break it away from its offensive social stigmas and instead try to make it empowering. Cameron questions the wisdom of this, by asking whether it can really be possible for women to empower themselves by using a swear word that reduces them to their genitalia alone. Attempts at breaking impolite language taboos include the stage show *The Vagina Monologues*, where audiences of women were encouraged to shout out 'cunt' as a collective group chant. Whilst the play was successful, trying to challenge deeply embedded societal politeness rules in this way is not overly effective in terms of bringing social change. Whilst this kind of chanting can happen in the very staged setting of a theatre, this does not then mean that every audience member will be able to leave the safe middle-class theatre and then integrate the word into their daily lives. Politeness norms and standards are heavily fixed by strong cultures and traditions, and they cannot simply be overturned, even if it can be empowering for some in the moment to shout out 'cunt' at a stage show.

The enduring power of the c-word to shock and offend is frequently discussed in the mass media. UK journalist Hannah Betts, who describes herself as a frequent user of the c-word and the f-word, tells an anecdote in a freelance magazine.[287] Describing a typically British experience she had when queuing, she explains that she was patiently waiting in an orderly taxi queue at Birmingham New Street station when queue jumpers started to get into cabs. Those who had been queuing patiently started to quietly bemoan queue jumpers for breaking queue rule etiquette. Betts, in her non-Birmingham, 'posh' accent, commented, 'They are complete cunts.' She describes how those who had been talking to her while patiently waiting in the queue were immediately shocked into silence. They then collectively decided to usher Betts into the next taxi that came along before she could swear again. Betts reports overhearing one of the group saying, 'That's it, let's help the posh c-bomber into a cab.' Betts describes swearing as expressive, creative and a 'rather beautiful thing'. What this also shows is that social class plays an important role here too, as class holds its own idealised representations of what it means to be a 'lady'.

Changing attitudes to swearing in public

Should speakers try and reclaim cunt, in a similar way to how 'queer' has been positively reclaimed by LGBTQI+ groups? For linguist Deborah Cameron,[288] the answer is a very clear and resounding no. In her view, cunt is far too sexist, misogynistic and insulting to attempt to rehabilitate it in a way that was envisioned by Eve Ensler in her stage show. However, some public figures do think that it should be reclaimed. In 2018, New Zealand MP and co-leader of the Green Party Marama Davidson[289] made this argument, demonstrating her conviction by using cunt in public at a political rally while giving a speech. Prior to this, she had received death threats calling her a cunt, and so she argued that treating cunt as such a powerful taboo gives it more power when it is used as a threat. This view split opinion. The opposition National Party's spokesperson for women, Paula Bennett, voiced her negative evaluation of Davidson's language in the following tweet:

> To do this in front of families and children is disgusting. You may want to 'reclaim the word' but you should not use your privileged position to decide for parents that their children should hear you repeatedly say it. There is no excuse for bad manners.[290]

Bennett calls here on politeness rules that Davidson has broken through her 'bad manners' and also critiques her for

270

exposing children to the expletive, drawing on the 'swearing causes damage to children' argument that we have seen earlier. We can conclude from this discussion, then, that cunt is still a very controversial and heavily loaded word. While it appears that some commentators and political figures want to try to change the meaning of cunt to make it more positive, or to strip it of some of its power, chances are that it is too politically loaded and controversial to be easily changed.

In 2017, when confronted with use of the word cunt as a direct insult towards her in her own courtroom, from a repeat offender who had been found guilty of racist abuse, Judge Patricia Lynch QC decided to retaliate. The offender first swore at her and said that she was 'a bit of a cunt'. Judge Lynch replied with, 'You are a bit of a cunt yourself.' The offender then decided to shout back, 'Go fuck yourself!' Again, Lynch responded, 'You too.'[291] She was eventually cleared of any misconduct following an investigation that was called into her language use. She later apologised for swearing. Though she was repeating an insult that the defendant had said to her, almost verbatim, her professional responsibility as a judge meant that she shouldn't have done this. And so, here we can see a prominent, highly respected judge use cunt in a courtroom setting, but she did not escape without an investigation into potential misconduct. This exemplifies that there is a different rule for the member of the profession than the offender, due to professional status and expectations around language formality. There is some evidence of changing attitudes in that the judge decided to use cunt in the courtroom in the first place, but this was not without its sanctions for her.

Turning now to think about changing attitudes towards swearing in a different context, this time involving the word 'fucking' and professional football manager Jürgen Klopp. On 7 May 2019, his Premier League team Liverpool played Barcelona in the Champions League semi-final. They were losing 3–0 from the first leg of the game and looked all but out of the competition. The only way they could get through to the final was to win 4–0 in the second leg. They almost miraculously managed to pull off the 4–0 victory and Klopp was clearly exuberant directly after the game in the post-match interview:

> **Klopp:** The whole performance was too much. It was over-whelming. I watched in my life so many football games but I can't remember any like this . . . I don't know how the boys did it [looks down at his watch]. It's ten past ten, most of the children are probably in bed, these – the boys are fucking mentality giants (interviewer puts his hand on his shoulder) – it's unbelievable, it's unbe-lievable.
>
> **Interviewer:** [laughing] sorry for the language.
>
> **Klopp:** If you have to fine me, fine me if you want. I'm not native so I don't have better words for it. It's unbeliev-able, they are mentality giants.[292]

Klopp voices his strong emotions and then moves on to articulate his full awareness that he will be breaking polite-ness broadcasting rules directly before he drops the f-bomb. He doesn't apologise (though the interviewer does on his behalf) and instead states that he doesn't care if he is fined – he is extremely proud of his players and wants to articulate his pride with full force. He gives them all the credit and uses 'fucking' to intensify his positive evaluation of them as a group of 'mentality giants'. By justifying his swearing breach by claiming not to have a large enough English vocabulary, he uses the populist poverty of vocabulary argument as an excuse, though he does manage to articulate his positive evaluation of his players as mentality giants a second time without the expletive.

There were no media reports of any complaints after-wards. The main reaction seemed to be amusement or viewers responding to Klopp being unable to control his use of emotional language. Head of digital platforms at the *Financial Times*, Matthew Garrahan,[293] evaluated this positively as the 'greatest post-match interview in sporting history' on Twitter. This comment demonstrates that context is everything. Swearing on live TV using a strong taboo word that cannot be censored as it was broadcast live would usually result in a demand for an apology. However, on this occasion, this did not happen. When the broadcast went back to the studio, the programme's host Gary Lineker had been asked by the broadcaster to apologise for the swearing on Klopp's behalf, but Lineker refused. Instead, he said, 'We'll give you that one, Jürgen.'[294] Lineker commented further that, because it was after the watershed, and as Klopp was so genuinely exhilarated by his team's performance, he couldn't help swearing uncensored on live television, he did not believe that he needed to apologise on Klopp's behalf. No complaints were received to Ofcom and so it appeared that viewers were in agreement with Lineker's opinion.

This was not the first time that Klopp had used the f-word on a live broadcast interview. Despite Klopp's justification that he swore due to a lack of English vocabulary, he has used other excuses before – in 2018, in a similar situation of exuberance where his Liverpool side had beaten Premier League champions Manchester City 4–3, when being interviewed by the US news channel NBC, he said, 'You can look at this game in different ways. You can look at it as a manager and say we could have done this and that. Or you can look at it as a football fan and say, "What the fuck was that?" Unbelievable.'[295]

Afterwards, he argued that because Donald Trump was now US president and Trump swore so much in public, he thought he could also swear openly on American TV.[296] This humorous, tongue-in-cheek excuse for breaking broadcasting rules and swearing on live TV was enough to get him off without a fine.

These examples show how speakers are pushing the boundaries of swearing in the broadcast media and in public spaces, and that, whilst such language would not have been tolerated historically, now it is being broadcast on mainstream TV and via social media.

Summary

As we have seen in this chapter, there are frequent and often vociferous discussions that take place around perceived standards in public life, and swearing is usually a key part of these conversations. However, swearing has been in existence for hundreds of years and has endured precisely because it fulfils a range of important social functions. Particular groups in society are frequently yet unfairly blamed for declining standards of behaviour in public.

This chapter has presented a topical survey of swearing and taboo informed by thorough sociolinguistics research, and it is important to bring the following arguments together to summarise the fresh approach that has been outlined here. Swearing does not automatically mean that a speaker is using impolite or distasteful language, or that the swearer lacks vocabulary or is lazy. This view has been categorically disproven as a social class-based stereotype and a politeness myth. Instead, it is important to acknowledge that people from all different social class backgrounds swear. Swearing can be expressive and creative, particularly when it is used to show solidarity and collegiality, and those who swear are proven to have more extensive vocabularies than those who do not.

We have also seen that the power that lies behind swearing, particularly in terms of how much offence can be caused, does change over time, and this can be related to shifting attitudes during different historical periods. As some countries and cultures have become more secular in recent times, blasphemous words have lost their power, becoming more commonplace and generally less frowned upon, though this does depend on context.

Swearing fulfils many different and useful social functions, though it is always important to remember that context and awareness of one's audience is everything. No one wants to find themselves in a situation where they are joining in with one of their friends, happily letting off the f-bomb in a show of solidarity, only to look behind to see someone senior to them whom they like and admire, but who detests swearing, within earshot. Repair work around swearing can be difficult once it has been overheard, though apologies may work.

Swearing can be used very effectively as a solidarity and collegiality-building device amongst groups, as well as a marker of aggression, exasperation and despair. Who swears, who gets stigmatised for swearing and who is more heavily sanctioned for swearing are critical issues which reveal a significant amount in terms of power and attitudes towards politeness, identity and cultural taboos in societies.

It is useful for us as language users to be able to gauge whether or not swearing will cause offence. As we have seen in this chapter, in some countries and cultures, swearing in public is illegal and so it is important to be able to think carefully about swearing, the context and form that it takes, and any consequences that swearing could have, such as being arrested or receiving a fine. If you are either swearing yourself or assessing other people's swearing, then the following points can act as a set of politeness measurements to predict any potential benefits or risks from swearing in the society and situation in which one finds oneself. To make informed judgements about the appropriacy of swearing it is useful to consider whether you are communicating face to face, in writing, via sign language or by gesture. If it is in writing, then there is a greater chance that someone other than your intended addressee could see. It is very important to consider who could potentially read it in future.

If in public, then consider where you are, including the rules of the country you are in, whom you are with, what the power relationship is between you and your interlocutor or audience, and why you are there. It is also worth assessing the impact that differing identity features could have. Consider age, gender, social class, religion, belief, sexuality, disability and any other relevant factors, including personality traits. It is also worth considering who else may overhear you and who could potentially be eavesdropping, even if you are not directly talking to them. Taking into account emotions can also be a good gauge of how likely people are to swear. From the para-linguistic cues that are available, including body language, we can make quite accurate assessments of whether people are angry, frustrated, in pain, happy, excited or exhilarated, for example, when they swear.

Overall, the aim of this chapter has been to break long-standing stereotypes and myths about swearing and improve understanding of swearing and the important role that it plays in cultivating many different types of interpersonal relation-ships. It can be used to express conflict and hostility, and as a form of verbal abuse, but it can also function as a creative and expressive form of language that can bring humour and camara-derie, enhancing interpersonal relationships in close-knit groups. Swearing is an aspect of language that many people value as a solidarity marker.

However, swearing continues to be controversial, and there are still taboos with some highly stigmatised terms. Communications regulators have strict rules in terms of what expletives can be used and at what times of day, to protect children from hearing words that are deemed to be inappropriate. Stigmatised forms of language such as swearing are rather tightly controlled in many places and swearing is illegal in public in some parts of the world.

It is important for speakers to be fully aware of when, how and why they are swearing to avoid being stigmatised or, in worst-case scenarios, being arrested or getting embroiled in physical or verbal violence due to swearing.

8

Saying Sorry Sincerely: How to Give an Effective Apology

Apologies play very important roles in our lives – relationships and careers can be saved or lost on the basis of the sincerity of an apology. Getting the rules of politeness right when giving an apology can make the crucial difference between its success or failure. This chapter presents a step-by-step guide for issuing your own apologies, to ensure that they stand the very best chances of success. Of course, I cannot promise you that every one of your future apologies will be successfully received and all will be forgiven. However, what I can do is share my knowledge of what good and bad apologies look like, building on over thirty years of research into apologies, and show how success and failure can be explained through sociolinguistics.

To bring this guide to life, we will analyse a wide range of different apologies, from those that were successful to those that failed. These include apologies issued by high-profile public figures, those issued on behalf of organisations, and those from friends, colleagues and complete strangers. One thing that is clear in this chapter is that apologies are far more complex than they first appear. There is a whole host of often complex strands of enquiry when thinking about how, why and when apologies are expected, given and received.

To help you, I've created a step-by-step guide to apologies in seven different stages, which we will go through chronologically:

1. When are apologies necessary?
2. Who should be apologising?
3. How should apologies be delivered?
4. How quickly should apologies be delivered?
5. How about responsibility or reparations?
6. Is the apology accepted?
7. What happens when apologies go wrong?

1. When are apologies necessary?

As a general rule of politeness, an apology is required when someone causes offence or harm to another. Whilst the need to give an apology for different offences will vary somewhat from culture to culture, apologies are a necessary part of repairing human relationships when things go wrong and they operate as a clear signal of where the boundaries of acceptable and unacceptable behaviour lie. To successfully follow the politeness rules, the type of apology will need to be appropriate to the seriousness of the offence that has been caused, and the cultural setting. There is, of course, a big difference between what would be required after losing someone's pen compared to if you borrowed someone's car and crashed it. Part of our assessment of the seriousness of an offence will depend on where the offence took place and the relationship between those involved. If an apology is not forthcoming when it is expected then one may well be demanded by a wronged party, particularly if the offence is more serious.

To examine when apologies are necessary and how detailed they need to be, we must first look at the concept of offence in more detail. New Zealand sociolinguist Janet Holmes[297] has devised a useful system for categorising different types of

282

offence, defining five types, which are useful to incorporate into our apologies guide:

Space offences
Talk offences
Time offences
Social gaffes
Offences against another's property

The first category, space offences, refers to when our personal space is invaded by another, such as accidentally bumping into one another on the street or inadvertently treading on someone's toes on public transport. In various cultures, if you are a pedestrian on a busy street and you see that you are directly on course to bump into another person, you may both end up trying to avoid one another in a rather awkward dance-like jig – it is cultural politeness norms that bring about these attempts to dodge past each other without collision. The uncomfortable jigging around may well be accompanied with a verbal 'sorry' in some cultural settings, particularly if you do end up colliding with one another anyway, regardless of who is deemed to be at fault. Anthropologist Kate Fox[298] reported that 80 per cent of people in the UK will say sorry in this situation and that, with the exception of Japan, no other country's speakers came close to this level of British apologising.

For British people, then, space offences are serious enough to break politeness rules and rank highly enough for verbal apologies to be seen as necessary, even when the apologiser bears no responsibility for the incident. In such contexts, the importance of re-establishing a social equilibrium and moving away from the embarrassment of bodies bumping into each other overrides the need to assign blame. If apologies are not given when they are expected for space offences, however, then this can potentially result in conflict and arguments on the street.

As well as cultural expectations, the weightiness of a space offence will depend on how much damage or harm is caused by the space invasion. There is a distinct difference between accidentally walking into someone with no pain or injury caused, which can be seen as a 'light' offence, versus banging into someone so hard that you cause them to fall over and break a bone – a 'heavy' offence, even if caused by complete accident. The amount of apologising and type of apology that would be needed for the heavy offence would be far greater, in any culture.

The second category, talk offences, refers to talking too much and not letting other people join in, or talking too little, too loudly or too quietly, which, again, is heavily culturally dependent. For example, if people dominate the conversational floor or interrupt too much, taking turns away from others who wish to speak, then this can be negatively evaluated and the need for an apology can occur. If you are asked a question and deliberately provide too little or too much information, or if you are deliberately evasive in your response, then this can also be identified as a talk offence and, again, an apology may be necessary.

As for our third category, time offences also vary in seriousness from culture to culture. Lateness is a good illustrator of this. In some cultures, lateness is a light offence; in others, it is heavy. Researcher Shoshana Blum-Kulka[299] found that, for Hebrew speakers in Israel, being late for work was not regarded as a heavy offence and therefore an apology was not always offered or expected. However, in cultures including Canada, the US and the UK, being late for work is considered a much heavier offence, and therefore more linguistic repair work is required, through apologies, to ensure that its seriousness is properly acknowledged.

Moving on to social gaffes, these refer to things that may happen to the body in public spaces, often in the form of bodily leakage, such as burping, crying, passing wind, coughing, sneezing or uncontrollable laughter. All of these may be considered rude to differing degrees in some cultural contexts, and therefore an apology may well be necessary. If we focus on sneezing, a recent UK YouGov poll – which took place before the Covid-19 pandemic – found that you would get fifteen more British people saying 'sorry' compared with the US response to sneezing in public. This shows that for British people, sneezing in public is a greater breach of politeness rules and thus the need for an apology is greater too.

Holmes's final category, offences against another's property, ranges in seriousness, from losing someone's pen or pencil, through to crashing someone's car. At the heavier end, it is likely that legal processes may well be invoked via insurance or litigation claims. As discussed further below, a verbal apology on these occasions may not be enough, and some form of repair or reparation may be needed.

So, if we think about Holmes's offence criteria in terms of our apologies guide, we can see that when something happens to us that we find offensive, the expectation of an apology occurs. If politeness rules are to be followed, the type of apology required will partly depend on the severity of the offence. Holmes uses a continuum of 'light', 'medium' and 'heavy' offences as a sliding scale of weightiness, to gauge the seriousness. Part of this weight-iness will depend on where the offence took place and the relationship between those involved.

2. Who should be apologising?

A vital factor in the success of an apology is whether the person apologising is the right person to be giving the apology in the first place. If they are not, then the apology stands very little chance of success and may well fall at the first hurdle. Ideally, the person who has committed the offence should be the one who apologises, so that this person can show how sorry they are. However, there are occasions when someone may legiti-mately apologise on behalf of another. For example, parents can apologise on behalf of young children who cannot articulate apologies for themselves. Apologies can also be legitimately delivered by political leaders on behalf of individuals in their government, and CEOs may apologise for the actions of the organisation they represent.

When a political scandal or mishandling is really serious, it may become important for a political leader to apologise on behalf of a member of their own government. For example, when former Prime Minister Harold Macmillan submitted a very formal written apology to Queen Elizabeth II for the Profumo Affair in 1963, arguably one of the biggest scandals in British political history. Macmillan's Secretary of State for War, John Profumo, had been caught having a sexual relationship with Christine Keeler, who was also having a sexual relationship with a Russian spy. This took place during the Cold War, within a year of the Cuban Missile Crisis, when nuclear war between the US and Russia had narrowly been avoided. This letter was eventually released into the public domain by the Public Records Office many years later and gives a unique insight into correspondence between a prime minister and the monarch, which is otherwise protected by strict protocols of privacy.

The private letter revealed that Macmillan had felt compelled to apologise in writing to the Queen for Profumo's behaviour: 'I feel that I ought to apologise to you for the undoubted injury done by the terrible behaviour of one of Your Majesty's Secretaries of State.'[300] Macmillan told Queen Elizabeth that, 'with hindsight', he might have handled things differently, but insisted he knew nothing about Profumo's behaviour.

The Profumo scandal ranks as exceptionally serious in terms of the weightiness of the offence and the potential harm it could have caused to British national security at the time. It was grave enough for Macmillan to apologise on behalf of another, one of his key government ministers. However, Macmillan was also trying to save his own skin here – whilst he used the apology to justify writing the letter in the first place, he then went on to explicitly protest his innocence and distance himself from any illegal or unethical behaviour. As part of the broader text around the apology, he said: 'I had of course no idea of the strange underworld in which other people, alas, besides Mr Profumo, have allowed themselves to become entrapped.'

However, the admission in his letter that he did not know anything drew intense criticism that he was out of touch with what was going on in his own government and that he had lost control of his ministers. Macmillan did end up resigning just a few months later and the Profumo Affair was deemed to have played a key role in his demise. His private apology to the monarch clearly was not enough to save him in the eyes of the media and the public. So, although the seriousness of the offence meant that Macmillan was absolutely the right person to apolo-gise in private, this was never going to be enough to save his political career in public. Often, politicians will issue apologies and, at the same time, sneak in a defence of their own actions to try to save their reputations. This decision really backfired on Macmillan here as not knowing what was going on made him look incompetent. Ultimately, he paid for this with his job and a loss of reputation.

Political leaders also have a legitimate responsibility to deliver historical apologies on behalf of previous governments, apolo-gising if a moral line had at some point been crossed. And so, if the need for issuing a historical apology arises, then it is the current prime minister or equivalent political leader who will be called upon to do so. In reality, though, it is much easier for politicians to apologise for events that have happened in the more distant past because they have had no direct control nor any personal culpability over events – which will not be directly related to current government policies or current politicians.

In 2021, then-New Zealand Prime Minister Jacinda Ardern apologised for historical racial profiling in the New Zealand police, which happened under previous governments in the 1970s. This profiling led to violent dawn raids of migrants from the Pasifika region who were in New Zealand. They were alleged to have broken visa rules and many people were instantly deported and families broken up without any warning. This was during a period of high unemployment in New Zealand and migrants were frequently blamed. Ardern's official apology[301] was seen to be successfully delivered and one part of its success was her use of four languages: te reo Māori, Tongan, Samoan and English. Through this she demonstrated her recognition of the importance of speaking to communities in their own native languages, not just using English. And in order to prove that she was the correct person to be issuing the apology, she stated, in Samoan, 'I stand before you as a representative of those who did you harm.' She then uttered the following, in English: 'I stand on behalf of the New Zealand government, to offer a formal and unreserved apology to Pacific communities.'

Canadian Prime Minister Justin Trudeau is another political leader who has apologised for various historical events, including to the relatives of Sikh, Muslim and Hindu families who were on board the Japanese boat *Komagata Maru* in 1914 – these passengers were denied entry to Vancouver and sent back to India due to the country's racist immigration laws. On return, Indian police boarded the vessel and a riot broke out, resulting in the deaths of twenty-two people. Trudeau has also apologised for the historical abuses of children of First Nations' communities in Canadian residential schools run by the Catholic Church, the expulsion of LGBT workers from Canadian public services and the relocation of Inuit communities from their original homes. He argued that, as the leader of Canada, he has a moral duty to apologise for past wrongs. He justified his decision to be the apologiser, stating that, 'Apologies for things past are important to make sure that we actually understand and know and share and don't repeat those mistakes.'

While this may all seem like good politics, some journalists have questioned whether Trudeau overuses apologies, particularly as there had been quite a flurry of them clustered together. In a BBC article in 2018, journalist Jessica Murphy[302] posed the question: 'Does Justin Trudeau apologise too much?', which was hotly debated by the media on both sides of the Atlantic. It opens up an interesting question – if a politician or a public figure apologises for a number of different historical events in short succession for which they bear no direct responsibility, other than being current head of state, do the apologies start to seem tokenistic and somewhat insincere? Another freelance Canadian journalist writing in the *Guardian* newspaper commented that, 'Even in Canada, where "I'm sorry" is a second national anthem, some wonder if the words are losing their meaning.'[303]

If politicians apologise many times in short succession, particularly when issuing historical apologies, then it may start to look insincere, which can undermine the strength and force of the historical apologies being made. It is important for apologies not to be overused as their sincerity will inevitably become in doubt. Politicians and their teams of political advisers need to be acutely aware that any historical apologies they give whilst in office may well be critically scrutinised from many different angles, including if they are believed to be over-apologising.

At the opposite end of the scale, in rarer cases, some politicians have refused to take part in any apologies, and this break with politeness expectations and the moral standards that go along with apologies is particularly noticeable if the person who is refusing is in a prominent position of power. During Donald Trump's presidency in the US, he explicitly refused to apologise for multiple incidents on multiple occasions – this included for historical events and for things that he himself had done that were deemed inappropriate in the media and by the general public (his 'grabbing women by the pussy' quote is just one example from a very long list of potential examples). Many news outlets published stories and commentary pieces on Trump's lack of apologies – CNN ran a news report with the headline 'Donald Trump is not sorry. Ever.' The *Washington Post* published an article titled 'Donald Trump never apologises for his controversial remarks' and news outlet Axios headlined an article: 'Why Trump's White House never says sorry'.

A spokesperson from the White House claimed that not apologising was 'a core operating principle' for Donald Trump. Another journalist commented that 'once you've worked for Trump for a while you know that the worst thing you can do, the biggest show of weakness, is to apologise'. By not apologising, Trump marks himself out as very different from all other politicians and presidents that have come before him. As one of his traits is to be different from establishment political figures, in refusing to apologise, he is rejecting taking part in an established political communication strategy that would be expected to be a part of his role as president. He changes the rules with apologies by completely refusing to utter them.

When Joe Biden took over as US president, it seemed that the political apologies equilibrium had returned: Biden apologised for his own actions when called upon to do so, but also, notably, he apologised on behalf of Trump for some of Trump's actions before him, including apologising for Trump's withdrawal from the Paris climate change agreement.

3. How should apologies be delivered?

In English, one of the most commonly accepted ways of communicating an apology is to utter 'sorry', either on its own or as part of a longer utterance. 'Sorry' tends to be the favoured way of apologising in more informal situations, when an offence is fairly small. Sometimes, a fully accepted, successful apology can simply be the one-word utterance 'sorry', providing that this fits the offence that has taken place and the relationship between those involved, such as accidentally brushing up against a stranger lightly in the street. On other occasions, it will be part of an 'I'm sorry' or 'we're sorry' construction, which may be followed by a reason – 'I'm sorry, I didn't see you there!'

When analysing what apologies look like linguistically, uttering 'sorry' does not automatically mean that an apology has been given. 'Sorry' can also be used to express sympathy or regret without any apology being present. If your friend's cat has died, you may say 'I'm sorry about your cat'. Assuming that you are not in any way responsible for the cat's demise, you are not apologising here; instead, you are expressing a sense of sympathy for the sadness that the death may have caused. This is a form of politeness as you are paying attention to the needs of others in expressing sorrow and sympathy, and this shows that you care about another person's feelings, though it is not an apology.

'Sorry' can also be used to describe a bad situation or an un-favourable condition that someone may have got themselves into, as in oft-heard phrases including 'what a sorry state of affairs' or 'he was in a sorry mess'. It is also possible to use 'sorry' as a challenge. Consider if someone says to you 'Sorry, no! That's not true!' in response to a statement that you have just made and that you firmly believe in – in such cases, 'sorry' is primarily being used as a way of gaining the conversational floor and to express disagreement, not as part of an apology. So, sorry needs to be looked at carefully in context, to ascertain how sorry is being used and if it is genuinely being used as part of an apology.

If 'sorry' is not used, then the other most common way to express an apology in English is to use the verb 'apologise', which tends to be the favoured choice in more formal situations and settings. Saying the words 'I/we apologise' is known in linguistics as a 'performative' speech act, because the apology comes into existence as it is uttered – the speaker brings the apology to life through the act of speaking it. Other forms that can be used to issue apologies include the phrases 'pardon me', 'forgive me' or 'excuse me'. Some English speakers will also borrow *'mea culpa'*, from Latin, which literally translates as 'through my fault' and has been brought into English through the Catholic Church. The latter tends to be used as part of a more formal apology if the offence is deemed to be high. However, although 'sorry' and 'apologise' are the most explicit and common ways of apologising in English, if these words are missing, then the authenticity or sincerity of the apology may well be questioned by the person(s) receiving it. Linguists refer to the use of 'I'm sorry' or 'I apologise' rather grandly as 'illocutionary force indicating devices' (IFIDs). This can be defined as the speaker's intention which lies behind the words. So, when an apology is intended, it is described as having the illocutionary force of being an apology.

Depending upon what has happened, apologies can be made stronger in their delivery by adding in words to intensify how sorry someone is for any offence that has been committed. The amount of intensification that is used will depend on how serious the offence is, as well as on the relationship between the apologiser and the person(s) receiving the apology. If the offence is towards the heavier end of the scale, intensification may well be out in force, and you may end up with a cluster of intensifiers from the apologiser to ensure the apology comes across as genuine and authentic – such as 'I am so very sorry', 'I am extremely sorry', 'we deeply regret what happened and send you our sincerest apologies'.

Of course, another important part of how apologies are delivered is not just the words that are spoken but the ways in which they are delivered, as this tells us how genuine someone is when they apologise. As we have touched upon earlier in the book in chapter four, if we think about young children learning to apologise, we frequently hear parents commanding their child to 'say sorry'. The child will often do this through gritted teeth, with the wrong intonation and body language, which undermines the sincerity of their apology (for example, not making eye contact, standing with folded arms, turning away from the person to whom they are apologising). At a surface level, they have literally fulfilled the parent's request – they have said sorry. In reality, though, sincerity is absent. The more children learn about politeness norms and conventions, what linguists refer to as achieving 'pragmatic competence', the better they get at delivering more authentic-sounding apologies.

Also, just because someone states 'I'm sorry' or 'we apologise', it does not automatically mean that an apology has *genuinely* been given and received as such. When we receive apologies, we subconsciously observe all of the metacommunication that takes places around the apology – the communication cues that accompany the language used which are part of the delivery of the apology. If it is a spoken apology, this includes body language, gesture, tone and pitch, as well as paying very close attention to any other speech that is delivered as part of the main apology phrase. As receivers, we then make a judgement about the sincerity of any apology.

We can learn a great deal about morality within a particular culture by observing how apologies are delivered. Key components that make up authentic and genuine apologies include sincerity, taking responsibility and accountability, including who is actually to blame for particular events and what should happen in future to prevent similar situations recurring.

Whilst we have just considered exactly how successful apologies can be delivered, we will now move on to detail a series of other important considerations which need to be taken into account if an apology is to be seen as genuine and is to be accepted by the receiver(s) of the apology.

4. How quickly should apologies be delivered?

Many commentators have argued that we are living in an age of the apology.[304] When things go wrong, politicians and public figures are immediately held to account by the mass media, members of the public, other politicians and public figures, and they are called upon to apologise as soon as is possible. If apologies, or events leading up to an apology, are particularly high profile, the mass media, including citizen journalists (self-appointed members of the public on social media), will often debate whether or not an apology was genuine or sufficient for the offence that has been committed.

With historical apologies, there has obviously been a neglect of delivering an apology quickly as, by their nature, these most often take place after a significant amount of time has passed. Sometimes, decades or even centuries can pass, as in the case of many recent apologies for the slave trade. And so, in these cases, political leaders and public figures will often try to bring some additional poignancy to the apology by timing its delivery carefully to coincide with poignant anniversaries or with publications from official inquiries to help enhance the apology's meaning and force, the sense of thoughtfulness and genuineness that lies behind it. For instance, UK Prime Minister David Cameron[305] apologised on behalf of the UK government in the House of Commons for the Bloody Sunday massacre in Northern Ireland in 1972 on the day of the publication in 2010 of a long-awaited official report, which investigated the Bloody Sunday deaths nearly forty years after the massacre took place.

Calls for apologies may also come directly from within the pages of reports of official inquires. For example, a recent inquiry conducted by the Joint Committee on Human Rights[306] in the UK investigated how 185,000 pregnant, single teenagers were forced to give up their babies in the 1950s, '60s and '70s. The report states that these women and their children (who are now in their forties and fifties) were owed an apology from the government for their mistreatment, reflecting that hundreds of birth mothers and children who were adopted have campaigned for a public apology for a substantial period of time, and yet were still waiting. Chair of the committee, Harriet Harman, said that 'the least the government can do is recognise that this should never have happened and it would never happen now, and it's right for the government to apologise'.[307] Despite such prompting and the timing being appropriate in terms of the investigative report being published, no apology was forthcoming.

5. How about responsibility or reparations?

In addition to thinking about who the apologiser is and how quickly apologies need to be delivered, in some cases, there is also a need not just to apologise through an explicit act ('I'm sorry', 'I apologise'), but also to accompany an apology with an explanation as to why the offence happened in the first place. It is only really for minor offences that you can utter a quick 'I'm sorry' and get away with it. Let's think about time offences again to illustrate.

If apologising for being late, the apologiser may well offer an explanation as to why the lateness happened, if the cultural norms and the weightiness of the situation demands it. The apologiser can take responsibility, using a strategy of self-blame: 'so sorry, completely my fault'; or self-deficiency: 'I slept through my alarm'; or they can give a denial of fault by blaming another person and/or a situation beyond one's own control: 'the bus was late', 'the traffic was awful', 'there's been an accident'.

Alongside any explanation is the need for the apologiser to take genuine responsibility for the offence – not just speak the words but come across as really meaning them. In the following example, Jacinda Ardern clearly takes responsibility on behalf of her government when she issues the historical apology to the Pasifika migrant community:

> I stand on behalf of the New Zealand government, to offer a formal and unreserved apology to Pacific communities for the discriminatory implementation of the immigration laws of the 1970s that led to the events of the dawn raids. The government expresses its sorrow, remorse and regret that the dawn raids and random police checks occurred and that these actions were ever considered appropriate. May my words today be received in the spirit of humility that I convey in them.[308]

Ardern actively expresses 'sorrow, remorse and regret' on behalf of the government, employing the power of metacommunication (talking about her own language, when she says 'may my words') to explicitly mark out that her apologetic words, and to further emphasise the genuineness and sincerity of the apology.

In cases such as these, where the offence is very heavy, then an apology on its own is not enough. The apologiser will also need to offer a form of reparation or repair. Ardern offered a clear form of reparation on behalf of her government, announcing that $3.1 million of scholarships would be created for Pacific students to study in New Zealand and the region, which she metaphorically stated would 'pave a new dawn' for Pasifika communities. Additional financial support would also be offered to artists and historians to create exhibitions reflecting upon the racist events. These financial investments operate as gestures of repair, put forward as a form of closure, to draw a line under past deeds and to move forward with newer generations. Additionally, as a promise of future forbearance, Ardern announced that her government would ensure that the dawn raids were taught as part of the New Zealand school history curriculum as a miscarriage of justice, and the exhibitions created by artists and historians would play a role here in learning from past events to prevent a similar situation ever recurring.

Even at the much lighter end of the offence scale, there may still also be a need for some reparation, but on an equitably small scale. For instance, if you have borrowed and broken someone's stapler, as part of your apology, you may present a form of reparation by offering to buy a new one to minimise the inconvenience of your actions.

Reparation can also involve formal legal proceedings, as in medical litigation cases, which can result in financial awards of compensation for medical malpractice, or in cases where an organisation has responsibility for people's health and safety, with compensation given for injuries or death sustained due to an organisation's negligence. In some cases, there may need to be a promise that the situation will not recur and that lessons have been learnt, so that others will not suffer in the same way in future.

If we consider medical litigation claims in the US, for example, apologies play a key role – so much so that there are formal 'apology laws'. In almost forty out of fifty states, these laws prevent apologies from being subsequently used by patients as evidence of culpability. The laws have been brought in to encourage more physicians to apologise in an attempt to cut the overall number of malpractice suits occurring – evidence shows that if patients receive an apology, then they are less likely to want to pursue legal action. In the case of malpractice suits that do go ahead, patients consistently cite the lack of an apology as critical in their decision to pursue a legal route instead of settling outside of court, alongside a sense that medical professionals were withholding information from them and their families by failing to communicate clearly or transparently. And so, what we can see here is that an apology can be so powerful it sometimes negates the need for reparations.

The first 'apology law' was brought in during 1986 in Massachusetts.[309] Apology laws can be split into two types – 'full' or 'partial', depending on the US state. Full apology laws are rarer (only eight out of fifty states have these at the time of writing); they cover every aspect of language that can be seen as part of an apology, including any disclosure of error, statements of responsibility and statements of sympathy or regret. In contrast, partial apology laws cover only expressions of sympathy/regret, leaving statements of error uncovered and thus medical practitioners unprotected. Psychiatrists Nina Ross and William Newman[310] report that, whilst statements of sympathy and regret are protected in the majority of states, expressions of fault are not, and extensions to give full coverage in all states is critical if apologies are to result in significantly fewer malpractice suits being issued.

In the UK, the National Health Service (NHS) has a body called NHS Resolution, whose role it is to provide expertise on NHS disputes and complaints between medical practitioners and patients, with the aim of resolving any disputes fairly. NHS Resolution has produced a four-page training booklet titled 'Saying Sorry'[311] for medical practitioners. In this booklet, it is clearly emphasised that saying sorry does not mean an admission of liability. Instead, saying sorry sincerely should happen as soon as possible, both because morally it is the right thing to do and because it can reduce legal claims.

Here is a sample template letter suggested as a starting point by NHS Resolution for an appropriate formal written apology letter to a patient and their family:

> I wish to assure you that I am deeply sorry for the poor care you have been given and that we are all truly committed to learning from what happened. I apologise unreservedly for the distress this has caused you and your family.[312]

The template contains the two explicit acts of 'sorry' and 'apologise', with the use of the personal pronoun 'I' to clearly show who is issuing the apology, along with intensification: 'deeply sorry' and 'apologise unreservedly'. It acknowledges that poor care has been given and there is the explicit promise of commitment to 'learning' to ensure that the same mistake does not recur. There is no offer of reparation here, as part of the aim of this route to resolution is to avoid financial litigation in the first instance.

NHS Resolution also advises that the following phrases should always be avoided:

We're sorry if you are offended.
I'm sorry you feel like that.
I'm sorry you took it that way.[313]

All three examples demonstrate the apologiser avoiding taking any responsibility. They are classic deflection strategies, often used by politicians and other public figures when they are deliberately trying to avoid being blamed for something. Although these three examples use the sorry-based unit and personal pronouns, ('I'm/we're sorry)', this is not enough as the language that comes directly after the phrase implies that the problem lies with the person to whom the apology is being issued and not with the person who is claiming to apologise. Using the conditional 'if', as in the first example, implies that other people would not be offended in the same circumstances, including the person who is 'apologising'. The use of the second person pronoun 'you' in the remaining two examples similarly act as social distancing devices – the speaker distances themselves from the perspective the hearer has taken and makes it clear that this is not shared, emphasising that different interpretations of events exist. These phrases work to deny that any real pain has been caused, and are thus lacking in sincerity and genuineness.

Another important observation made in the NHS Resolution booklet, which applies in all contexts and with all apologies, is the issue of the timing. NHS Resolution states that apologies should be given immediately, after clinicians first become aware that there has been an issue, without any delay. It is common to hear of people in many different situations where offence or harm has been caused 'still waiting' for an apology, and often the length of time it takes for an apology to be issued when it is expected can cause additional upset and distress. Apologies will be viewed as less effective if the person(s) receiving the apology feels as if the other person has been forced to apologise, instead of apologising of their own volition, and as promptly as possible.

The overarching aim for any genuine apology is for it to bring a sense of resolution and ideally a sense of closure to a situation in which harm or offence has been caused, so that those who have been negatively affected can move on. If we consider politicians and public figures who offer apologies for serious offences relating to situations of their own making, then the ultimate way to offer reparation and a promise that such situations will not happen again is to resign. Resignations can be seen as the ultimate resolution to a public apology if an offence is serious enough; it may be the only way that the situation can be reconciled appropriately. Often in high-profile, public roles, apologies on their own are seen to not go far enough, particularly if there are any doubts raised about sincerity. Often, there follows demands for resignations by the mass media and affected members of the public, which may or may not happen. Politicians may also reject the need for resignation for as long as possible to try to wait until the matter has passed out of public consciousness.

6. Is the apology accepted?

An apology may be accepted or rejected by the target audience; if it is rejected, then the apologiser's integrity and authenticity may be further questioned. If an apology is accepted, then a sense of repair and ideally a resolution can be brought about, which can hopefully include forgiveness and/or a sense of closure for those concerned. The successful delivery of an apology represents an important social act – it demonstrates remorse and, as such, it can be seen as upholding the moral fabric of the culture and society where the apology takes place.

To illustrate a successful apology, we will go back to the world of sport. In 2015, English Premier League football manager Nigel Pearson,[314] who was managing Leicester City at the time, lost his temper at a post-match press conference with a local journalist, Ian Baker. Leicester were embroiled in a relegation battle at the time and they had just lost an important match. Pearson was under increasing pressure and his job was on the line.

Ian Baker had denied that journalists (including himself) had been criticising the abilities of the Leicester City players during the season. This infuriated Pearson who believed that Baker was being unreasonable and refusing to acknowledge the truth that regular criticism had been received from Baker and others. The press conference ended up turning into quite a farcical affair, with Pearson becoming more and more impolite and insulting. He directed a number of impolite comments at Baker, many of which called Baker's professional integrity and his ability as a journalist into question. He did this through asking whether Barker was mentally capable of asking questions (the most fundamental part of a journalist's job), belittling him for not being able to speak clearly and mocking him for not being fluent enough because he used 'erm'. The most bizarre insult, though, was when he asked Baker if he was an ostrich because he must have his head in the sand if he had not seen that the Leicester players had been criticised by the media all season.

Pearson ended up walking out of the press conference because he had become so angry. Unsurprisingly, the clip of him asking Baker if he was an ostrich went viral and gathered a great deal of media attention. Baker sarcastically commented on the insult from Pearson on social media on his Twitter feed: 'If being called an ostrich by Nigel Pearson is not a career high-light, I don't know what is.'[315] At the press conference the next day, Pearson came in and sat down calmly at the seat he had left to storm out the night before. He delivered the following apology to Ian Baker, who was sitting close to the front, at the very beginning of the press conference, before any questions were asked:

> **Pearson:** Before we start, Ian, because you are here, apolo-gies for last night.
> **Baker:** Apologies accepted, Nigel.
> **Pearson:** Thank you. I think it's right to do it in front of the cameras rather than pulling you to the side so I apologise for that and, errr [pause], hope it doesn't ruin our relationship. Okay? Thank you. [looks away]
> **Baker:** All right, Nigel, thank you.
> **Pearson:** Okay, no problem.[316]

Ian Baker then later posted on Twitter: 'I have accepted the apology. Fair play to him for being big enough to apologise.'[317]

This is a very clearly expressed apology and a straightforward acceptance by Ian Baker, and so repair has taken place and the matter has clearly been brought to a close. Pearson does not offer an explanation or any reparation at this point but, due to the power imbalance between the two of them – although Baker is the interviewer who asks the questions, as an elite football manager, Pearson has more status – the short and very public nature of the apology (which is more threatening to Pearson's status) seems appropriate in these circumstances and is certainly evaluated as such by Baker. Baker then also clarifies that he has accepted the apology on Twitter and that he appreciated it.

We will now explore whether politicians' apologies have been accepted by analysing how they were received by those to whom they were addressed, alongside how they were evaluated and judged by the mass media and, ultimately, whether or not the politician survived in their role.

As we've seen, apologies given by politicians and public figures most often fall into the heavy or serious category of offence. Their professional responsibilities make them directly account-able to members of the public and often there is a significant amount of work that goes into apologising, given that they are a leader in a position of responsibility in public life.

I worked in collaboration with my colleagues Karen Grainger and Sandra Harris to publish an academic article in which we examined how politicians can get away with not resigning, even in instances when they hold ultimate responsibility, and how they do this is through their strategic use of apologies. We exam-ined the case of Steven Roberts, a soldier killed in the Iraq War because he did not have the correct military equipment, which should have been provided by the British Army. His widow, Samantha Roberts, presented clear evidence that her husband had been asked to give his flak jacket to someone closer to the front line, meaning he was not protected when he was attacked.

Samantha Roberts demanded an apology from Defence Secretary Geoff Hoon for her husband's death. Hoon had said, 'I'm sorry that your husband was killed in the war.' However, although 'sorry' was used, it is clearly 'sorry' to express regret in this instance, and not to apologise. This apology attempt was rejected outright by Roberts as being inauthentic, as there was no sense that Hoon was taking any responsibility or providing any real explanation as to how this situation had arisen. There was also no offer of reparation and no promise that such a situation would not recur. Roberts therefore continued to demand a public apology from Hoon. Under pressure, Hoon then issued the following:

I am extremely sorry that Sgt Roberts did not have the enhanced body armour which we expected that he would receive. Some 38,000 sets of that enhanced body armour were sent to theatre. We wanted him to have that equipment. I'm extremely sorry that he did not have it. But – I think this is a crucial issue – ministers were assured that our armed forces were ready for battle . . . It is a military judgement as to whether soldiers are ready for battle. You would rightly criticise any minister who interfered in such a judgement.'[318]

At a surface level at least, this looks more like a formal apology – more so than Hoon's previous expressions of 'sorry', which came across insincerely, just as an expression of Hoon's regret, not as something that he was genuinely sorry for. He repeats the intensification phrase 'I am extremely sorry' and offers an explanation and account. However, notably, he still does not take responsibility for what happened. Instead, he uses 'but' to introduce his view that blame lay with the 'armed forces' and their 'judgement' to move equipment and not himself or the government, because 'ministers were assured that our armed forces were ready for battle'. He claims that this was the 'most crucial issue', a form of metacommunication to emphasise where he believes blame lay, which was not, as Sgt Roberts's widow was alleging, with him. So, although he is arguably going beyond just an expression of regret here, his 'apology' still lacks many of the characteristics that would be required for it to be evaluated as genuine.

In our study, we also looked at how the mass media had

interpreted this newer 'apology' from Hoon and found varied responses. The *Daily Mail* rejected it outright as an apology: 'Grieving widow still waits for Hoon apology'. The *Guardian* stated that an apology was given, but it failed to include blame: 'Hoon apologises over soldier's death, but sidesteps blame', thus implicitly questioning the genuineness of the apology. The *Daily Express* claimed that Hoon had been 'shamed' into 'an apology' and picked up on the issue of timing: 'Nine months to say "sorry"',[319] thus implying a lack of sincerity and that he only apologised because he had been forced to – something he should have done without any prompting months before. The differences between these newspaper interpretations of whether or not an apology had taken place show the ambiguity with which the apology was given. It is notable that, despite calls to resign, Hoon did not – and he was not forced out of office. The 'apology' he had issued protected him enough to retain his job.

There were multiple calls for Tony Blair to apologise for misleading Parliament over weapons of mass destruction, along with calls for him to resign due to the seriousness of the offence. Blair famously stated the following at a Labour Party conference speech: 'I can apologise for the information that turned out to be wrong, but I can't, sincerely at least, apologise for removing Saddam.'[320] Blair avoids taking full responsibility here through the use of 'can', which interrupts the usual 'I apologise' frame. The 'can' here acts more as a statement of his ability to be able to apologise – it does not mean that he is genuinely apologising. He then follows this up with 'I can't, sincerely at least, apologise' – refusing to 'sincerely' apologise for removing Saddam Hussein from office, as well as implying that some apologies are insincere.

Blair's use of 'can' brings real ambiguity as to whether or not an apology has been given. The *Independent* newspaper interpreted this sorry as an expression of Blair's regret, and they make the point that it cannot be an apology because regret is easy to show, and is something different from being genuinely apologetic and taking full responsibility for what has happened: 'He won't say he's sorry; he just says he regrets what has happened'.[321] Other areas of the media also questioned whether or not an apology had taken place – again, due to the lack of explanation and responsibility. If you are going to deliver a successful and genuine apology, then there should be no room for any ambiguity about the apology being delivered. Tony Blair declined to apologise further and instead called for a military inquiry. Despite numerous calls for his resignation, Blair managed to stay in his post and went on to be re-elected as prime minister at the next general election.

Continuing to look at politics, as it is such an important and fruitful arena in which to examine apologies, we will now turn our attention to how apologies were used strategically in the UK government's Partygate scandal during the Covid-19 pandemic. It is worth tracking key events as they unfolded chronologically, as a flurry of political apologies took place in very quick succession. The first apology that Prime Minister Boris Johnson delivered was after a rather damaging clip of his press officer, Allegra Stratton, joking about a breach of lockdown rules, became public. In addition to Stratton's apology and resignation, the prime minister apologised in the House of Commons for the behaviour of his Downing Street staff, stating the following: 'I understand and share the anger up and down the country at seeing Number 10 staff seeming to make light of lockdown measures. I apologise unreservedly for the offence that it has caused up and down the country and I apologise for the impression that it gives.'[322]

It was initially thought that the breach of the rules was restricted to this 'gathering' of a handful of staff, including Johnson. Although it was undeniably damaging for Boris Johnson to apologise, on this occasion, he apologises for his staff's behaviour, rather than for the 'gathering' itself, which he had continually insisted was within the rules. He uses 'I apologise' twice and then immediately distances himself from Stratton by sharing in the 'anger' of people 'up and down the country'. Johnson takes no responsibility, instead leaving this with Stratton. Because the ultimate act of resigning took place, there was an implication that the bad behaviour would go with her. Whilst somewhat damaging to Boris Johnson and the government, this incident appeared to have been brought to an end with the resignation.

However, then more compelling evidence of many more parties began to emerge – twelve in total were investigated by the Metropolitan Police and sixteen were investigated by Sue Gray (the senior civil servant who headed up an inquiry into the lockdown 'gatherings' at Number 10). On 12 January 2022, Boris Johnson had to apologise again in the House of Commons for a garden party in May 2020, to which approximately 200 people were invited, with the invitation informing staff to 'bring your own booze'. There was clear evidence that Johnson was present at this party. He stated the following in his apology speech:

I want to apologise. I know that millions of people across this country have made extraordinary sacrifices over the last 18 months . . . I know the rage they feel with me and with the government I lead when they think, in Downing Street itself, the rules are not being properly followed by the people who make the rules. And though I cannot anticipate the conclusions of the current inquiry, I have learned enough to know there were things we simply did not get right and I must take responsibility . . . When I went into that garden just after 6pm on 20 May 2020, to thank groups of staff before going back into my office twenty-five minutes later to continue working, I believed implicitly that this was a work event . . . with hindsight, . . . I should have recognised that even if it could be said technically to fall within the guidance, there are millions and millions of people who simply would not see it that way, people who have suffered terribly, people who were forbidden from meeting loved ones at all inside or outside, and to them and to this House I offer my heartfelt apologies.[323]

Johnson again uses the 'I apologise' structure twice, including his intensified 'heartfelt' apologies. In contrast to the first example, he explicitly and directly states his responsibility: 'I must take responsibility' and 'in hindsight' he should have sent everyone back inside. He makes sure that points out how he was only present for twenty-five minutes and that this would not happen again with 'hindsight'.

He also includes his defence in his explanation and account, which works to weaken the overall force of the apology – he says firstly that he cannot anticipate the findings of the inquiry; he then states his belief that 'implicitly' it was 'a work event', suggesting 'it could be said technically to fall within the guidance' – he thus repeats his view that he has not 'technically' broken the rules or the law, though he does hedge this using 'if' and 'could be said', and he does admit that 'there are millions and millions of people' who 'would not see it that way'.

In terms of reactions to the apology, from within Johnson's own political party, Scottish Conservative leader Douglas Ross called for the prime minister to resign, focusing on the part of the apology where Johnson talked about 'hindsight':

He has admitted he was there, he has also apologised for that and, crucially for me, he said in hindsight if he had his time again he would have done things differently, and that to me is an acceptance from the prime minister that he did wrong, and therefore I don't believe that his position is tenable and therefore he does need to resign.[324]

Similarly, the SNP's Westminster leader Ian Blackford commented that, 'If he has any decency, any dignity, he would not just apologise, he would resign.' A female member of the public whose father had died from Covid who was interviewed by the BBC[325] questioned the authenticity of the apology and stated that Johnson was only apologising for being caught, not because he was genuinely sorry about what had happened, thus undermining the sincerity of the apology. Johnson's request at the end of his speech was for Sue Gray to be allowed to complete her inquiry so that 'the full facts' could be established, thus setting up the publication of the Gray report as the next stage in the Partygate saga, but also crucially buying him some time.

On 12 April 2022, Johnson announced that he had received a fixed penalty notice fine from the Metropolitan Police for a party which had taken place on 19 June for his birthday, organised by his wife Carrie, who was also fined, along with the then Chancellor Rishi Sunak, who later became prime minister. From this point, Johnson could no longer legitimately state that these gatherings were 'technically' within the guidance as the police fine proved otherwise. The following apology was delivered from him in a scripted political speech to camera, read from a piece of paper:

Today, I've received a fixed penalty notice from the Metropolitan Police relating to an event in Downing Street on 19 June 2020 and let me say immediately that I've paid the fine and I once again offer a full apology and I accept in all sincerity that people had the right to expect better. Now I feel an even greater sense of obligation to deliver on the priorities of the British people.

The Gray report was published a week after the police fines were issued. Her report concluded that there were 'failures of leadership and judgement in Number 10 and the Cabinet Office' and 'the senior leadership at the centre, both political and official, must bear responsibility'. She makes it explicitly clear here, by choosing the word 'responsibility', that this lies with Johnson and other senior leaders. Johnson again apologised in the House of Commons. On this occasion, there was no sign of events being 'technically' within the rules – he could no longer state this position, due to both the police fine and the findings of the report that he had urged people to wait for in order to establish the facts.

At this point, there remained many questions about Johnson's morality, integrity and suitability for office. So much so that a vote of no confidence was called by his own party. He survived the vote and thus appeared to have survived as leader and prime minister. However, it was another event outside of Partygate that led to his actual resignation just a few weeks later, relating again to his morality, integrity and ultimately his trustworthiness as prime minister, but it took more than fifty of his own government ministers to resign first.

Just as the Partygate dust was beginning to settle, a new story broke, focusing on Boris Johnson's deputy chief whip, Chris Pincher. Pincher was accused of groping two men at a private members' club. It emerged that Pincher had previously been investigated for 'inappropriate behaviour' and misconduct when he was at the Foreign Office, three years earlier. The prime minister denied he had any knowledge about this when he appointed him as deputy chief whip. However, this turned out not to be true. Lord McDonald stated in public that Johnson had been briefed in person about a complaint that had been made against Mr Pincher when he was in the Foreign Office.[326] Johnson was fully aware of this information, but he still went on to appoint him. Johnson thus issued yet another apology in a media interview:

I think it was a mistake and I apologise for it in hindsight. I think it was the wrong thing to do, err, I apologise to everybody who's been badly affected by it and I just want to make absolutely clear that there's no place in this government for anybody who, err, is predatory or who, err, abuses their position of power.[327]

There is a familiar pattern here, with Johnson issuing two 'I apologise' performatives and highlighting that 'in hindsight' he should have done things differently. On the back of the damage to trust, integrity and morality caused by Partygate, serious questions remained about the PM's honesty and integrity, and the Pincher incident became a step too far. The fifty ministers who then resigned included those previously most loyal to him – most notably, Chancellor Rishi Sunak and Health Secretary Sajid Javid. Ultimately, this was what made Johnson's position as PM untenable and forced him to resign.

Notably, in his resignation speech, there was no sign of any apology at all, but one was very much expected from the voting public and the mass media. So much so, that multiple news agencies commented directly on the audacity of Johnson to leave office without apologising: 'UK PM bows out with regrets but no apologies'[328] (Reuters); 'No remorse and no apologies as Boris Johnson finally loses his grip' (*Scottish Herald*);[329] 'There was not even a hint of an apology for the chaotic melodrama he had dragged his party and the public through' (*Guardian*);[330] 'There was no apology for his misjudgements over Partygate or Pinchergate. Typically, the only expression of "regret" was that he was being forced out of office' (*Independent*).[331]

Despite the multiple apologies in the last few months of Johnson's reign, they were not enough to save him as he was forced out of office by members of his own party. The lack of any apology in Johnson's resignation speech questions how much responsibility he took for his actions and how genuinely sorry he was for Partygate and the Pincher affair.

However, one thing that is for sure is that political apologies are highly complex and significant speech acts – they play a critical role in the careers of politicians and public figures when it comes to assessing sincerity and morality in different cultures, as well as playing an important role in helping to repair relationships when things go wrong.

7. What happens when apologies go wrong?

As is evident from the detail of the above discussion, delivering apologies, particularly in public spheres, is fraught with complexity. When they go wrong, it is not unheard of for people to have to issue an apology for their initial apology. One prominent example of this is from the CEO of British Petroleum (BP), Tony Hayward. In April 2010, there was an explosion on BP's Deepwater Horizon oilrig platform, which caused an extensive oil spill into the Gulf of Mexico. This is still the largest oil spill on record at the time of writing, with billions of gallons of oil entering the ocean. In a TV interview broadcast a few weeks after the initial spill, whilst the spill was still uncontained, and seriously affecting the lives of local people and killing wildlife, CEO Tony Hayward gave the following 'apology' to people living in the area:

> I'm sorry. We're sorry for [pauses] the massive disruption it's caused to their lives and, you know, we're— There's no one who wants this over more than I do, you know; I'd like my life back. So there's no one that wants this thing done more than I do. We're doing everything we can to contain the oil offshore, defend the shoreline and return people's lives to normal as fast as we can.[332]

He utters sorry twice but then makes a major mistake, as he decides to talk about himself and the negative impact that the explosion has had on his life, which he wants 'back'. He then reiterates this desire to get 'this over' in the next utterance, referring to the largest oil spill ever dismissively and vaguely as 'this thing'. This is a significant failing when issuing any apology – particularly one when the harm committed has been so serious and long-lasting: the initial Deepwater Horizon explosion which resulted in the spill caused the deaths of eleven BP employees and injured seventeen, as well as killing and injuring countless birds, fish and marine life, both at the time and for many years afterwards. As the CEO at the time, Hayward was the figurehead of the business and he needed to apologise and take responsibility, but in addition to his major gaffes, there is also no offer of an explanation, no expression of responsibility or any offer of reparation for any of the victims.

The backlash to this 'apology' was so fierce that Hayward had to issue a second apology for the first apology he had given. This time, he decided to play it safe and not speak to the camera at all, instead opting to apologise in writing, via a written statement, presumably so that the apology could be planned out, most likely co-authored, ensuring that it was much more carefully crafted and less likely to backfire on him. Instead of being let loose on live TV, he released the apology for the initial apology – on BP's Facebook social media site. As this second apology was scripted and written down, there was no opportunity to engage with Hayward directly, so this is a much safer way to deliver an apology than putting Hayward in front of a TV camera.

Hayward describes himself as being 'appalled' by his own behaviour during his initial apology, and then delivers the second apology using the more formal, performative 'I apologise' to the families of the men who died. He offers part of an explanation, stating that the words he spoke in his first apology do not represent how he really feels or how the company really feels. Then he moves on to this, arguably the most important part of the apology:

> I made a hurtful and thoughtless comment on Sunday when I said that 'I wanted my life back.' When I read that recently, I was appalled. I apologize, especially to the families of the 11 men who lost their lives in this tragic accident. Those words don't represent how I feel about this tragedy, and certainly don't represent the hearts of the people of BP – many of whom live and work in the Gulf – who are doing everything they can to make things right. My first priority is doing all we can to restore the lives of the people of the Gulf region and their families – to restore their lives, not mine.[333]

He does not go any further and, at this point, there is no offer of any reparation through resignation. This apology saga was an undeniable public relations disaster for BP. Having to issue an apology for an apology seriously damages the reputation of the CEO, as well as causing even further damage to the public image of the organisation. The intense negative publicity that had been received for his 'apology' comments became very damaging for BP. On 17 July, BP issued a statement announcing that Hayward would step down as CEO by 'mutual agreement'.

In another written statement following this announcement, Hayward thankfully steers clear of issuing any further apologies but, interestingly, on this occasion, he directly mentions 'responsibility': 'The Gulf of Mexico explosion was a terrible tragedy for which – as the man in charge of BP when it happened – I will always feel a deep responsibility, regardless of where blame is ultimately found to lie.'[334]

He explicitly communicates that he feels responsibility here, intensified by his choice of the word 'deep', but it is still

314

delivered with a caveat that 'ultimately' blame may lie elsewhere. However, the blame was found to lie with BP. Following an extensive inquiry and court ruling, the company was ordered to pay a record fine of $20.8 billion for gross negligence and reckless conduct.

The key lesson to be learnt here is that, as far as any apologies are concerned and for corporate and public apologies in particular, it is crucial to focus predominantly on the victim of the offence. If there is any suggestion that the perpetrator has suffered, then this will not be received well at all. It is critical for the focus to be on those who have suffered and for the apologiser to show genuine contrition and sincerity. In this case, the focus needed to be on the families of the dead workers and all of the other people whose lives and livelihoods had been significantly altered by the oil explosion.

Also, when CEOs are occupying and being interviewed in their official corporate role, there is a golden rule that attention should never be given to bemoaning the negative impact on the personal life of the person apologising. It is imperative not to attempt to save one's own reputation in such situations, but instead concentrate on delivering a genuine apology to repair the relationship with those who have been harmed and affected, as well as repairing relationships with the general public at large. Even if leaders manage to do this successfully, if events are serious, like they were in this case, then there will be an expectation that someone should resign and, whilst this may take a while, if damage to a company's reputation is significant enough it can be very difficult to continue in the public sphere. So, very often, resignation or pressure to step down will result.

Another example from the corporate world of how not to apologise can be seen in the following apology attempts, taken from the CEO of United Airlines, Oscar Munoz. A flight operated by the company had been overbooked and staff on board had decided to try to resolve this situation by removing paying passengers who had valid tickets. When one passenger refused to leave the plane, the staff violently dragged him off the flight. The incident was filmed by concerned passengers on multiple mobile phones and these clips then went viral as they were shared on multiple social media platforms. Oscar Munoz initially issued the following apology on Twitter:

> This is an unsettling event for all of us here at United. I apologize for having to re-accommodate these customers. Our team is moving with a sense of urgency to work with the authorities and conduct a review of what happened. We are also reaching out to this passenger to talk directly to him and further address and resolve this situation.[335]

Munoz uses the phrase 'I apologise' but then follows this with the language choice of 'reaccommodate', which denies the violent nature and sidesteps both blame and responsibility for the removal of the passenger. Also, by evaluating the event as 'unsettling' for United staff and not even mentioning the victim of the attack, instead opting to just refer to generic, plural 'customers', Munoz is again avoiding taking responsibility and also trying to underplay what happened. There is an implicit suggestion here that the passenger may have been responsible for what happened to him, despite video evidence to the contrary having been viewed around the world. This first apology resulted in vociferous criticism and Munoz was forced to apologise a second time, which he did again on Twitter:

> The truly horrific event that occurred on this flight has elicited many responses from all of us: outrage, anger, disappointment. I share all of those sentiments, and one above all: my deepest apologies for what happened. Like you, I continue to be disturbed by what happened on

this flight and I deeply apologize to the customer forcibly removed and to all the customers aboard. No one should ever be mistreated this way. I want you to know that we take full responsibility and we will work to make it right.[336]

In this second apology, he reframes what happened on the flight, beginning straight away with the evaluative phrase 'the truly horrific event'. He uses the 'I apologise' construction twice with intensifiers – 'my deepest apologies' and 'I deeply apologise' – and one of these apologies is explicitly addressed to the passenger who was attacked and injured. The verb 'reaccommodate' has been reconceptualised as 'forcibly removed', which, as the videos had all shown, is a much more accurate description of what happened. There is also a very clear and explicit statement of responsibility – 'we take full responsibility' – and this is delivered as part of a corporate reassurance that 'we' will make things right in future.

Summary

Overall, this chapter has aimed to present a guide to apologies which can be used either to plan the delivery of apologies or to evaluate them when they are received. Many of the ways in which we devise and deliver apologies takes place subconsciously and the aim here has been to draw on academic research and frameworks so that some of these processes can be demystified. We have looked at the successful and unsuccessful delivery of apologies in many different spheres, from very high-profile leaders through to apologies delivered by and given to members of the public and strangers.

There are many lessons that can be learnt from the analysis

of real-life apologies. The first of these is that getting apologies right is not always easy and delivering them appropriately is a complex process. Furthermore, apologies may not always land well, despite what speakers may originally intend. As language users, we engage in a complex process of weighing up how, when and why we need to give and receive apologies, based on our perceptions of levels of offence in terms of seriousness, the type of offence and the levels of power, solidarity and social distance that exist between us and our addressees. The ways in which the apologies that we issue are received and responded to may be different to what we originally intended. If this is the case and we get our apologies wrong, then we need to be prepared to reissue them differently, using alternative language. We will all be expected to apologise from time to time as we go about our daily lives, and carefully observing how intended recipient(s) react to any apologies that we issue can be a good way to track how apologies have been received. Additionally, interpreting and evaluating apologies delivered to large audiences by politicians and high-profile leaders through the mass media, including social media, should also enable you to make informed decisions about whether or not such public apologies are authentic, appropriate or trustworthy.

In order for our apologies to be accepted, we need to make sure that we are perceived to be sincere and authentic when giving them. Part of this authenticity is making sure that the right person apologises and that the apology appropriately fits the offence or the amount of harm that has been caused. It is important to use the 'I'm/we're sorry' and/or 'I/we apologise' constructions, but on their own they may not be enough. It is also crucial that we go beyond expressions of regret and, often, depending on the seriousness of the offence, provide an explanation, take responsibility and give an offer of reparation or a promise of future forbearance to repair relationships and bring events to a close. In some cases, financial compensation may be appropriate. In others, in very severe and serious circumstances, such as causing a death, receiving forgiveness from bereaved people who are left behind may be unachievable.

9

State of the Art: Politeness, Cyberspace and Artificial Intelligence

This book has taken you on a journey of discovery, drawing upon real-life language as it is used at home, at work and in many public settings to assess how our communication can become more effective when we raise our conscious awareness of what's happening when we communicate politeness with one another as human beings in different contexts, communities and cultures. We have decoded politeness and examined various ways in which it is constantly around us through the scientific tools offered by the last fifty years of sociolinguistic politeness research. We have identified conversational and written strategies, as well as examining how politeness and impoliteness can be effectively communicated through body language, gesture and other paralinguistics, and via digital communication in cyberspace.

We have looked at politeness and impoliteness in our homes and at work, including in corporate businesses, in healthcare settings, at the airport, in the world of law, in courtrooms and in litigation cases, in politics, at the Olympics, on sports fields, in dressing rooms, in *dojos*, in TV and radio interviews, in meetings, when driving, on the street, in playgrounds, when waiting in queues – to mention just some of the key contexts. We have also seen how politeness rules and etiquette codes play key roles during important life stages, such as naming a child, on marriage or when changing identities, as well as investigating what happens when life ends, including the role of politeness and indirectness in black box communications in plane crashes.

The importance of how our identities are shaped by the politeness in the communities and cultures where we live, work, play sport and engage in other leisure activities has been emphasised at various stages. We have also seen how politeness norms and expectations can vary quite dramatically from culture to culture, as well as recognising the importance of going beyond cultural stereotypes of politeness and nationality to ensure that more subtle and nuanced understandings of the relationships between politeness and culture are made, as in the examples of improving workplace productivity by unpicking cultural stereotypes in Mike Handford and Hiro Tanaka's long-term linguistic consultancy work in Japan.

We have also uncovered a series of deeply ingrained stereotypes and long-held myths surrounding politeness and impoliteness, particularly around social class and gender. We have seen how these can do a lot of damage, but also how they can be unpicked and questioned. They directly affect how individuals, groups and cultures are judged, and they can cause prejudice, bias and social exclusion. By learning to recognise class, gender and race-based stereotypes and politeness myths, our understanding of politeness can become much more enriched. The subtleties of what binds us together as humans can hopefully be seen more clearly.

We have also seen how, over the last two decades, many more routes to researching politeness and impoliteness have developed, due to the explosion of electronic communication in our everyday lives. Cyberspace has undeniably transformed the ways in which people connect with each other and with popular culture every day, no matter where they are in the world. At the same time, it has also changed the ways in which communicators can be polite, rude, abusive and offensive to one another, including engaging in illegal behaviour, such as revenge porn and online hate crimes. Because of this, cyberspace has become a common focus for impoliteness researchers. With the vast increase in the amount of time that we spend online, for many people, interacting in cyberspace has resulted in an increase in impoliteness and hostilities in everyday life. On the internet, identities can remain hidden and so individuals are able to take advantage of this anonymity to engage in abusive and sometimes illegal behaviours. This has changed the dynamic of public life and in such spheres, there has been significant fusion between private and public identities, as well as private and public spaces. The boundaries between home, work and public life have become increasingly blurred.

What we have learnt

Overall, this book has taught us how we first acquire politeness as very young children, and how it continues to develop and change through the various stages of our lives, at home, at work and in public. The importance of having polite communication within the home and in our close-knit friendship groups places a critical emphasis on the value of having strong, supportive networks of friends and/or families in our lives. Being the recipient of positive politeness, such as receiving compliments, expressions of admiration and approval, and communicating how much we like, admire and want to be with one another plays a critical role in our health and well-being, which in turn helps to create harmonious and co-operative societies. It is critical for us to seek to have supportive and cordial relationships with those with whom we have the deepest social bonds, those whom we trust and respect.

Impoliteness and conflict in these backstage relationships in private spaces can be difficult to navigate as it is ideally at home where a great deal of our politeness and identity processing work takes place, so that we can rationalise, reflect and learn from our frontstage performances of politeness, impoliteness and identity. This is the place where we get chance to reset and to work through any difficult challenges with which we have been presented frontstage, so that we can recharge and go again.

As we saw in the chapter on politeness with family and friends, the importance of friends acting like therapists cannot be overestimated. Engaging in talk with each other lies at the heart of many mental health campaigns in the UK and elsewhere in the world, so the ability to show solidarity, care and respect with friends and family cannot be overestimated either.

One of the worrying aspects and potential disruptors to the home setting and these relationships is the invasion of social media and mobile devices into every aspect of our lives, including backstage. As we've seen in chapter four's discussion of how digital media affects politeness and young people's communication, the amount of time that young people are spending communicating with adults in their lives is diminishing and social bonds are breaking at an earlier age.[337] And with it, we are losing valuable opportunities to talk, build social bonds and work through the everyday experiences that we have of politeness and impoliteness encountered at school, at work or in public settings. It is not just young people but also many adults who spend more time on social media than ever before, and often this can be at the expense of human-to-human, face-to-face communication.

To brighten the mood, it is not all doom and gloom, as with digital communication, advancements have been made in terms of the speed and creativity with which we can build solidarity and social bonds with others and have given us access to a larger global network of people than would ever previously have been possible.

In chapter five, we have focused on leadership and how leaders can use strategies of politeness to succeed. We have covered many different areas of politeness communication, including the communication acts that leaders need to successfully deliver to do an effective job, as well as the importance of less commonly examined features of business communication, including humour and small talk. A range of communication from different workplace cultures has been included, and we have also examined what happens when cultural politeness norms clash and miscommunication and impoliteness result. Ways of repairing relationships in these tricky and culturally sensitive situations are also examined. Finally, this chapter presents a practical model for using politeness to run successful meetings, which I have named AGENDAS. It incorporates my observations from analysing linguistic politeness and leadership during the last twenty-five years in organisations of many different types and sizes.

We have then examined politeness and impoliteness in the public domain of sport. Chapter six moved us from the workplace to more leisure and community-based activities – though, of course, for professional athletes, coaches and those who work in sports full-time, this is also their workplace. We have witnessed how politeness is at the heart of sporting values, including respect, friendship and fostering excellence in training practices. We have examined how positive and negative politeness strategies are effectively used in sports communication, including the essential role of rituals, solidarity-building and the role of respect and friendship in teams, and how sports coaches can build successful teams. We looked at a range of sports, including rugby, football (soccer), Gaelic football, Australian Rules football, volleyball, hockey, basketball, tennis and martial arts, including judo and aikido.

Our detailed focus on martial arts shows us that, although martial arts are based on dealing with conflict through combat, etiquette is fundamentally important in how combat is approached and dealt with. Continually abiding by politeness

327

and etiquette codes when training in self-defence is so integral
to the art of combat that, without them, martial arts cannot be
said to exist. We have seen how martial arts are based on *budo*,
the spiritual path leading to harmony and how a goal of aikido
is to strive for more harmonious relationships with others in
the wider world, as well as a continual focus on gaining victory
over oneself. This can be attained by striving for unity, harmony
respect and peace with others.[338] We have also focused on what
happens when impoliteness and conflict occur in sport and how
some sports have had to resort to running campaigns dedicated
to instilling respect by targeting players, coaches, caregivers
and spectators, particularly in children's sport. In aikido, we
have seen how children learn politeness principles that they
can apply both inside and outside of the *dojo* to avoid abusive
and offensive behaviour in all aspects of their lives, as well as
practising politeness in their listening, speaking and observa-
tional politeness skills when training.

In the remaining two chapters, we have focused on two
essential linguistic features which encode a significant amount
of social, cultural and historical detail when considering politeness: swearing and apologies. By focusing on swearing, we can
dispel powerful stereotypes and myths that have long circulated
about swearing, based on social class, gender and race. We have
looked at changing attitudes towards swearing through different
historical traditions, as well as the levels of offence that can be
caused by different swear words and how these can change over
time. We have come up with a set of key criteria that can be used
as predictive tools to see if swearing will be viewed as desirable
or undesirable depending upon group norms. The importance
of swearing as a key indicator of positive politeness and as a
device to strength social bonds, which is often overlooked, is
highlighted.

In our consideration of apologies, I presented a how-to guide,
so that readers can assess and also deliver their own apologies,

giving these the best chances of success, providing that they are delivered sincerely and authentically. We looked at the over-arching importance of apologies as devices of linguistic repair, and how integral apologies are to healing interpersonal relationships that have suffered due to offence being caused. We extensively examined the importance of apologies in the world of politics, which is particularly important as we are said to be living in the age of the apology in public life. We have also assessed the consequences of what happens when things go wrong with apologies. Apologies have to be delivered by the right person who has responsibility for the offence and they have to be sincerely delivered with appropriate tone, body language and gestures. We have shown how the ultimate price to pay is losing one's job if an apology is unsuccessful, and how this could be due to a lack of sincerity or demonstrating inappropriate care and a lack of respect for victims.

Apologies restore the moral order and civility of a society, bringing back a sense of balance and equilibrium to heal previous conflictual situations, and so it is essential to the survival of interpersonal and professional relationships that apologies are well delivered. And if apologies are given in the public domain, then the potential audience reach and the scope for criticism is huge, and so the stakes are often very high. Relationships may suffer further under the watchful eye of the media, which may seek to magnify the damage, which can often result in more harm and offence being caused.

By following the step-by-step guide to apologies presented in chapter eight, it is the intention that readers will give themselves the best chances of success with delivery of future apologies. Of course, no guarantees can be made as there are too many unknown variables to predict how future apologies may land, but providing that the person delivering the apology is the right person, they have responsibility for what happened, they are genuinely and sincerely sorry and that appropriate reparations and promises of future forbearance are in place, then an apology stands a decent chance of success.

Politeness and recent developments in cyberspace

We have witnessed how the role that electronic communication plays in our lives went through a seismic shift as the world unexpectedly entered the Covid-19 pandemic in 2020.

During the global pandemic, many of the usual forms of communication that had been dominant in societies around the world were changed almost overnight, and with them, so were politeness norms and conventions. Many people ended up spending large chunks of their lives online, communicating via Zoom, Microsoft Teams, FaceTime and other online platforms that bring communities and groups of people together, as many forms of face-to-face conversation became illegal. Body language and gestures were considerably reduced, and facial expressions became unreliable due to cameras freezing, often instead catching people at rather unfavourable angles. The online transition happened with such speed that many workplaces had no time to plan or set out any politeness or 'netiquette' guidelines for how to communicate appropriately in these spaces. Lockdown e-meetings, online group gatherings and other online encounters were a steep learning curve, and politeness norms, etiquette and behavioural guidelines emerged as time progressed.

One of the difficulties of homeworking was the sudden blurring of frontstage and backstage, as physical workplace locations were closed and, instead, people's homes, their usual 'safe' backstage environment, immediately became their frontstage work context. Work video calls were frequently disrupted by children barging into rooms, pets, family members wandering around in the background, summons to answer the front door and a number of other distractions. What would previously have been seen as breaking politeness rules and etiquette codes, particularly in workplaces, became commonplace disruptions.

In the early stages of lockdown, videos went viral on social media of people in online workplace meetings on Zoom who had not turned off their cameras and gone to the bathroom in full view of co-workers, and partners of people accidentally running into the video shot in their underwear, resulting in much embarrassment to those who had experienced such mishaps and much hilarity to other viewers. These examples illustrate the many social faux pas that may occur when people are able to see into one another's homes and the reputational damage that can be caused, in a manner different to anything that had gone before. Meetings, teaching sessions, job interviews and a range of other face-to-face speech events, including conferences and training sessions, moved online and some have stayed there. Post-pandemic, businesses and organisations have retained several elements of flexible working, at least for some days of the week, and working from home has become an accepted norm in many workplaces.

One of the most obvious ways in which politeness becomes more difficult in online conversations is with turn-taking and, in particular, turn allocation. On Zoom and Teams, there is a significant reduction in the non-verbal cues which are present face to face, and so you will often get people speaking simultaneously to try to gain the conversational floor. The timing of pauses and speaker intonation, which are used meticulously in face-to-face conversations to signal where turn-taking would be appropriate, are heavily disrupted online.

Transition-relevant places (TRPs) are when the conversational floor is up for grabs and someone else can come in as speaker. As the timing of pauses is very difficult to judge (silences may or may not be present, depending on people's broadband connection), it is not unusual for two or three people to start talking at the same time as it is very difficult to work out how not to talk over one another to change speakers. You then often get apologies and a bout of metacommentary often involving an apology ('sorry, I thought you'd finished', 'sorry, I didn't meant to interrupt', 'you carry on', 'no, no, it's okay, you go'), with speakers trying to allocate turns politely, but continuing to talk over each other. It can take some time to sort out and, during these periods, talk becomes messy, unstructured and ultimately these complex transitions can make meetings run for longer.

Turn-taking often works more effectively online when the current speaker can successfully select the next speaker by directly signalling that they are handing the floor over, often through direct naming. This can work well if you know each other already and if you use each other's first names. Online platforms at least have name prompts at the bottom of screens and, providing these are accurate, this at least gives us people's terms of address so that we do not have to rely on our own memories of people's names.

Whatever turn-taking strategy is used online, it is common for the person whose turn it is to forget to turn on their microphone. The indirect command 'You're on mute!' has become an incredibly common exclamation which happens in almost every meeting, often resulting in humour and/or laughter, accompanied with an apology and a metacomment about forgetting ('sorry, I'm always doing that!', 'sorry, I'll start again', 'sorry, there's always one, isn't there!').

Post-pandemic, it is now quite usual for online etiquette rules to be announced by meeting chairs or organisers, either verbally or posted in chat as a written set of rules for appropriate behaviour online to avoid impoliteness – often this includes a request for ensuring that participants have their microphones switched off to avoid unnecessary background noise when not speaking. The microphone rule also ensures that people who want to slurp hot beverages loudly or eat snacks noisily in front of their computers are not doing this into everyone's eardrums!

Microsoft Teams and Zoom have brought in a number of other function buttons that represent particular emotions, which are encoded with politeness. Some of these give positive politeness, such as clapping hands to show approval or congratulations, hearts and thumbs up emojis to show that something is liked or loved, an emoji wave to perform the basic politeness conventions of hello and goodbye, and the hand raise function to politely ask a question without having to interrupt or jump in.

As workplaces are now actively choosing to hold meetings online as opposed to being legally forced to do so, it's useful to consider how online meetings and gatherings can continue to be improved. Despite the functional tools of platform providers, online meetings still have glitches, and are still reduced forms of communication compared with face-to-face meetings, where we can observe, analyse and take cues from whole bodies interacting in time and space, which opens up possibilities for far more paralinguistic communication: gaze and detailed facial expressions – which are hard to see online – touch and physical space, body positioning, seating and reactions to the wider environment can be seen beyond a small contained screen. Anxieties about being impolite due to accidentally broadcasting private chats or private interaction if microphones are accidentally left on still abound.

To try to address this issue, a team of psychology researchers from University College London and Exeter University[339] in the UK have conducted experimental studies to address anxieties about appearing impolite in online meetings. They argue that the functional emoji buttons are not as effective as they need to be; in some situations, they can make communication worse by causing more confusion than they resolve.

As an alternative to function buttons, the research team came up with a system of physical gestures that need to be actively performed by those at meetings onscreen through their video cameras. The crucial difference here is that participants are not using any function buttons at all. Physically performing gestures is a much more active way of getting people to engage and not get sidetracked by multitasking, as for it to work everyone needs to have their cameras on. The gestures include giving a literal thumbs up to show support, recognition or that you are listening, or putting your hand to your heart to show empathy or kindness.

The scheme also attempted to address the problems with turn-taking online, as discussed above. In a recent interview, the two academics heading up the project, Hills and Jones,[340] drew on a sports metaphor to explain their paralinguistic choices. They argued that people need to think about meetings as very similar to being part of a sports team. If you have a good team, then they will be looking for you to pass the ball to them, so other meeting participants need to work on their timing and look to receive the topic. To signal this, participants should give a physical wave above their heads meaning 'please pass to me'. The current speaker notices and indicates that the turn is coming to the person who is waving by using their first name, as in 'I'll now pass to James', so that James and everyone else in the meeting knows exactly whom the turn has been given to.

Another strategy to gain the floor would be to bang your hands together in a building motion to show that you want to support and build upon what the current speaker is saying, and, therefore, if they pass the turn to you, they know that you will support them with your contribution. If you would like to ask a question, then the team argues that you should visibly scratch your head. They describe these tools as super-charged gestures. They conducted experiments with their student body, in which half of them had been trained in the video gestures and the other half had not. Those who had done the training found the meeting more enjoyable and used far more positive words during the meeting than the control group, who had not had any training.

In the real world outside of a laboratory setting, for such schemes to work, people would need to have sufficient broadband to enable the cameras to be on all the time, which may preclude some users taking part. Also, meeting etiquette would need to be very clear about everyone having their cameras on all at the same time. In larger meetings, the need for everyone to be visible on the screen may also prove problematic. However, these are really interesting ideas to avoid impoliteness in online meetings. They are appealing as they address the need for both practical, transactional talk, as well as the ability to express emotions, support and the more social aspects of talk. As we have seen in this chapter, both are critical to the success of workplace talk. The research team is also very clear that the gestures need to be trialled over a period of time to give meeting participants time to adjust – they suggest a minimum of five meetings as a good length trial period.

Towards the future: AI and politeness programming

This book has illustrated the overall importance of politeness in everyday communication in the widest range of settings. We have examined various forms of spoken, written and digital communication that we encounter as we go about our everyday lives, from a range of different global locations. It is the intention that by reading about the linguistics of politeness, reflecting on your own use of politeness and freeze-framing real-life examples of communication that you will have become more consciously aware language users. One of the overall intentions of this book has been to show how significant politeness is in everyday communication. It is not something that is just associated with morality and civility, but instead it plays a fundamental role in governing how we communicate with one another in the widest range of contexts. As was stated right at the beginning of chapter one, politeness is everywhere and it is hoped that the various chapters in this book have illustrated how important politeness is in all of the different contexts and different ways in which we communicate with one another on a day-to-day basis.

Wherever we are interacting, politeness norms will be present, as will be the boundaries of impolite behaviour. We are continually making assessments of our own and other people's behaviour in light of the levels of power, social distance and formality that exists between us and our fellow communicators. Our use of politeness and impoliteness is continually influenced by our social class, age, gender, race, ethnicity and many other social identity variables that may be relevant during any interaction that takes place.

The definition of communication has been taken far and wide in the book to include interactions with pets in the private, backstage world of the family, as well as looking at interactions at various life stages, such as parents talking to babies and children, friendship groups and workplace groups, with a wide variety of different age groups. We have also considered the important role played by the mass media in politeness and impoliteness, ranging from television programmes, advertisements, sports media interviews and interactions and engagements on social media platforms and feeds, through to very formal interactions in official settings, when thinking about legal communication, for example, around healthcare litigation, as well as considering formal public settings where important decisions are made. We have also investigated the important role that etiquette and etiquette guides and codes can play in the everyday lives of people in terms of how they are assessed and evaluated, as well as including the importance of etiquette as a connection to important historical traditions and practices.

The study of impoliteness is particularly powerful for revealing the boundaries of politeness and where these lie, and we have looked at a wide variety of contexts in which impoliteness regularly occurs, such as workplaces where adversarial talk is common, including the example of traffic wardens, as well as impoliteness in more conventional settings like in business meetings, on television shows and on social media platforms.

Looking to the future, one of the areas of discussion which promises to be significant moving forward is the role of politeness in artificial intelligence. Many of us are already interacting with multiple personalised AI devices in societies where technology has advanced enough, including the personal assistants Siri on smartphones and Siri and Alexa in our homes. We regularly interact with these devices as if we are engaging in human-to-human communication, and it is important to consider how these artificial voices are pre-programmed with details about politeness and the boundaries of avoiding impoliteness in conversation with human voices. This affects how authentically we will experience this communication and how it will make us feel in terms of emotional connections to the device.

One recent academic study that sits in this space has considered how communication with AI devices can affect children's perceptions of politeness and their understanding of politeness norms. Pooja Mandagere's[341] work has found that many children are now growing up in homes where the adults around them are engaging in communication with various robotic voices and devices. And so what effects will this have on how they acquire the norms of politeness? Will this affect the ways in which they talk to humans, including adults and their own peer groups? Many parents complain that using Alexa or Google Assistant means that children are not acquiring politeness when they talk to these virtual assistants.

Mandagere has also discussed whether children are learning rudeness from listening to how adults interact with Alexa, with children imitating angry voices and not learning to use politeness strategies as much as they would do if they were hearing adults interacting with other humans, where politeness norms are more dominant. Adult speech patterns are mostly transactional when interacting with AI devices such as Alexa, and this misses out crucial parts of affective or social talk, which, as we have seen at various stages in this book, is crucial, not just for establishing solidarity and strengthening bonds between people, but also in terms of playing a crucial role in the facilitation of getting tasks done.

Mandagere draws attention to how technology giants Amazon and Google have created technology as part of their AI assistants that would enable AI to recognise when conventional politeness markers including 'please' and 'thank you' are said, and the technology will then provide positive reinforcement as a part of its reply. Mandagere points out that Google recently released its AI assistant's 'Pretty Please' feature and claims that this technology has been designed to encourage polite behaviour in children, so it will be interesting to see how this develops.

Recently, *Forbes*[342] has reported that, whilst initial attempts at AI did not use politeness and instead tried to base conversation around transactional talk only, it quickly became very clear to people that they were just communicating with robots and that there was an inauthentic feel to the interaction. Now, many language processing systems have added in politeness, including backchanneling noises such as mmm, mhm, or uh-huh, which give the impression that the AI is really listening and is engaged with what we are saying. However, whilst this is thought to be positive in the sense that it will make people feel more comfortable, or at the very least more at ease communicating with machines, the reverse side of this is that people may end up with false and misleading impressions of what the AI can achieve. It may also lead to a sense of AI as sentient, which presents significant ethical dilemmas as technology moves forward.

As leading AI and machine learning researcher Lance Eliot[343] points out, 'Politeness is a dual-edged sword that provides an added indicator potentially of human qualities and thus could be considered part of the anthropomorphising tendency sway. Using politeness in AI is a darned if you do, darned if you don't, kind of challenge.' Eliot also poses a fascinating question for the future of self-driving cars. He draws attention to the question that as cars become fully self-driving, what should the AI politeness system be like? As he explains, when we are passengers in human-driven cars, our drivers may be polite or impolite towards us, and at present, AI software engineers are experimenting with different systems to try to replicate this experience as authentically as possible.

All of these issues will be fascinating to watch develop from a politeness perspective. And despite the many uncertainties that the future holds, one thing is definitely for sure – politeness is everywhere and it is here to stay. Regardless of what technological forms of communication we end up interacting with in the future, there will still be a fundamental need for successful communication to be based on politeness, through which human co-operation and harmony can be achieved.

ENDNOTES

1   Cameron, Deborah (1995) *Verbal Hygiene*. London: Routledge.
2   See Mullany, L. (2020) *Professional Communication: Consultancy, Advocacy, Activism*. Palgrave.
3   Brown, P. (2015) 'Politeness and Language'. In *International Encyclopaedia of the Social & Behavioral Sciences*, 2nd edition, Volume 18.
    http://dx.doi.org/10.1016/B978-0-08-097086-8.53072-4.
4   Mills, Sara (2017) *Politeness and Social Class*. Cambridge University Press.
5   Watts, R (2003) *Politeness*. Cambridge University Press, p. 23.
6   Allen, K. and K. Burridge (2006) *Forbidden Words: Taboo and the Censoring of Language*. Cambridge University Press. p. 65.
7   Brown, P. and S. Levinson (1987) *Politeness: Universals in Language Usage*. Cambridge University Press.
8   Brown and Levinson (1987: 12) ibid.
9   Culpeper, J. (2010) *Impoliteness: Using Language to Cause Offence*. Cambridge University Press.
10 Ibid.
11 Culpeper, J., D. Bousfield & A. Wichmann (2003) 'Impoliteness revisited'. *Journal of Pragmatics* 35: 1545–79.
12 Ibid.

13   Beebe, L. (1995) 'Polite fictions: instrumental rudeness as pragmatic competence'. In: *Linguistics and the Education of Language Teachers: Ethnolinguistic, Psycholinguistics and Sociolinguistic Aspects.* Georgetown University Press, pp. 154–68. Cited in Culpeper, J., D. Bousfield & A. Wichmann (2003: 1550).

14   Culpeper, J., D. Bousfield & A. Wichmann (2003) 'Impoliteness revisited'. *Journal of Pragmatics* 35: 1545–79.

15   Ibid, p. 1565.

16   Scott, F. (2016) 'Foul-mouthed parking attendant suspended'. Mail Online 08/06/16. https://www.dailymail.co.uk/news/article-3631152/Foul-mouthed-parking-warden-suspended-telling-driver-f-threatening-arrested-recording-camera.html/ accessed 10/06/23.

17   *Daily Mail* (2016) 'Foul-mouthed parking warden suspended after expletive-laced encounter'. https://www.youtube.com/watch?v=umGPrbOevfE/ accessed 23/06/23.

18   Scott, F. (2016) 'Foul-mouthed parking attendant suspended'. Mail Online 08/06/16. https://www.dailymail.co.uk/news/article-3631152/Foul-mouthed-parking-warden-suspended-telling-driver-f-threatening-arrested-recording-camera.html accessed 01/11/23.

19   Culpeper, J. (2005) 'Impoliteness and entertainment in the TV quiz show'. *Journal of Politeness Research,* 1(1): 35–72.

20   See Holmes, J., M. Stubbe & B. Vine (1999) 'Constructing professional identity'. In S. Sarangi and C. Roberts (eds) *Talk, Work and Institutional Order.* Mouton, pp. 351–85, for further details on these three identity categories.

21   Spencer-Oatey, H. & D. Kadar (2021) *Intercultural Politeness: Managing Relations Across Cultures.* Cambridge University Press, p. 4.

22   Holliday, A. (1999) 'Small cultures'. *Applied Linguistics* 20(2): 237–64.

23   Giles, H. & T. Ogay (2007) 'Communication accommodation theory'. In B. Whaley & W. Samter (eds.) *Explaining*

Communication: Contemporary Theories and Exemplars.
Lawrence Erlbaum, pp. 293–310.

24   Goffman, E. (1967) 'Interaction Ritual'. Doubleday.

25   Eckert, P. (2000) *Linguistic Variation as Social Practice.*
Blackwell.

26   Eckert, P. & S. McConnell-Ginet (1999) 'New Explanations and
Generalisations in language and gender research'. *Language in
Society* 28(2): 185–201.

27   Ibid, p. 185–6.

28   Ibid, p. 186.

29   Au, S., F. Khandwala & H. Stelfox (2013) 'Physician Attire
in the Intensive Care Unit and Patient Family Perceptions of
Physician Professional Characteristics'. *JAMA Internal Medicine*
173(6): 1–2.

30   Johnson, S., M. Doi and L. Yamamato (2016) 'Adverse Effects
of Tattoos and Piercing on Parent/Patient Confidence in Health
Care Providers'. *Clinical Paediatrics*, 55(10).

31   Thomas, D. (2019) 'Tattoos at work: Are they still an issue?'
BBC News 16/06/19.
https://www.bbc.co.uk/news/business-48620528/ accessed
04/05/23.

32   Kirk, I. (2022) 'Should visible tattoos be allowed in the
workplace?' YouGovUK 05/08/22.
https://yougov.co.uk/society/articles/43350-should-visible-
tattoos-be-allowed-workplace accessed 02/09/23.

33   McNeil, D. (2006) 'Greetings Kill: Primer for a Pandemic'. *New
York Times* 12/02/06.
https://www.nytimes.com/2006/02/12/weekinreview/greetings-
kill-primer-for-a-pandemic.html accessed 15/02/24.

34   Tannen, D. (2005) *Conversational Style: Analyzing Talk Among
Friends.* Oxford University Press.

35   Wardhaugh, R. (2009) *An Introduction to Sociolinguistics.* 6th
Edition. Blackwell.

36   See Holmes (2000) for further detail on how phatic communion
is a part of 'small talk', where small talk is a broader category
consisting of both 'social talk' and 'phatic communion'. In

Holmes, J. (2000) 'Doing collegiality and keeping control at work: Small talk in government departments'. In J. Coupland (ed.) *Small Talk*. Longman, pp. 32–61.

37   Holmes, J. (2000) 'Doing collegiality and keeping control at work.' In J. Coupland (ed.) Small Talk. Longman, pp. 32-61.

38   Fox, K. (2004) *Watching the English*. Hodder & Stoughton.

39   Jenkins, R. (2018) 'British people will spend over four months of their lives talking about the weather, study says'. *Independent* 17/08/18.
https://www.independent.co.uk/extras/lifestyle/
british-people-time-spent-talking-weather-conversation-topic-
heatwave-a8496166.html accessed 23/10/23.

40   #verybritishproblems (2024)
http://www.verybritishproblems.com

41   Goffman, E. (1967) *Interaction Ritual*. Doubleday.

42   See Mullany and Stockwell (2015) for a broader discussion of these incidents of overhearing – In Mullany, L. & P. Stockwell (2015) *The English Language: A Resource Book for Students*. Second Edition. Routledge.

43   Wheatcroft, G. (2007) *Yo Blair!: Tony Blair's Disastrous Premiership*. Politico's Publishing.

44   For a broader examination of this incident, see Mullany (2011) 'Frontstage and backstage'. In: Linguistic Politeness Research Group (eds) *Discursive Approaches to Politeness*. Mouton de Gruyter, pp. 133–65.

45   See for example, Arcimaviciene, L., & S. H. Baglama, (2018). 'Migration, Metaphor and Myth in Media Representations: The Ideological Dichotomy of "Them" and "Us"'. *SAGE Open*. accessed 24/01/24.

46   Mullany, L. (2011: 140)

47   Smith, A. (2010) 'Brown apologises for "bigoted woman" comment.' *LabourList*.
https://labourlist.org/2010/04/brown-apologises-for-bigoted-
woman-comment/ accessed 21/01/24

48   Independent Team (2020) '"Bigotgate" 10 years on'. *Independent*
https://www.independent.co.uk/news/uk/politics/

bigotgate-gordon-brown-anniversary-gillian-duffy-transcript-full-read-1957274.html 28/04/20.

49   See
     https://www.deedpoll.org.uk/ for further details.

50   See Gov UK (2022) 'Names: Names that Cannot be Used in
     Passports' for further details. At
     https://assets.publishing.service.gov.uk/
     media/63999781e90e077c2502f71b/Names_-_names_
     that_cannot_be_used_in_passports__V9_FOR_GOV.
     UK_publication_.pdf accessed 14/02/24.

51   Allen, K. and K. Burridge (2006) *Forbidden Words: Taboo and
     the Censoring of Language.* Cambridge University Press.

52   Miller, M. (2011) 'Top ten baby names guaranteed to get your
     kid beaten up'. Huffington Post 20/09/11.
     https://www.huffpost.com/entry/top-10-baby-names-
     guarant_b_969157

53   Blum, S. (1997) 'Naming practices and the power of words in
     China'. *Language in Society* 26(3): 357 –379.

54   Evason, N. (2021) 'Chinese culture: Naming'. *Cultural Atlas.*
     https://culturalatlas.sbs.com.au/chinese-culture/chinese-culture-
     naming accessed 14/02/24.

55   Evason (2021)

56   Blum (1997: 372)

57   Blum (1997: 373)

58   Anadolu Agency (2015) 'The surname law: A profound change
     in Turkish history'. 22/06/15.
     **https://www.dailysabah.com/feature/2015/06/22/the-
     surname-law-a-profound-change-in-turkish-history**

59   Anadolu Agency (2015) 'The surname law: A profound change
     in Turkish history'. 22/06/15.
     https://www.dailysabah.com/feature/2015/06/22/the-surname-
     law-a-profound-change-in-turkish-history

60   *Oxford English Dictionary* (2021) Deadname. Accessed 14/02/24.
     https://www.oed.com/dictionary/deadname_n?tab=meaning_
     and_use#1223539050

61   Zoellner, Z. (2019) '"It's deeply, deeply traumatizing": Laverne

Cox blasts IMDb for "deadnaming" transgender stars by using their birth names - forcing the site to change its policy.' *Daily Mail* 15/08/19.
https://www.dailymail.co.uk/femail/article-7361133/Laverne-Cox-slams-IMDb-deadnaming-transgender-stars.html, accessed 23/01/24.

62 AikiTV (2022) Joe Thambu Shihan with Louise Mullany. *Keep the Flame Alive* interview series, AikiTV September 2022. https://aikitv.online/ accessed 27/02/23.

63 Ibid.

64 Ibid.

65 Ibid.

66 Holmes, J. (2001) *An Introduction to Sociolinguistics*. Blackwell.

67 Weale, S. (2023) 'London school drops Sir and Miss to fight cultural misogyny'. *Guardian* 6/06/23.
https://www.theguardian.com/education/2023/jun/06/london-school-drops-sir-and-miss-honorifics-to-fight-cultural-misogyny accessed 14/02/24.

68 BBC Magazine (2014) 'Who, what and why? How did it come to be Sir and Miss?' BBC Online 14/05/14.
https://www.bbc.co.uk/news/blogs-magazine-monitor-27407789 accessed 12/02/24.

69 Cook, H. M. & M. Burdelski (2017) '(Im)Politeness: Language Socialization'. In J. Culpeper, M. Haugh & D. Kadar (eds) *The Palgrave Handbook of Linguistic (Im)politeness*. Palgrave, pp. 461–88. Direct quote, p. 467.

70 Gleason, J. B., R. Perlmann, & E. B. Greif (1984) 'What's the magic word: Learning language through politeness routines'. *Discourse Processes* 7(4): 493–502.

71 Ibid. p. 495.

72 Ibid. p. 497.

73 Ibid. pp. 500–501.

74 Bates, E. (1976). *Language and Contexts: The acquisition of Pragmatics*. Academic Press.

75 Al-Abbas, L. (2023) 'Politeness strategies used by children in requests in relation to age and gender: a case study of Jordanian

elementary school students'. *Langauge, Culture and Diversity.* 8: 1–9.

76   Cook, H. M. & M. Burdelski (2017) '(Im)Politeness: Language Socialization'. In J. Culpeper, M. Haugh & D. Kadar (eds) *The Palgrave Handbook of Linguistic (Im)politeness.* Palgrave, pp. 461–88.

77   Cook, H. M. (2011) 'Language socialisation and stance-taking practices'. In A Duranti, E. Ochs & B. Schieffelin (eds) *The Handbook of Language Socialisation.* Blackwell. pp. 296–321.

78   Cook, H. M. & M. Burdelski (2017: 472).

79   As with all published linguistics studies, the names given here (Ami and Ken) to my knowledge are pseudonyms, as are all of the other names given in all of the other academic linguistic studies cited in the remainder of the chapter and throughout the rest of the book, as is in accordance with linguistics research ethics.

80   Blum-Kulka, S. (2000) 'Gossipy events at family dinners: Negotiating sociability, presence and the moral order'. In J. Coupland (ed.) *Small Talk.* Longman, pp. 213–40.

81   Ibid. p. 223.

82   Mills, S. (2017) 'Sociocultural approaches to (Im)politeness'. In Culpeper, J., M. Haugh & D. Kadar (eds) *The Handbook of (im)politeness.* Palgrave, pp. 41–60.

83   Mills (2017: 58) ibid.

84   Tovares, A. (2007) 'Family members interacting while watching TV'. In Tannen, D., S. Kendall & C. Gordon (eds) *Family Talk.* Oxford University Press, pp. 283–310.

85   Ibid, p. 296.

86   Ibid, p. 297.

87   Talbot, M. (1995) 'A synthetic sisterhood: False friends in a teenage magazine'. In M. Bucholtz & K. Hall (eds) *Gender Articulated: Language and the Socially Constructed Self.* Routledge, pp. 235–50.

88   Spanier, G. (2013) 'Watching you, watching me: why C4 show Gogglebox is set to go global'. *London Evening Standard.* 18/12/13, accessed 15/12/23.

89 Tannen, D. 'Talking the dog: Framing pets as interactional resources in family discourse'. In D. Tannen, S. Kendall and C. Gordon (eds.) *Family Talk*. Oxford University Press, pp. 49–69.

90 Tannen (2003: 175)

91 Coates, J. 'Small talk and subversion: Female speakers backstage'. In J. Coupland (ed.) *Small Talk*. Longman, pp. 241–263.

92 Coates (2000: 245) ibid.

93 Coates, J. (2000: 252) ibid.

94 Coates, J. (2000: 248) ibid.

95 Coates, J. (2000: 256) ibid.

96 Coates, J. (2003) *Men Talk*. Blackwell.

97 Coates, J. (2003: 43) ibid.

98 Connell, R. (2005) *Masculinities*. Second Edition. Routledge.

99 Cameron, D. (1997) 'Performing gender identity: Young men's talk and the construction of heterosexual masculinity'. In S. Johnson & U. H. Meinhof *Language and Masculinity*. Blackwell, pp. 47–64.

100 Cameron (1997: 53) ibid.

101 Cameron (1997: 54) ibid.

102 Sutherland, R. (2019) 'Tackling the root causes of suicide'. https://www.england.nhs.uk/blog/tackling-the-root-causes-of-suicide/ accessed 21/01/24.

103 Norwich City Football Club (2023) 'Check in on those around you': World Mental Health Day video. https://www.canaries.co.uk/content/mental-health-video-made-available-to-all accessed 12/12/23.

104 https://ittakesballstotalk.com/

105 West-Knights, I. (2023) 'Never unfollow, gossip with caution, and always ask before you post – how to behave online'. *Guardian* 14/04/23. https://www.theguardian.com/lifeandstyle/2023/apr/14/how-to-behave-online-expert-guide-avoid-making-an-ass-of-yourself-on-social-media

106 Chambers, D. (2013) *Social Media and Personal Relationships: Online Intimacies and Networked Friendship*. Palgrave.

107 Vogels, Emily (2023) 'Teens and Cyberbullying 2022'. Pew Research Centre. 15/12/22. https://www.pewresearch.org/internet/2022/12/15/teens-and-cyberbullying-2022/ accessed 12/11/23.

108 ONS (2023) Office for National Statistics: 'Cyberbullying study in young people'.

109 Adu, A. & D. Milmo (2023) 'Rishi Sunak considers curbing social media use for under 16s'. *Guardian* 14/12/23. https://www.theguardian.com/media/2023/dec/14/rishi-sunak-considers-curbing-social-media-use-under-16s#:~:text=While%20some%20sources%20told%20the,in%20particular%2C%E2%80%9D%20they%20said. accessed 22/02/24.

110 See for example, Holmes, J. & M. Stubbe (2003) *Power and Politeness in the Workplace.* Pearson.

111 See Schnurr, S. (2013) *Exploring Professional Communication.* Routledge.

112 Ibid.

113 Holmes, J. & M. Stubbe (2003) *Power and Politeness in the Workplace.* Pearson.

114 Holmes and Stubbe (2003: 34) ibid.

115 Owen, C., C. Scott, R. Adams & P. Parsons (2022) 'Leadership in crisis: developing beyond command and control'. *Disaster Resilient Australia.* https://knowledge.aidr.org.au/resources/ajem-jul-2015-leadership-in-crisis-developing-beyond-command-and-control/ accessed 16/02/24.

116 Linde, C. (1988) 'The Quantitative Study of Communicative Success: Politeness and Accidents in Aviation Discourse'. *Language in Society* 17(3): 375–99.

117 Mullany, L. (2007) 'Gendered Discourse in the Professional Workplace'. Palgrave, p. 165.

118 Mullany, L. (2010) 'Gendered identities in the professional workplace: negotiating the glass ceiling'. In C. Llamas & D. Watt (eds) *Language and Identities.* Edinburgh University Press, pp. 179–91.

119 Mullany (2007: 220) ibid.

120 Mullany, L. (2006) 'Narrative constructions of gendered and professional identities'. In G. White & T,. Omionyi (eds.) *The Sociolinguistics of Identity*. Continuum.

121 Mullany, L. (2010) 'Gendered identities in the professional workplace: negotiating the glass ceiling'. In C. Llamas & D. Watt (eds.) *Language and Identities*. Edinburgh University Press, pp. 179–91.

122 Mullany, L. (2007: 195) ibid.

123 Mullany, L. & S. Schnurr (2022) 'Globalisation, geopolitics and gender: Key issues for professional communication'. In Mullany, L. & S. Schnurr (eds.) *Globalisation, Geopolitics and Gender in Professional Communication*. Routledge. pp. 1–16.

124 Holmes, J. & S. Schnurr (2017) '(Im)politeness in the workplace'. In J. Culpeper, M. Haugh & D. Kadar (eds.) *The Handbook of Linguistics (im)politeness*. Palgrave, pp. 635–60.

125 Holmes and Schnurr (2017: 650) ibid.

126 Holmes and Schnurr (2017: 649) ibid.

127 Schnurr, S., M. Marra and J. Holmes (2007) 'Being (im)polite in New Zealand workplaces'. *Journal of Pragmatics* 39(4): 712–39.

128 Schnurr, Marra and Holmes (2007: 730) ibid.

129 Spencer-Oatey, H. & T. Xing (2003) 'Managing Rapport in Intercultural Business Interactions: A Comparison of Two Chinese-British Welcome Meeting'. *Journal of Intercultural Studies* 24(1): 33–46.

130 Spencer-Oatey and Xing (2003: 40) ibid.

131 Handford, M. (2020) In Mullany, L. (ed.) *Professional Communication: Consultancy, Advocacy, Activism*. Palgrave, pp. 29–46.

132 Handford (2020: 37) ibid.

133 Handford (2020: 39) ibid.

134 Handford, M. (2020: 42) ibid.

135 Handford (2000: 34)

136 Mullany, L. (2007) *Gendered Discourse in the Professional Workplace*. Palgrave.

137 Plester, B. & J. Sayers (2007) '"Taking the piss": Functions of banter in the IT industry'. *Humor: International Journal of Humor Research* 20(2): 157–87.

138 Austin, P. (1990) 'Politeness Revisited – The Dark Side', in Allan Bell and Janet Holmes (eds.) *New Zealand Ways of Speaking English*, pp. 277–93. Multilingual Matters.

139 Brown, A. & R. Woodfield (2024) 'Banter and beyond'. *Gender, Work and Organization*. 1–17.

140 Plester, B. & J. Sayers (2007) '"Taking the piss": Functions of banter in the IT industry'. *Humor: International Journal of Humor Research* 20(2): 157–187.

141 Clarke, T. (2022) '"It's just banter mate!", but when does a joke at work cross the line?' Hay & Kilner https://www.hay-kilner.co.uk/insights/when-does-a-joke-at-work-cross-the-line/ July 2022 accessed 12/10/23.

142 Plester, B. & J. Sayers (2007) '"Taking the piss": Functions of banter in the IT industry'. *Humor: International Journal of Humor Research* 20(2): 157–87.

143 Clarke, T. (2022) '"It's just banter mate!", but when does a joke at work cross the line?' Hay & Kilner July 2022. https://www.hay-kilner.co.uk/insights/when-does-a-joke-at-work-cross-the-line/ accessed 12/10/23.

144 Schnurr, S., M. Marra & J. Holmes (2007) 'Being (im)polite in New Zealand workplaces'. *Journal of Pragmatics* 39(4): 712–39.

145 Schnurr, Marra & Holmes (2007: 736) ibid.

146 See Mullany, L. (2007) *Gendered Discourse in the Professional Workplace*. Palgrave, p. 234 for a discussion of humour from a gender-based perspective in these data.

147 Archer, D. C. Lansley & A. Garner (2020) 'Keeping airports safe: The value of small talk'. In D. Archer, K. Grainger & P. Jagodzinski (eds.) *Politeness in Professional Contexts*, pp. 273–97.

148 Archer, Lansley & Garner (2020: 287) ibid.

149 Archer, Lansley & Garner (2020: 287) ibid.

150 McCarthy, M. (2000) 'Mutually captive audiences: Small talk and the gender of close-contact service encounters'. In J. Coupland *Small Talk* Pearson, pp. 84–109.

151 McCarthy, M. (2000: 94) ibid.

152 McCarthy, M. (2000: 101) ibid.

153 McCarthy, M. (2000: 101) ibid.

154 See Boden, D. (1997) *The Business of Talk: Organizations in Action*. Polity Press.

155 Spencer-Oatey, H. & T. Xing (2003) 'Managing Rapport in Intercultural Business Interactions: A Comparison of Two Chinese-British Welcome Meetings'. *Journal of Intercultural Studies* 24(1): 33–46.

156 Debray, C. (2020) 'Managing rapport in team conflicts'. In D. Archer, K. Grainger & P. Jagodzinski (eds.) *Politeness in Professional Contexts*. Benjamins, pp. 129–50.

157 Debray (2020: 140) ibid.

158 Debray (2020: 144) ibid.

159 Debray (2020: 137–8) ibid.

160 IOC (2024) 'Olympic Values'. https://olympics.com/ioc/olympic-values accessed 12/10/23.

161 See File, K. (2015) 'The strategic enactment of a media identity by professional team sports players'. *Discourse & Communication*, 9(4): 441-464, for further discussion.

162 Reuters (2016) 'Egyptian judoka sent home for refusing to shake Israeli opponent's hand'. *Guardian* 15/08/16. https://www.theguardian.com/sport/2016/aug/15/egyptian-judoka-sent-home-israeli-opponent-hand-shake-olympics accessed 11/11/23.

163 File, K. (2015) 'The strategic enactment of a media identity by professional team sports players'. *Discourse & Communication* 9(4): 441–464.

164 File (2015: 451) ibid.

165 File (2015: 453) ibid.

166 File (2015: 455) ibid.

167 File (2015: 469) ibid.

168 Wilson, N. (2010) 'Bros, Boys and Guys: address term function and communities of practice in a New Zealand rugby team'. *New Zealand English Journal* 24: 33–54.

169 Wilson (2010: 16) ibid.

170 All Blacks (2024) Home page.
     https://www.experienceallblacks.com/ accessed 14/02/24.

171 All Blacks (2024) 'History of haka'.
     https://www.experienceallblacks.com/insider-information/haka/
     history-of-haka/ accessed 16/02/24.

172 Kelly, V. (2022) 'The Science behind the haka'.
     https://habs.uq.edu.au/article/2017/08/science-behind-haka
     accessed 23/02/2024.

173 Murol, M. (2022) 'Do the All Blacks get an advantage from the
     haka? Science says yes'. *Sydney Morning Herald* 14/09/22.
     https://www.smh.com.au/sport/rugby-union/
     do-the-all-blacks-get-an-advantage-from-the-haka-science-says-
     yes-20220815-p5b9u6.html accessed 12/10/23.

174 Kelly, V. (2022), reported in: Murol, M (2022) 'Do the All
     Blacks get an advantage from the haka? Science says yes'. *Sydney
     Morning Herald* 14/09/22.
     https://www.smh.com.au/sport/rugby-union/
     do-the-all-blacks-get-an-advantage-from-the-haka-science-says-
     yes-20220815-p5b9u6.html accessed 12/10/23.

175 Murol, M. (2022) 'Do the All Blacks get an advantage from the
     haka? Science says yes'. *Sydney Morning Herald* 14/09/22.
     https://www.smh.com.au/sport/rugby-union/
     do-the-all-blacks-get-an-advantage-from-the-haka-science-says-
     yes-20220815-p5b9u6.html accessed 12/10/23.

176 O'Dwyer, F. (2022). 'The functions of collegial humour in
     male–only sporting interactions.' *Te Reo: The Journal of the
     Linguistic Society of New Zealand*, 64(2), 15–36.
     https://nzlingsoc.org/wp-content/uploads/2022/03/1-ODwyer-
     pg-16-36.pdf.

177 O'Dwyer, F. (2022: 28) ibid.

178 O'Dwyer, F. (2022: 30) ibid.

179 Kuiper, K. (1997) 'Sporting formulae in New Zealand English:
     two models of male solidarity'. In J. Coates *Language and
     Gender: A Reader*. Blackwell. pp. 285–94.

180 Scott, J. (2022) Women's Euros victory interview. Talk Sport 9/08/22.
https://talksport.com/football/1166777/jill-scott-swearing-euro-2022-england-germany-womens-lionesses/

181 @BBCFootball (2022) 'The politest man in football is back in the Premier League' Twitter 7/11/22.
https://twitter.com/bbcsport/status/1589518010867326976?lang=en-GB accessed 10/10/23.

182 BBC Online (2022) Premier League: Unai Emery's first post-match interview, Aston Villa v Manchester United. Twitter 6/11/22.
https://twitter.com/bbcsport/status/1589518010867326976?lang=en-GB accessed 12/11/23.
From bbc.co.uk
https://www.bbc.co.uk/sport/football/63535339 accessed 12/11/23.

183 BBC Online (2022) Premier League: Unai Emery's first post-match interview, Aston Villa v Manchester United. Twitter 6/11/22.
https://twitter.com/bbcsport/status/1589518010867326976?lang=en-GB accessed 12/11/23.

184 Football on TNT Sports (2019) Unai Emery: Good evening 28/05/19 Twitter @footballontnt
https://twitter.com/footballontnt/status/1133387722394132482 accesssed 14/02/24.

185 Emery, U. (2023)
https://www.instagram.com/unaiemery_/p/Cqgh4MNNU0Q/ Instagram. Posted 01/04/23, accessed 10/09/23.

186 Youll, R. (2023) 'Aston Villa 'like a family' says Ezri Konsa'. *Shropshire Star* 09/08/23.
https://www.shropshirestar.com/sport/football/2023/08/09/aston-villa-like-a-family-says-ezri-konsa/, accessed 12/10/23.

187 Townley, J. (2024) 'Emi Buendía speaks out on ACL recovery and reveals what Unai Emery told him after devastating blow'. *Birmingham Mail*, 25/01/24.
https://www.birminghammail.co.uk/sport/football/football-news/emi-buendia-speaks-out-acl-28513720 accessed 14/02/24.

188 Northcroft, J. (2023) Unai Emery Interview: 'I told the Villa players: I'm not here to waste my time'. *The Times* https://www.thetimes.co.uk/article/noai-emery-i-told-villa-players-i-am-not-here-to-waste-my-time-l60dqlrnb accessed 21/12/23.

189 Emery, U. (2024) 'It's not for me, it's for our work' @AVFCOfficial Twitter 12/01/24. https://twitter.com/AVFCOfficial/status/1745815500746113309 accessed 23/01/24.

190 There is a banner on the Holte End at Aston Villa's Villa Park stadium which reads 'Holte End, The 12th Man'. This was there before Emery arrived, but his reference to it is a direct acknowledgement to the fans that he notices and appreciates the banners and encouragement of the crowd to help their team.

191 Townley, J. (2024) Unai Emery Q&A: Every word Aston Villa said about 'heart of the club', Konsa update and 5-0 thrashing. *Birmingham Mail*, 04/02/24. https://www.birminghammail.co.uk/sport/football/football-news/unai-emery-qa-every-word-28563687 accessed 14/02/24.

192 Jackson, J. (2018) 'Respect? Following José Mourinho at Manchester United was a crazy ride'. 22/12/18. *Guardian* https://www.theguardian.com/football/2018/dec/22/respect-covering-jose-mourinho-manchester-united-wild-ride accessed 27/02/24.

193 Lawrence, A. (2015) 'Arsène Wenger accuses José Mourinho of disrespecting other manager'. *Guardian* 01/05/15, https://www.theguardian.com/football/2015/may/01/wenger-accuses-mourinho-disrespecting-managers accessed 27/02/24.

194 Miller, C. (2023) Jose Mourinho sent off yet AGAIN for telling the opposition manager you cry too much. *The Mirror* 6/11/22. https://www.mirror.co.uk/sport/football/news/jose-mourinho-roma-red-card-31251074#Accesssed 02/02/24.

195 The FA (2015) Chelsea boss José Mourinho charged for misconduct. The FA, 08/01/15. https://www.thefa.com/news/2015/jan/08/jose-mourinho-charged-080115 accessed 26/02/24.

See also Swanson, B. (2016) FA confirms José Mourinho fined for 'putting extra pressure' on referee Anthony Taylor, 16/11/16. https://www.skysports.com/football/news/11667/10659558/ fa-confirms-jose-mourinho-fined-for-putting-extra-pressure-on-referee-anthony-taylor accessed 27/02/24.

196 Schlachter, T. (2023) 'José Mourinho sent off after making 'crying' gesture as Roma scores dramatic winner'. CNN News 23/10/23. https://edition.cnn.com/2023/10/23/sport/jose-mourinho-red-card-roma-winner-spt-intl/index.html#:~:text=José%20 Mourinho%20was%20sent%20off,was%20shown%20a%20 red%20card accessed 24/11/23.

197 Sky News (2020) José Mourinho: I was rude to an idiot, says Spurs boss after booking. 02/01/20. https://news.sky.com/story/jose-mourinho-i-was-rude-to-an-idiotsays-spurs-boss-after-booking-11899672 accessed 23/11/23.

198 Ibid.

199 Sky Sports News Retro (2022) '"I'm a special one" – José Mourinho's first Chelsea press conference'. 23/04/20; Originally broadcast 04/06/13. https://www.youtube.com/watch?v=hkZFko2Vsa8 accessed 27/02/24.

200 Press Association (2016) 'From "voyeur" to "specialist failure": Every dig and jibe from years of Mourinho vs Wenger spats'. *The Mirror* 27/04/16. https://www.mirror.co.uk/sport/football/news/voyeur-specialist-failure-every-dig-12435994 accessed 2/02/23.

201 Sky Sports Retro (2022) 'José Mourinho calling Frank de Boer the worst Premier League manager of all time'. 30/08/22. https://www.youtube.com/watch?v=yxQ2khkXyM8 accessed 12/05/23.

202 All Football (2020) 'José Mourinho and Pep Guardiola's War of Words through the years'. 25/02/19. https://m.allfootballapp.com/news/EPL/Jose-Mourinho-and-Pep-Guardiolas-War-of-Words-through-the-years/1118697 accessed 23/11/23.

203 Sky Sports Retro (2019) '"3 for me & 2 for them!" – José Mourinho reminds everyone about his Premier League titles'. 08/05/20. https://www.youtube.com/watch?v=Kh9cJ9xydmI, accessed 12/07/23.

204 BBC (2005) Mourinho accused as Frisk quits. BBC Online 14/03/05. http://news.bbc.co.uk/sport1/hi/football/teams/c/chelsea/4346509.stm accessed 14/02/24.

205 Ibid.

206 *Guardian* (2005) 'UEFA Clears Mourinho' 17/03/05. https://www.theguardian.com/football/2005/mar/17/newsstory.sport5 accessed 28/02/24.

207 BBC Sport (2005) 'Mourinho accused as Frisk quits'. BBC Online 14/03/05. http://news.bbc.co.uk/sport1/hi/football/teams/c/chelsea/4346509.stm accessed 27/02/24.

208 Davis, D. & L. Augustus (2022) 'José Mourinho has a long history of falling out with players . . . and now Roma's stars are getting a taste after he blasted their "psychological complex"'. Mail Online. https://www.dailymail.co.uk/sport/football/article-10386617/Jose-Mourinhos-long-history-falling-players-criticising-weak-Roma.html accessed 24/01/23.

209 Wenger, A. (2021) PUT TO BED: Chelsea ended Arsenal rivalry when José Mourinho oversaw 6-0 win on Arsène Wenger's 1000th game. Talk Sport 21/08/21. https://talksport.com/football/930218/chelsea-vs-arsenal-mohamed-salah-arsene-wenger-jose-mourinho/ accessed 01/02/24.

210 Wayne Rooney, post-match interview, reported in the *Coventry Telegraph*, Wayne Rooney threat to Birmingham players as miserable run continues ahead of Coventry City clash. 06/12/23. https://www.coventrytelegraph.net/sport/football/football-news/coventry-city-birmingham-wayne-rooney-28238272 accessed 10/01/24.

211   Football Hub UK (2023) Wayne Rooney 'grow a pair of balls' Instagram 03/12/23.
https://www.instagram.com/bcfc_.hub/p/
C0aGsmnISsF/?next=%2Fkac_polaskova%2F&hl=af Dec 2023 accessed 17/01/24.

212   Eustace, J. (2023) John Eustace Statement. League Managers Association 16/10/23.
https://www.leaguemanagers.com/latest-news/john-eustace-statement accessed 17/01/24.

213   Guyett, M. (2023) 'Erik ten Hag has lost 50% of the Manchester United dressing room as players make their feelings known to the under-pressure boss'. Sportskeeda 04/12/23.
https://www.sportskeeda.com/football/rumor-erik-ten-hag-lost-50-manchester-united-dressing-room-players-make-feelings-known-under-pressure-boss-reports accessed 27/02/24.

214   Leeks, J. (2023) 'Jadon Sancho has "no relationship" with Erik ten Hag and "barely speaking" to Man Utd boss'. *The Mirror* 11/10/23.
https://www.mirror.co.uk/sport/football/news/manutd-jadon-sancho-ten-hag-31157593 accessed 27/02/24.

215   Dakers, A. (2023) 'Jadon Sancho forced to train alone after criticising Man Utd manager', *i news* 14/09/23.
https://inews.co.uk/sport/football/jadon-sando-forced-train-alone-man-utd-manager-erik-ten-hag-2617702 accessed 27/02/24.

216   Dawson, R. (2023) 'Sancho's career at risk due to no apology', ESPN 09/10/23.
https://www.espn.co.uk/football/story/_/id/38613149/sancho-man-utd-career-risk-no-apology-sources accessed 27/02/24.

217   Wood, L. (2023) 'Jadon Sancho deletes social media post hitting out at Manchester United manager Erik ten Hag'. *Manchester Evening News* 12/09/23.
https://www.manchestereveningnews.co.uk/sport/football/football-news/manchester-united-sancho-ten-hag-27702817 accessed 27/02/24.

218 King, K. (2023) 'Four Man Utd stars in dressing room bust-ups with each other following Brighton humiliation'. *The Mirror* 19/09/23.
https://www.mirror.co.uk/sport/football/news/man-utd-fernandes-mctominay-brighton-30973641 accessed 27/02/24.

219 Deeney, T. (2023) 'Man Utd are ordinary, scared and lack leaders'. *The Sun* 15/12/23.
https://www.thesun.co.uk/sport/25071764/man-utd-erik-ten-hag-liverpool-sack-troy-deeney/ accessed 28/02/24.

220 Parsons, T. (2023) 'Man Utd owners the Glazers told to sack Erik ten Hag over team selection'. *Express* 07/09/23.
https://www.express.co.uk/sport/football/1810162/Man-Utd-Glazers-Erik-ten-Hag-Rasmus-Hojlund accessed 27/02/24.

221 Solhekol, K. & M. Reddy (2023) 'Jadon Sancho: Manchester United manager Erik ten Hag will not back down in stand-off with winger'. Sky Sports 27/09/23.
https://www.skysports.com/football/news/11095/12970359/jadon-sancho-manchester-united-manager-erik-ten-hag-will-not-back-down-in-stand-off-with-winger accessed 27/02/24.

222 The FA (2024) 'Respect'. The Football Association.
https://www.englandfootball.com/participate/explore/inclusive-football/Respect accessed 21/01/24.

223 The FA (2024) 'Respect: We Only do Positive'. The Football Association.
https://www.thefa.com/get.involved/respect accessed 21/01/24.

224 The FA (2024) 'Positivity always wins'.
https://www.englandfootball.com/participate/explore/inclusive-football/Respect/Positivity-Always-Wins accessed 27/02/24.

225 Tate, J. (2022) 'Footballers need to show referees some respect – we are in short supply'. *Guardian* 13/01/22.
https://www.theguardian.com/football/when-saturday-comes-blog/2022/jan/13/footballers-need-to-show-referees-some-respect-we-are-in-short-supply accessed 27/02/24.

226 The FA (2024) 'Pledge of Positivity'.
https://www.thefa.com/get.involved/respect accessed 21/01/24.

227 The FA (2018) 'Create a fun, safe and inclusive environment for all the players'. https://www.thefa.com/get.involved/respect/we-only-do-positive accessed 27/02/24.

228 Kellett. P. & D. Shilbury (2007) 'Umpire participation: Is abuse really the issue?' *Sports Management Review* 10(3): 209–29.

229 Ridinger, L., S. Warner , J. Tingle & K. Kim (2017) Referee recruitment and retention. *Global Sport Business Journal,* 5(3) p. 30.

230 Tingle, J., S. Warner & M. Satore-Baldwin (2014) 'The experience of former women officials and the impact on the sporting community'. *Sex Roles* 7197): 7–20.

231 Kellett. P. & D. Shilbury (2007) 'Umpire participation: Is abuse really the issue?' *Sports Management Review* 10(3): 209–29.

232 International Judo Federation (2021) Judo Values: Politeness. https://www.youtube.com/watch?v=6KC0LyREKJE, accessed 21/02/24.

233 Aiki TV interview (2022) Joe Thambu Shihan with Louise Mullany. *Keep the Flame Alive* interview series, Aikido Shudokan. September 2022. https://aikitv.online accessed 27/02/24

234 Shioda, G. (1991) Translated version (2002) *Aikido Shugyo: Harmony in Confrontation.* Translated by J. Payet & C. Johnston. Shindokan Books.

235 Ueshiba, M. (2007, translated version) *The Art of Peace.* Translated by J. Stevens. Shambhala Pocket Classics.

236 Ueshiba, M. 'Aikido isn't about defeating one's enemy, it's the way to unite human beings'. Cited in: Budgen, M. (2023) Aikido: A Japanese martial art practiced by millions. BBC Travel 01/9/23 https://www.bbc.com/travel/article/20230831-aikido-a-japanese-martial-art-practiced-by-millions accessed 27/02/24.

237 Ibid.

238 Aiki TV interview (2022) Joe Thambu Shihan with Louise Mullany. *Keep the Flame Alive* interview series, Aikido Shudokan. September 2022. https://aikitv.online accessed 27/02/24.

239 Ibid.

240 Ibid.

241 Ibid.

242 Thambu, J. & M. Oka (2023) *Budo: The Art of Being*. Aikido Shudokan, p. 64.

243 Ibid., p. 65.

244 Aiki TV interview (2022) Joe Thambu Shihan with Louise Mullany. *Keep the Flame Alive* interview series, Aikido Shudokan. September 2022. https://aikitv.online accessed 27/02/24

245 Ibid.

246 See http://www.nottinghamaikido.com

247 The Eagle Dojo (2024) *Student Creed*. Dragon's Induction Pack. Nottingham, UK.

248 British Aikido Board, 'Supporting your child in aikido'. https://bab.org.uk/safeguarding/supporting-your-child-in-aikido/ accessed 21/01/24.

249 Hua, W. Li and D. Jankowicz-Pytel. (2020) 'Whose Karate? Language and cultural learning in a multilingual Karate club in London'. *Applied Linguistics* 41(1): 52–83.

250 Jay, K. and Jay, T. (2015) 'Swearing and fluency. Taboo word fluency and knowledge of slurs and general pejoratives: deconstructing the poverty-of-vocabulary myth'. *Language Sciences* 1–9.

251 Jay, T. (2003) *The Psychology of Language*. Benjamins.

252 Love, R. (2021) 'Swearing in informal spoken English: 1990s–2010s'. *Text and Talk, 41* (5–6): 739–62.

253 McEnery, A. & Z. Xiao. (2004) 'Swearing in Modern British English: The Case of Fuck in the BNC'. *Language and Literature*, 13(3), 235–68.

254 Fry S. https://www.goodreads.com/quotes/715054-the-sort-of-twee-person-who-thinks-swearing-is-in

255 Allen, K. and K. Burridge (2006) 'Forbidden Words: Taboo and the Censoring of Language'. Cambridge University Press.

256 Stephens, R., D. Spierer & E. Katehis (2017) 'Effect of swearing on strength and power performance'. *Psychology of Sport and Exercise,* 35: 111–17.

257 Omissi, A. (2015) 'Swear words, etymology, and the history of English'. *Academic Insights for the Thinking World.* Oxford University Press 11/07/15.
https://blog.oup.com/2015/07/english-swear-words-etymology/ accessed 14/04/23.

258 Buckley, O. & J. Coles (2021) 'Woman detained for swearing In Dubai after sending single word in WhatsApp message'. *The Mirror* 04/02/21.
https://www.mirror.co.uk/news/world-news/brit-woman-detained-dubai-after-23436409 accessed 26/09/23.

259 Gulf News (2019) 'Using the "F" word is a criminal offence in the UAE'. *Gulf News* 24/01/19.
https://gulfnews.com/uae/using-the-f-word-is-a-criminal-offence-in-the-uae-1.61621180 accessed 02/02/24.

260 LY Lawyers, Queensland Government legislation.
https://cabinet.qld.gov.au/documents/2008/nov/summary%20 offences%20bill/Attachments/5208T3542.pdf.

261 Curtis, K. (2022) 'Pocock reprimanded for swearing in parliament, but what is allowed?' *Sydney Morning Herald* 08/09/22.
https://www.smh.com.au/politics/federal/parliamentary-ears-protected-from-colourful-language-in-the-chamber-20220908-p5bgi5.html accessed 21/09/23.

262 Australian Parliament Hansard record:
https://www.aph.gov.au/Parliamentary_Business/Hansard/Hansard_Display?bid=chamber/hansards/27150/&sid=0018.

263 Reuters (2021) 'Get the F**K out! Philippines foreign minister blasts Beijing for 'illegal' activity in the disputed South China Sea'. *Daily Mail* 03/05/21.
https://www.dailymail.co.uk/news/article-9537307/Philippines-foreign-minister-tells-Beijing-f-South-China-Sea.html accessed 10/11/23.

264 Jain, A. (2021) 'China calls for "basic etiquette" after Philippine "get the f*** out" remark'. *Independent* 04/05/21. https://www.independent.co.uk/asia/china/philippines-china-locsin-jr-b1841777.html, accessed 10/11/23.

265 Locsin T. (2021) Tweet, reported in Jain, A. (2021) "China calls for "basic etiquette" after Philippine "get the f*** out" remark'. *Independent* https://www.independent.co.uk/asia/china/philippines-china-locsin-jr-b1841777.html, accessed 10/11/23.

266 Lemon, J. (2019) 'Trump Once Called Chinese "Motherf***ers" in a Speech', Newsweek 06/01/19. https://www.newsweek.com/trump-chinese-motherfuckers-speech-tlaib-1280860 accessed 26/10/23.

267 Vitali, A, K. Hunt & F. Thorp (2018) 'Trump referred to Haiti and African nations as "shithole" countries', NBC News 11/06/18. https://www.nbcnews.com/politics/white-house/trump-referred-haiti-african-countries-shithole-nations-n836946 accessed 28/10/23.

268 'The Profanity President: Trump's four letter vocabulary'. *New York Times* 19/05/19. https://www.nytimes.com/2019/05/19/us/politics/trump-language.html#:~:text=In%20a%20single%20speech%20on,did%20not%20seem%20to%20mind. accessed 10/10/23.

269 Baruch, Y., R. Prouska, A. Ollier-Malaterre & J. Bunk (2017) 'Swearing at work: the mixed outcomes of profanity'. *Journal of Managerial Psychology* 32(2): 149–62.

270 Mullany, L. (2010) 'Ice-Road Truckers'. In D. Kadar and F. Bargiela-Chiappini (eds) *Politeness Across Cultures*. Palgrave pp. xx-xx.

271 Daly, N,. J. Holmes, R. Newton & M. Stubbe (2004) Expletives as solidarity signals in FTAs on factory floors. *Journal of Pragmatics*, 36(5): 946-964.

272 Love, R. (2021) 'Swearing in informal spoken English: 1990s–2010s' *Text & Talk*, 41 (5–6): 739–62.

273 Jay, K. and T. Jay (2015) 'Swearing and fluency. Taboo word fluency and knowledge of slurs and general pejoratives: deconstructing the poverty-of-vocabulary myth'. Language Sciences 1- 9.

274 Interview with Elyse Methven (2015) Anti-swearing laws redundant and ineffective at protecting children: legal researcher. ABC Radio Sydney. https://www.abc.net.au/news/2015-07-23/anti-swearing-laws-redundant-says-researcher/6642888 accessed 23/06/23

275 Palacios Martinez, I. (2021) Taboo vocatives in the language of London teenagers. *Pragmatics 31*(2): 250-277.

276 Love, R. (2023) Schools could teach students about swearing to promote responsible language use. Aston University Podcasts, https://www.aston.ac.uk/latest-news/podcast-schools-could-teach-students-about-swearing-promote-responsible-language-use#:~:text=Dr%20Robbie%20Love%20said%20having,language%20such%20as%20racial%20slurs accessed 29/12/23.

277 Jay, K. and T. Jay (2015) 'Swearing and fluency. Taboo word fluency and knowledge of slurs and general pejoratives: deconstructing the poverty- of-vocabulary myth'. Language Sciences 1- 9.

278 Lakoff, R. (1975) *Language and Woman's Place.* HarperCollins.

279 Morgan M. (2005) 'The Angry black woman stereotype'. In M. Bucholtz (ed.) Lakoff Revisited. Oxford University Press. https://hbr.org/2022/01/the-angry-black-woman-stereotype-at-work

280 Ibid.

281 Ensler, E. (2000) *The Vagina Monologues*, Virago.

282 Kerri, A. (2019) 'Nice girls don't swear, right? This trans lady says fiuck that'. *Advocate* 11/09/19. https://www.advocate.com/commentary/2019/9/11/nice-girls-dont-swear-right-trans-lady-says-fck accessed on 12/12/23.

283 Lakoff, R. (1975) *Language and Woman's Place.*

284 Ofcom (2021) 'Public attitudes towards offensive language on TV and radio'. Ofcom September 2021.

https://www.ofcom.org.uk/__data/assets/pdf_file/0020/225335/
offensive-language-quick-reference-guide.pdf; accessed
15/09/23.

285 Dent, S. (2022) 'Susie Dent's Introduction to Swearing: The
C-Word'. *Why Now* 22/01/22.
https://whynow.co.uk/read/susie-dents-introduction-to-
swearing-the-c-word accessed 23/05/23.
Staake, J. (2019) 'When a Student Drops the F-Bomb: Dealing
With Cursing in the Classroom'. *We Are Teachers* 13/09/19.
https://www.weareteachers.com/cursing-in-the-classroom/
accessed 11/09/23.

286 Cameron, D. (2018) 'Cuntroversy: On Samantha Bee and the
C-word. Language: A Feminist Guide'. 03/06/18.
https://debuk.wordpress.com/2018/06/03/cuntroversy-on-
samantha-bee-and-the-c-word/ accessed 12/03/23.

287 Betts, H. (2022) 'The C Spot'. *Airmail* 11/11/23.
https://airmail.news/issues/2023-11-11/the-c-spot accessed
12/12/23.

288 Cameron, D. (2018) 'Cuntroversy: On Samantha Bee and the
C-word. Language: A Feminist Guide'. 03/06/18.
https://debuk.wordpress.com/2018/06/03/cuntroversy-on-
samantha-bee-and-the-c-word/ accessed 12/03/23.

289 Zhao, C. (2018) 'Political Leader Says Women Must Reclaim the
C-word: 'I Stand by Using That Word . . . We Have to Disarm
and Reclaim'. Newsweek 08/08/18
https://www.newsweek.com/political-leader-says-women-must-
reclaim-c-word-i-stand-using-word-we-have-1062965 accessed
23/09/23.

290 Roy, E. (2018) 'New Zealand MP uses C-word at rally in call to
reclaim it from abusers'. *Guardian* 09/08/18
https://www.theguardian.com/world/2018/aug/09/new-zealand-
mp-uses-c-word-at-rally-in-call-to-reclaim-it-from-abusers
accessed 12/07/23.

291 Bowcott, O. (2017) 'Judge who swore at abusive defendant
cleared of misconduct'. *Guardian* 09/01/17.

https://www.theguardian.com/law/2017/jan/09/judge-who-swore-at-abusive-defendant-cleared-of-misconduct accessed 12/07/23.

292 BT Sport (2019) 'Jürgen Klopp swears in interview after beating Barcelona 4-0'. YouTube 07/05/19. https://www.youtube.com/watch?v=ELhLR2iEYmg accessed 05/07/23.

293 Garrahan, M. (2019) Twitter. https://twitter.com/DanGarrahan

294 Harrison, E. (2018) 'Gary Lineker refuses to apologise for Jürgen Klopp'. *Radio Times* 08/05/19. https://www.radiotimes.com/tv/sport/football/liverpool-barcelona-jurgen-klopp-swearing-gary-lineker-bt-sport/ accessed 05/07/23.

295 Liverpool manager Jürgen Klopp curses in postgame interview, says 'I thought in America it's OK'. The Comeback. https://thecomeback.com/soccer/liverpool-manager-jurgen-klopp-curses-postgame-interview-says-thought-america-ok-2-2.html accessed 14/01/24.

296 Ibid.

297 Holmes, J. (1995) *Women, Men and Politeness.* Longman.

298 Fox, K. (2005) *Watching the English.* Hodder & Stoughton.

299 Blum-Kulka, S. (1992) In R. Watts, S. Ide & K. Ehlich (eds) *Politeness in Language: Studies in its History, Theory and Practice.* Mouton.

300 Wales Online (2003) Profumo letter: Macmillan's apology over sex scandal. Wales Online 07/03/03. https://www.walesonline.co.uk/news/uk-news/macmillans-apology-over-sex-scandal-2489525 accessed 14/02/23.

301 Australian Associated Press (2021) 'Jacinda Ardern apologises for New Zealand dawn raids on Pasifika people in 1970s'. *Guardian* 02/08/21. https://www.theguardian.com/world/2021/aug/02/jacinda-ardern-apologises-for-new-zealand-dawn-raids-on-pasifika-people-in-1970s accessed 23/08/23.

302 Murphy, J. (2018) 'Does Justin Trudeau apologise too much?'
    BBC 28/03/18.
    https://www.bbc.co.uk/news/world-us-canada-43560817
    accessed 12/02/23.

303 Besner, L. (2018) 'Is Canada apologising too much?' *Guardian*
    16/05/18.
    https://www.theguardian.com/commentisfree/2018/may/16/
    canada-justin-trudeau-apologising-too-much accessed 25/01/23

304 See Harris S., K. Grainger & L. Mullany (2006) 'The Pragmatics
    of political apologies'. *Discourse & Society* 17(6): 715-737.

305 McDonald, H., O Bowcott & H. Mullholland (2010) 'David
    Cameron apologies for 'unjustifiable' shootings'. *Guardian*
    15/06/10.
    https://www.theguardian.com/uk/2010/jun/15/bloody-sunday-
    report-saville-inquiry, accessed 14/02/23.

306 Joint Committee on Human Rights (2022) Official apology
    sought in recognition of lasting suffering caused by adoption
    practices in 1950s-1970s involving unmarried mothers. UK
    Parliament Committees.
    https://committees.parliament.uk/work/1522/the-right-to-
    family-life-adoption-of-children-of-unmarried-women-19491976/
    news/172077/official-apology-sought-in-recognition-of-lasting-
    suffering-caused-by-adoption-practices-in-1950s1970s-involving-
    unmarried-mothers-jchr/ accessed 23/05/23

307 Harman, H. (2022) Quote appeared in: Official apology sought
    in recognition of lasting suffering caused by adoption practices
    in 1950s-1970s involving unmarried mothers. UK Parliament
    Committees.
    https://committees.parliament.uk/work/1522/the-right-to-
    family-life-adoption-of-children-of-unmarried-women-19491976/
    news/172077/official-apology-sought-in-recognition-of-lasting-
    suffering-caused-by-adoption-practices-in-1950s1970s-involving-
    unmarried-mothers-jchr/ accessed 23/05/23.

308 Australian Associated Press (2021) 'Jacinda Ardern apologises
    for New Zealand 'dawn raids' on Pasifika people in 1970s'.
    Guardian 02/08/21.

https://www.theguardian.com/world/2021/aug/02/
jacinda-ardern-apologises-for-new-zealand-dawn-raids-on-
pasifika-people-in-1970s accessed 23/07/23.

309 Ho, B. (2011) 'What's an apology worth?' Journal of Empirical
Legal Studies. 8(1): 179-199.

310 Ross, N., & P. Newman (2021) 'The Role of Apology Laws in
Medical Malpractice'. The Journal of American Academy of
Psychiatry and Law, 49(3): 1-9.

311 NHS Resolution (2017) 'Saying Sorry'. June 2017.
https://resolution.nhs.uk/wp-content/uploads/2018/09/Saying-
sorry-leaflet-2019.pdf accessed 27/02/23.

312 NHS Resolution (2017) 'Saying Sorry'. June 2017, p.3.
https://resolution.nhs.uk/wp-content/uploads/2018/09/Saying-
sorry-leaflet-2019.pdf accessed 27/02/23.

313 Ibid, p. 3.

314 Sky Sports Retro (2015) '"You are an ostrich!" – Nigel Pearson's
infamous ostrich rant'. 12/01/21.
https://www.youtube.com/watch?v=4xfdk3MliFc accessed
12/09/23.

315 Press Association (2015) 'Nigel Pearson draws line in sand, says
sorry to journalist he called "an ostrich"'. *Guardian* 12/04/15.
https://www.theguardian.com/football/2015/apr/30/nigel-
pearson-leicester-city-ostrich-rant accessed 27/02/24.

316 BBC (2015) Nigel Pearson: Leicester boss apologies after
'ostrich' rant. BBC Online 30/04/15.
https://wwnw.bbc.co.uk/sport/football/32537484 accessed
24/10/23.

317 Press Association (2015) 'Nigel Pearson draws line in sand, says
sorry to journalist he called "an ostrich"'. *Guardian* 12/04/15.
https://www.theguardian.com/football/2015/apr/30/nigel-
pearson-leicester-city-ostrich-rant accessed 27/02/24.

318 *Guardian* (17/01/04) cited in Harris, S., K. Grainger & L.
Mullany (2006: 744) 'The pragmatics of political apologies'.
Discourse & Society 17(6): 715–37.

319 Harris, Grainger and Mullany (2006: 730) ibid.

320 Blair, A. (2005) Labour Party Conference speech on Saddam Hussein. In Harris, Grainger and Mullany (2006: 765) 'The pragmatics of political apologies'. *Discourse & Society* 17(6): 715–37.

321 *Independent* (29/09/04). Cited in: Harris Grainger and Mullany (2006: 747) 'The pragmatics of political apologies'. *Discourse & Society* 17(6): 715–37.

322 Hughes. D. (2022) 'Johnson apologies and Stratton quits'. *Independent* 05/07/22. https://www.independent.co.uk/news/uk/allegra-stratton-boris-johnson-downing-street-itv-news-prime-minister-b1972224.html accessed 15/08/23.

323 NBC News (2022) Boris Johnson Offers 'Wholehearted Apology' After Covid 'Partygate' Fine. https://www.youtube.com/watch?v=Jk07s_Bxr6M accessed 15/02/24.

324 BBC Online (2022) 'Boris Johnson vote: Douglas Ross says PM has to think about resigning'. https://www.bbc.co.uk/news/uk-scotland-scotland-politics-61718741 Scottish leader Douglas Ross – he should resign, accessed 23/08/23.

325 ITV News (2021) 'PM faces fierce questions after leaked video adds fuel to No 10 Christmas party row'. 08/12/21. https://www.itv.com/news/2021-12-08/pm-in-for-grilling-as-leaked-video-heaps-fresh-pressure-over-no-10-party-claims accessed 17/01/24.

326 Brown, F. (2022) 'Probe launched into Chris Pincher after scandal which ended Boris Johnson's premiership'. Sky News 24/10/22. https://news.sky.com/story/probe-launched-into-chris-pincher-after-scandal-which-ended-boris-johnsons-premiership-12729141 accessed 14/12/23.

327 Hughes, D. (2022) 'Johnson apologises for handling of Pincher row as he faces Tory backlash'. *Independent* 05/07/22. https://www.independent.co.uk/news/uk/boris-johnson-chris-pincher-prime-minister-government-commons-b2116383.html, accessed 23/07/23.

328 Smout, A. (2022) 'Bye bye Boris: UK PM Johnson bows out with regrets but no apologies'. *Reuters* 07/07/22. https://www.reuters.com/world/uk/bye-bye-boris-uk-pm-johnson-bows-out-with-regrets-no-apologies-2022-07-07/ accessed 15/11/23.

329 Bol, D. (2022) 'Boris Johnson resigns: Prime Minister quits "best job in the world"'. *The Herald* 07/07/22. https://www.heraldscotland.com/politics/20263071.boris-johnson-resigns-prime-minister-quits-best-job-world/ accessed 12/03/23.

330 Stewart, H. (2022) 'Boris Johnson's resignation speech: what he said, and what he meant'. *Guardian* 07/07/22. https://www.theguardian.com/politics/2022/jul/07/boris-johnsons-resignation-speech-what-he-said-and-what-he-meant accessed 23/11/23.

331 Stone, J. (2023) 'Boris Johnson's resignation statement in full'. *Independent* 10/06/23. https://www.independent.co.uk/news/uk/politics/boris-johnson-resignation-statement-full-text-b2354893.html, accessed 24/11/23.

332 Hayward, T. (2010) Interview with CNN. https://www.youtube.com/watch?v=_zs_06Dwl_k accessed 27/03/23.

333 Rubin, G. (2010) Tony Hayward apologies for his idiotic comment. *Business Insider* 02/06/10. https://www.businessinsider.com/bp-ceo-tony-hayward-apologizes-for-saying-id-like-my-life-back-2010-6/ accessed 12/09/23.

334 BP (2010) 'CEO Tony Hayward to step down.' BP Website. https://www.bp.com/en/global/corporate/news-and-insights/press-releases/bp-ceo-tony-hayward-to-step-down-and-be-succeeded-by-robert-dudley.html#/ accessed 13/03/23.

335 Thomas, L. (2017) 'United CEO says airline had to "re-accommodate" passenger, and the reaction was wild'. CNBC 10/04/17.

https://www.cnbc.com/2017/04/10/united-ceo-says-airline-had-to-re-accommodate-passenger-and-twitter-is-having-a-riot.html/ accessed 14/06/23.

336 Rushie, D. & D. Smith (2017) 'United Airlines CEO offers softer apology after stock nosedives' *Guardian* 12/04/17. https://www.theguardian.com/us-news/2017/apr/11/united-airlines-shares-plummet-passenger-removal-controversy accessed 17/10/23.

337 Chambers, D. (2017) *Social Media and Personal Relationships: Online Intimacies and Networked Friendship.* Palgrave.

338 Ueshiba, M. (translated version 2007) *The Art of Peace.* Translated by J. Stevens. Shambhala Pocket Classics.

339 Hills and Jones (2021) UCL podcasts: Meetings and impoliteness. https://www.ucl.ac.uk/news/2022/jul/our-top-ten-ucl-podcasts, accessed 23/10/23.

340 Ibid.

341 Mandagere, P. (2020) 'The Effects of AI on Children's Politeness'. PhD thesis, Western Michigan University. https://scholarworks.wmich.edu/honors_theses/3279/ accessed 22/12/23.

342 Forbes (2023) 'The power of AI in modelling healthy communications'. 17/08/23. https://www.forbes.com/sites/forbesbusinesscouncil/2023/08/17/the-power-of-ai-in-modeling-healthy-communications/ accessed 27/02/24.

343 Eliot, L. (2023) 'Why Excessive AI Politeness Could Be Oddly Inconsiderate: Implications too for Self-Driving Cars'. *Forbes Innovation* 22/08/20. https://www.forbes.com/sites/lanceeliot/2020/08/17/why-excessive-ai-politeness-could-be-oddly-inconsiderate-implications-too-for-self-driving-cars/?sh=e8e27f367523/ accessed 12/01/23.

ACKNOWLEDGEMENTS

The initial idea for this book started life over coffee with my editor Oliver Holden-Rea in the London Review of Books café in late 2019, just before the Covid-19 pandemic hit. Despite being pulled in different directions with university teaching and research during the various periods of lockdown, finding the time to write this book at a point in the future remained at the forefront of my mind. Thank you, Oli, for being the most patient and supportive editor that one could hope to work with. There have been a few storms along the way and your unwavering enthusiasm, belief and patience with this project has made it happen. I'll be forever grateful to you.

One of the great dangers of writing a book about politeness is being unintentionally impolite by leaving names out of the acknowledgements, so apologies in advance if I have done this to anyone. I will say that I have met and worked with many wonderful staff and students over the years and I have learnt a great deal from them all. Thanks in particular to the following politeness researchers and sociolinguists with whom I have had the pleasure of working with: Christine Christie, Erika Darics, Francesca Bargiela-Chiappini, Derek Bousfield, Jonathan Culpeper, Bethan Davies, Kieran File, Karen Grainger, Sandra

Harris, Michael Haugh, Janet Holmes, Agnes Kang, Veronika Koller, Miriam Locher, Peter Masibo Lumala, Meredith Marra, Andrew Merrison, Stephanie Schnurr and Olga Zayts. Special thanks to Sara Mills, who has been a source of great inspiration for me over the years. Although one of my PhD supervisors, Sandra Harris, is no longer with us, her research influence lives on in my work and is a part of this book. To Ron Carter, another much missed colleague and the best mentor that anyone could ever wish to have – I still hear your voice and your laugh every time I come into work and I would like to think that you would have enjoyed reading this book.

At the University of Nottingham, I wish to thank my other fantastic colleagues past and present, who have talked through politeness ideas with me over the years: Gavin Brookes, Luke Collins, Malgorzata Chalupnik, Jacqueline Cordell, Sarah Grandage, Kevin Harvey, Victoria Howard, Leigh Harrington, Daniel Hunt, Lucy Jones, Thomas Legendre, Jai McKenzie, Peter Stockwell, Matt Welton and Melissa Yoong. Special thanks to Lucy Jones and Claire Stripp for taking the time to read parts of this manuscript. Any errors of course remain my own. Heartfelt thanks also to Lucy Halberstam for your encouragement and belief in this project, and to Bryony Dunn and Ali Langton for your help, ideas and enthusiasm.

Sections of the sport chapter have been inspired by the years I have spent at the Aikido Eagle Dojo in Nottingham. Sensei Phil Musson, you have taught me so much about resilience, timing and *budo* and I feel very privileged to be a part of your dojo. Deepest thanks to you for all of the conversations that we have had about politeness and etiquette for this book and for your feedback on earlier drafts. Sincerest thanks also to Sensei Joe Thambu for the time I spent with you and your aikidoka at the Aikido Shudokan Hombu dojo in Melbourne and for the interview for your *Keep the Flame Alive* series, which has informed different parts of this book.

Lastly, to Sally Squires, thanks so much for holding me together and for your unrelenting belief in me and this project – our many conversations have helped greatly. To Nicola Burton, thanks so much for the laughter and friendship. To Matt, Abbie and Tommy, deepest gratitude for creating the time for me to work on this project, particularly for your patience as things took way longer than expected. Your humour, feedback and unrelenting belief have been invaluable and without your love, this book would not exist.

Every effort has been made to contact copyright holders. Please advise the publisher of any errors or omissions and these will be corrected in subsequent editions.